THE MATTER OF HONOR
(a novel)

THE MATTER OF HONOR
(a novel)

A. S. White

Three Towers Press
Milwaukee, Wisconsin

Copyright © 2024 by Arnold S. White
All rights reserved.

No part of this publication may be reproduced, stored in a retrieval system, or transmitted, in any form or by any means, electronic, mechanical, photocopying, recording, or otherwise, without the written permission of the author or publisher.
Pen and ink art by the author.

This book is a work of fiction. Places, events, and situations in this book are purely fictional and any resemblance to actual persons, living or dead, is coincidental.

Published by Three Towers Press
An imprint of HenschelHAUS Publishing, Inc.
www.henschelHAUSbooks.com
Milwaukee, Wisconsin

ISBN (paperback): 979-8-9908-203-5-7
ISBN (hardcover): 979-8-9908-203-0-2
LCCN: 2024938575

Author portrait by Evan Moore (2023)

Printed in the United States of America.

*This book is dedicated to the hundreds of thousands
who are incarcerated while awaiting trial,
particularly women with children,
and cannot pay a cash bond to be released.*

CHAPTER 1

"Progress is impossible without change and those who cannot change their minds cannot change anything."
—George Bernard Shaw

GOLD'S FAVORITE COLOR WAS GRAY, like his eyes that bleached his view of life in a shade of tedium. He rubbed them, closed a file in a case where he was supposed to oppose a trial date motion, and turned off his office lamp. He was weary of protecting Cynthia Carlton, his best-paying client, from her daddy, a greedy multi-millionaire bastard she claimed cheated her. She wanted him to oppose postponing the trial after her father's recent heart surgery because the new trial date conflicted with a vacation she was thinking about. Settlement of her case seemed as unlikely as surviving Jonestown, and Gold desperately wanted out of it.

He was bored with his practice. Bored with most of his clients. Seemed like the only interesting people he met were his criminal defendants, a small part of his practice that represented the last vestige of the law school ideals he cherished twenty-five years ago. Helping the Public Defender's office, where he had worked briefly in the sixties as an idealistic hippie, justified coming to work. Unfortunately, he spent little time with these court appointed clients because he encouraged them to avoid trial by pleading guilty to lesser charges he negotiated with prosecutors. After sentencing, it was sayonara and on to the next.

Before leaving, he glanced at a stack of new criminal appointment files from the court. After Frannie added them to his new-client list, he would take an afternoon to visit those locked up.

His practice was quite ordinary. He'd never tried a big case (and sought desperately to find a way out of Cynthia's), created an outstanding business entity, handled a complex trust, filed a complicated bankruptcy, or discovered a significant tax loophole. Gold's routine had been the same for years, not so much because it satisfied him but from sheer inertia. He could always find enough friction to stop himself from changing. He didn't really decide to keep things as they were. He wasn't into decision-making. Instead, he simply drifted along the shore of placid Lake Mediocrity, floating nowhere.

But every Tuesday night since before Kennedy was elected, he played poker. He hurried his old Mercedes home to his 8th-floor condo in The Park Towers, barely paying attention to radio news of unconfirmed reports of finding Etan Patz, the kidnapped 6-year-old "Boy on the Milk Carton"; a giant oil rig blowout in the Gulf of Mexico; or the death of a local inmate who may have OD'd at the Women's Correctional Institution. They fluttered about aimlessly in his tired brain, so he switched to music.

As soon as he stepped into his condo, he shed his gray suit and donned a plain T-shirt and a pair of khakis. He had set the table, shuffled the cards, and chilled the beer before he went to work, just like always.

Smoke hovered above his living room card table as Alan dealt. Fred, a dentist, was always a sucker who telegraphed winning hands by tapping his fingers. Barry, who owned a junkyard, often raised big, holding only two pairs, making him both a big winner and a huge loser in the same evening.

Betting was getting crazy when the avocado green phone on the kitchen wall rang. Al, as he was known to his friends, threw in his cards and answered the call.

The Matter of Honor

"Is this Alan Gold, the lawyer?"

"Yes, it is. How may I help you?"

"My name is Millie Rivers. I'm sorry to bother you again, but I don't know who else to call. Do you remember me calling you a while back about my daughter, Honor Wilson. She was arrested and put in jail."

"Oh, yes, I believe I told you I had not yet received her paperwork. They are extremely backed up at the defender's office. Well, yesterday, they sent me a stack of court appointments, and your daughter's file is probably among them. Don't worry, Ms. Rivers. Frannie, my paralegal, is already processing them, and I'll see your daughter as soon as I can."

She sobbed, "The prison called last week. My daughter is dead."

"Oh, my God. I'm so sorry. My deepest sympathies. Was she sick? An accident?"

"No. Like I told you before, she recently had a stillborn baby. She was getting a little stronger when they arrested her. I called the jail a few times, and they kept saying she was fine. Then, they called back the other night and told me she was dead. Now, I keep asking myself, how can that be? First, she's fine; then, she's dead. My other kids are still in shock, and my church friends keep calling me. I don't know what to do. Can you help me?"

"Please come to my office tomorrow at nine. We'll talk about it then."

"Thank you. I'll be there, but I've got to be to work at the nursing home by 11."

"We won't be long. See you then."

The guys looked at him when he took his seat, tacitly asking him, "Who was that?"

"Some lady. Said her daughter died at the Women's Correctional Institution."

"Oh, I heard the story on the radio coming over here," said Steve, a professor at Denison University east of Columbus. "A black woman awaiting trial. Didn't hear the cause of death."

Barry said, "Drugs. She overdosed, I'll bet. Let me tell you, kids these days; they can't stay away from them. They don't want to work. They just want to have babies to get more welfare and spend it on drugs. I only wish we had politicians who'd crack down and turn this country around before it's too late."

"Wow, Barry. Sounds like you got her all figured out. You condemn her and her entire lazy generation and pull out a jeremiad of the world going to hell before you even know why she died. Good job," said Steve. "My students at Denison are neither better nor worse than those I taught a decade ago in the sixties, except perhaps for a decline in English and math skills. Drugs are a problem, but not the end of the world."

"Maybe not at your private school in the suburbs, but down in the 'hood where I work, it's another story. Day in and day out, truant kids walk past my salvage yard higher than a kite, looking for trouble. We had to add barbed wire on top of our fence, along with a mean and hungry Rottweiler. I'm telling you, they'd steal the shirt off my back if I didn't keep it buttoned," said Barry.

"And why do you think that is?" asked Fred.

"It's the drugs. Takes away their brains. Today's kids live for the high. It's out of control, and it's not getting better," Barry said.

"Don't you think there's an economic side to this, Barry?" asked Steve, pushing his point. "Aren't drugs and theft more likely among the poor than those who are better off?"

"Sure," said Barry, "but why do you think they're poor? Because they're spending all their god-damned welfare money on drugs."

Steve refused to back down. "Don't you think other factors are at work? What about discrimination? What about poor schools in black communities? What about the effects of slavery on black society? What about..."

Barry interrupted, "Oh, you bleeding-heart liberals are all the same, making excuses for their lack of effort. Jobs are always available to those who want to work."

"Will you two knock it off and play?" Fred said, tapping his fingers on the table. "I didn't come for a lecture. If I wanted that, I'd have stayed home and listened to my wife tell me how much better her first husband was. Besides, I've got a good hand." For a change, Alan didn't fold when Fred went all in. His three kings defeated Fred's two pairs.

"Well," said Alan. "Her daughter is dead. It's all I've got right now. Stay tuned."

CHAPTER 2

ON WEDNESDAY, FRANNIE ushered into his office a short, stocky black woman wearing light blue medical scrubs under a blue rain jacket.

"Mr. Gold, this is Ms. Millie Rivers."

He rose. "Nice to meet you. I'm very sorry to hear about your daughter."

"Thank you. I hope you can help me find out how she died. We haven't had her funeral yet because the coroner won't give her to me."

They sat down and settled in. Alan took out a yellow legal pad and said, "Oh, how sad. So young. She never had a chance. Like I told you, I never met her. I was appointed to defend her against criminal charges, not investigate her death. I don't do that sort of work. Please let me suggest that other attorneys far more skilled in these matters might be of greater service to you. If you like, I will gladly share the names of a few I know. Better yet, I'll refer you to the bar association. They have a list of attorneys better suited for this type of case. It's not my area of practice."

"I understand. Please tell me, what type of case is this?"

"To be honest, I'm not sure. I guess it's either a personal injury or a civil rights case. The first thing an attorney would do is look for anything improperly done. If not, he would probably close his file. I assume the coroner is examining her body to discover the cause of death. When he completes his exam, you'll be able to schedule the funeral. Waiting for her must be so painful," Alan said.

"Yes, but what hurts most is not knowing what happened. Honor was my firstborn. She'd never been arrested or used drugs. I still don't understand why they locked her up. I was at Bible study when she got picked up. My kids told me she'd complained of a headache, so she went over to Benny's Quick Stop to buy some aspirin and never came back.

"The worst thing she ever did was quit school after she got pregnant. I don't know why she got pregnant the second time when she wasn't getting along with her husband. I told her, another child isn't going to fix your marriage. Now, I've got to raise her son, Winston. Don't know how we're going to get by. None of my kids are old enough to make any real money. The authorities told me she overdosed, but she never touched drugs, except marijuana sometimes. I just want to know why she died.

She tightened her jacket over her scrubs and continued. Gold made notes.

"Now, don't get me wrong. Honor was no angel. She could be foolish and sometimes stubborn, like when she refused to marry Reginald Wilson Jr., Winston's father. But we got her married to him despite a fuss from his light-skinned mother. They moved to Chicago. Honor tried to make a man out of that mama's boy, but he couldn't be changed. He is what he is.

"She didn't give up on herself even when they made her quit school. Got her GED by doing homework long into the night. When she moved back from Chicago and in with us a few months ago, she started raising both her child and my kids, even though she wasn't yet strong enough. She was like a second mother to them. I got four others, but none like my Honor.

"People tell me jails can be mean. She told me she tried to see the prison doctor, but they refused to let her. You were her lawyer. Have they told you anything? Her death makes no sense, and that's making me lose my perspective. You know what I mean, Mr. Gold?" She was out of breath. "You'll find out what happened to her, can't you? "

"Well, let me try to get you the autopsy report, Ms. Rivers. That should tell you the cause of her death. I don't know that I could do much more."

With that, he walked her out his office door and into the hallway. Turning back toward his desk, he thought, *I never wanted kids, but my God, what would it be like to lose one, especially like she did?*

On his way back, he picked up the morning's *Citizen Journal* from the lobby coffee table and scanned a little story on page 4 of the local section. Inmate died at the Women's Correction Institution for no apparent reason. Coroner investigating. superintendent says they followed procedures. Guard says she might have overdosed. Local black leader says his community prays for the family. Not much there. Gold wondered, *Will reporters run with her story or instead cover whether Clark Kellogg will return to play OSU basketball next year? Oh, well, I'll mail her mother the autopsy report when I get it and go back to my other cases. Interesting, but not for me.*

Later that morning, reviewing his stack of newly appointed cases, he found Honor's file, including discovery materials the prosecutor had provided to the Public Defender's Office. He found perhaps some minor irregularities in her arrest but nothing of significance. The arresting officer's report showed that Honor had been shopping in Benny's Quick Stop when the cops raided it and arrested Benny for selling drugs to an undercover cop.

Even though police found no drugs, Honor was charged anyway. When booked at WCI, she had a few dollars, plus an unopened box of aspirin, in her handbag. Her background check disclosed no criminal record in Illinois or Ohio and no connections to Benny. Surprisingly, Alan found nothing at all to suggest Honor had committed a crime at all.

Gold called the coroner's office for a copy of the preliminary autopsy report. *Guess there is not much more I can do now but wait for the report,* thought Gold, as he put aside the appointments and opened another file to draft a will. *No reason to suspect anything will come of this. Lots of people die for no reason. Is there ever a reason for death?* As he shuffled through the will papers in his hands, he kept thinking about Honor Wilson, someone he'd never met and now would never talk to.

When he stood inside the crowded gas station to pay for gas on Broad Street near Sherman Avenue on his way home that night, he glanced at newspapers on the counter, frowning when he compared local press headlines. The *Call and Post,* a paper read mainly in the black community, read "BLACK SISTER DIES IN CITY HANDS," while *The Columbus Dispatch,* the largest paper in town, contained no headlines about Honor at all.

A few days later, he received a copy of the preliminary autopsy report. The coroner found the cause of Honor's death was choriocarcinoma, a fast-growing cancer that occurs in the uterus that had metastasized to the brain. Gold checked the toxicology section but found no mention of drugs in her system, except for marijuana. *Why had they told her mother of a possible overdose when the actual cause of death was cancer?*

CHAPTER 3

MEDICAL TEXTS HE REVIEWED briefly at the county law library later showed that symptoms of metastatic choriocarcinoma were headaches, vaginal bleeding, and fatigue.

Later that evening, he dialed Millie. "Ms. Rivers, I received the coroner's preliminary report, and I am sorry to say he found that your daughter died of cancer that began in her uterus and spread to her brain. It started with her stillborn."

"She didn't die from an overdose?"

"They found no drugs in her system, except a trace of marijuana."

"I knew it. My daughter was not an addict. I think the mayor should apologize to me and my family and tell everybody that she was not an addict."

"Let me ask you, Ms. Rivers. Do you know if she suffered from either headaches or vaginal bleeding?"

"On the night she was arrested, the kids said she went Benny's to buy something for a headache. When I visited her at the prison, Honor also told me her head hurt. Said she complained to the nurse there, and that's why she wanted to see a doctor. They just gave her aspirin. Don't recall her mentioning any bleeding."

"She told prison staff she was having headaches, and they ignored her?"

"Yes. She said she also told them about her baby being born dead, but they didn't believe her."

"I see. You know anything more?"

"Not that I can think of. Oh, she looked worse each time over the weeks I visited."

"The coroner's office also told me you can now retrieve her body. I suggest you call the funeral home for pick-up. Ms. Rivers, let me see if I can find someone to help you if that's okay with you."

"Thank you. I don't know what to do," Millie said in a quiet voice.

"Maybe I can find an attorney who can advise you. I'll just check a few possibilities for you. No promises."

"Thanks, Mr. Gold. I need possibilities."

The next day, Alan called several personal injury attorneys he knew, asking if any would consider taking the case. He told them it was not his practice area, but suggested that they might get the family a few bucks in a quick settlement. To his surprise, after he told them the client was black, awaiting trial at the Women's Correctional Institution, the prison doctor was on contract with the city, his white nurses were city employees, and the cause of death was choriocarcinoma metastatic to the brain, they thanked him politely. None was interested.

At the same time, friends and church members were giving Millie the names of black attorneys who might want to take her case. When she called, she told them she was angry at newspaper reports of a guard suggesting her daughter was a drug addict. All she wanted was to restore the good names of her daughter and her family. Their responses were the same as those received by Gold. None of the lawyers could handle the financial burden of fronting the thousands of dollars it would cost for experts, tests, depositions, etc. All expressed sympathy; none wanted the case.

A few days later, she called Gold's office for an appointment. Frannie squeezed her in the following day for 15 minutes between other clients. When Millie arrived, Frannie quickly ushered her into Alan's office.

"Good morning, Ms. Rivers. Thank you for stopping by. I was about to call you anyway. I want to let you know that I telephoned a few colleagues who are personal injury and civil rights attorneys to see if they might be interested in exploring your case for a possible suit. I'm sorry, but no one wanted to meet with you. So, after sending you the autopsy report as promised and trying unsuccessfully to find you a lawyer, it looks like we have come to the end of our road together. I wish you the best of luck and hope you will give me a call sometime to let me know what happened." He arose from his chair and extended his hand.

Millie Rivers did not move.

"Mr. Gold, I don't know you very well, but you seem like someone who cares about folks. I want to ask you a question. What would you do if it were your daughter? Would you just let it go? Could you? Because I can't, and I need a little help to find out why she died."

Gold withdrew his hand and put it to his chin as he thought about her question. His better judgment agreed with what he had heard from more experienced attorneys. At the same time, Millie made a compelling argument that she and her family should not be left without knowing at least what happened. Once again, he reminded himself he was not suited for the job. He had taken and settled only one malpractice case against a doctor in his entire career. He had never sued a government entity. Litigation, he found, was too stressful. It disturbed his routine. While he too was curious about how and why Honor had died, his poker games taught him the price sometimes of learning what's in another's hand is not worth it.

"I do very little litigation, Ms. Rivers, but I suppose I can make a few calls and talk to some inmates to see if anyone knows what happened. Once I do that, I will be done. But, let me be clear. That's all I will do. Is that agreeable?"

"Yes. I want everyone to know my daughter was not a drug addict."

"I'll send you a letter advising you of my limited role. In the meantime, please look for other counsel. I will share whatever I learn with the attorney you select. You may also want to look outside the city. Sometimes, lawyers from elsewhere with no local connections can serve you better. This case could get political. At any rate, I want you to understand that I will only make a few calls and ask a few questions. That's all. Understood?"

"I understand, Mr. Gold. Look, this may sound crazy, but just in case you change your mind or things change, let me ask you something. You may say no, but I'll ask it just the same. Would you come to her funeral?"

"Thank you for asking, Ms. Rivers. Call me when you know the time and place, and I'll try."

CHAPTER 4

MAYOR JONATHON BLANDFORD was already having second thoughts about his re-election run that November as he walked toward his office from the basement garage of City Hall—candidate's remorse. On the campaign trail, he spoke passionately about erecting towering skyscrapers downtown and using federal money to pour concrete freeways across the city. Sometimes, though, he longed to sit in his small library at home with a pipeful of Prince Albert mix, and travel with James Michener to Japan, Hawaii, or Afghanistan or scheme with his favorite writer, Niccolò di Bernardo dei Machiavelli, in great political intrigues. It was better than reviewing the *carte du jour* in Columbus politics, trash collection, snow clearance, and police and fire department maintenance.

Working on his election campaign this season, like his others, impaired his ability to govern and prevented him from focusing on more significant issues. Several years before, he tried to avoid election politics by retaining Terry Prince, a nationally known political campaign advisor, to free him from political matters. It was not working out well. To Terry, everything was political, and Blandford found himself revisiting scuffles he'd hoped to avoid.

As he rounded the corner, the clicks from his leather heels reverberated off the marble-lined walls. Portraits of his predecessors hanging on marble walls, white men dressed in formal black jackets of bygone eras, wordlessly warned him of lurking political dangers. He opened the door to his offices and walked into a silent lobby of sound-absorbing ceiling tiles and thick, dull red carpet. Polly Gibson, his secretary, was busy typing thank-you letters.

"Good morning, Mr. Mayor. Your cup of coffee is on your desk, the safety director is waiting in your office, and Terry will be here at 9:30 to review his latest polling. You must leave for your Chamber of Commerce meeting at 10 o'clock sharp before your lunch speech."

"Thanks, Polly. Please hold all calls."

On a seat cut into a soft dull cube, beneath a portrait of Gov. James Rhodes, sat Bruno Puchik, Blandford's Safety Director, reading *The Columbus Dispatch*.

"Good morning, Mayor. Says here that the disorder last week on the Near East Side almost turned into a riot when those people claimed the fire department took too long to get to an apartment house blaze. The *Dispatch* seems to be insinuating we don't care about Negras just because we don't have many in the fire department.

"Maybe you should have a little talk with Mr. Foxx about his cub reporters. He may not know how agitating those remarks are to my cops and firefighters. They could cause a loss of confidence in the Safety Department.

"When I commanded troops invading Germany, I saw what Army Intelligence did to Nazi control of towns. As soon as anybody complained about anything, they'd use it to start an insurrection. Now I'm on the other side, and I can tell you, Mayor, it's a helluva lot easier to start a riot than to stop one."

"Well, you're not in Germany, Bruno, and last week's incident was not an insurrection. Some folks don't understand that public hiring means selecting the most qualified, not favoring those of a particular skin color. Some don't believe me when I say we fill city jobs in an orderly fashion, selecting only the best-qualified people. I agree it's because of what they hear in the media. President Carter made a speech not too long ago actually advocating a policy favoring blacks for jobs in government. At a mayors' conference a few months ago, I heard mayors making proposals to set aside government contracts for minorities. Talk about free-for-alls! Where will it all end?" he said, raising his hands to the heavens.

"That reminds me, Mayor. We had a little incident last night at WCI. My superintendent reported this morning a Negra inmate died last night after guards sent her to OSU Hospital. The coroner is doing an autopsy. Now watch, someone will try to make something of this, too. I'm not complaining, Mr. Mayor, but our jobs aren't getting any easier.

"Also, I wanted to report back when you asked me the other day to investigate those agitators on the Near East Side. Well, we're keeping close tabs on several leaders from the clergy, and I can say with some confidence we'll be able to stick something on them if we need to."

"Bruno, tell Terry about any blowback from that death. I want to stay away from political stuff as much as possible. I'm hoping it will go away. We'll provide the media with a simple explanation for why she died and be done with it. Oh, I also want to do a press conference on employment discrimination in a week or so. I'll need some numbers from you to back me up. Check minority hires in your department—police, fire, and the men's and women's prisons. I want to assure the public we do not discriminate in hiring. And let me know why that fire truck took so long. Thanks, Bruno."

Puchik nodded and left.

Blandford turned to his intercom, "Polly, send Terry in."

Terry Prince, Special Assistant to the Mayor (campaign manager), bounced into his boss's office with an ever-present smile pasted across his well-tanned face. He sat on one of the stuffed square chairs in front of the mayor's large mahogany desk.

"Good morning, Mayor."

"Good morning, Terry. How are we doing?"

"Our first polling numbers look tremendous. We're ahead in every district that is above medium income. Your name recognition is strong, and your favorability is over 68 percent."

"Well, it's only January, Terry. A lot can happen between now and election day. By the way, Bruno reported a black inmate's death at WCI, and we received complaints that a fire truck took too long to get to a fire on the East Side. Neither may mean much, but I wanted to let you know, Mr. Politico. You didn't tell me how we are doing in districts below medium income."

"Not as well as I hoped. There seems to be a gap, but I'm on it. Locally, I'm finding that civil rights concerns are rising among lower-income voters, consistent with national demographics. I am planning a fall initiative to boost your approval rating among them. Maybe a hot appointment or a call for some new program might juice things up. Still working on it. I've got you addressing the Ohio Conference of the AME Church next week. A few words to them also might help us with the black vote."

"Yes, I know. I plan to spend some time preparing for it. Church leaders are concerned about incarceration issues. Maybe I'll say something about arrest rates in those communities and what we're doing about it. Add some black hiring data that Bruno is working on. I hear they also believe laws like prostitution, vagrancy, and bail bond practices unfairly discriminate against blacks. Some even have said our laws have incarcerated so many of them that we are splitting into two societies, black and white. Another told me they are also worried that the state legislature might pass some kind of public protection bill like California, where they tripled jail time for repeat offenders.

"I've wanted to talk about incarceration, prison, and freedom for a long time. I want to say something memorable," the mayor thought aloud as he struck a pensive pose, standing and looking out a window facing the Scioto River, imagining the black ministers cheering his historic oration that might lead him to national recognition.

"Oh, I'm sure your comments on incarceration to a black audience will be a big hit, Mr. Mayor," said Terry, picking a barely noticeable piece of lint from his blue serge blazer. "But if you go ahead with that idea, please let me take a peek at your speech before you deliver your discourse. Anyway, I think the election might depend on what happens this summer. Have to keep things under control, particularly teenagers. A few more crazies like those on the East Side last week could cost us six to eight points within this demographic. We've got to keep folks happy, Mr. Mayor. Just talking about civil rights hurts us. Bad for our numbers. Instead, how about hosting a community picnic? Maybe some soul music, a few prizes, something quick and easy. I'll make some arrangements.

"By the way, Mayor, Bruno is working on a new police class this fall. You may have heard that Mabel Bright's son wants to be a cop. Barely passed the civil service test. You remember Mabel. She is the white ward committeeman for the Hilltop district. A big vote-getter. You might want to say something to Bruno to pick her boy. The kid's name is Freddie Bright. You want me to handle it?"

"Yes, go ahead, please," said the mayor, still thinking about his speech. "Mabel has worked hard on our campaigns."

CHAPTER 5

AFTER MEETING WITH THE MAYOR, Bruno Puchik returned to his headquarters in the old Public Safety Building. His metal shoe clips pounding on hardwood floors announced his arrival as he walked through the outer office. Magazines from the Ohio Association of Chiefs of Police and a few old copies of *Guns and Ammo* lay on the table. Standing guard around them were old, leather-covered chairs with wooden arms. As he marched in with his chin up, his communications officer barked, "Morning, sir. Nothing to report at this time. All quiet, sir."

He nodded, eyes ahead, advancing to his field command. Unlike the mayor's cozy surroundings, his office was like a war room. He favored police over his firefighters. Officers were his troops in his endless battle against incorrigibles. A large street map of Columbus (updated weekly) hung on one wall and was dotted with various colored pins reflecting reported crimes and personnel and equipment deployment. He had removed thick carpet and sound-absorbing ceilings to expose old wooden beams and hardwood floors. Likewise, instead of elevator music, he listened to police radio chatter.

He closed his door and put his Smith and Wesson original model 39 and its holster in a desk drawer. An old nine-foot walnut-stained table with a few metal chairs around it served as his conference room. Through the intercom, he instructed his communications officer to commence establishing telephone contact with his immediate subordinates ASAP. While he waited, he glanced at four of the piles of papers scattered about the table.

After instructing his chief of police, fire chief, and superintendent of the men's prison of the mayor's request for employment numbers, Bruno spoke to the acting superintendent of the Women Correctional Institution, Haskel Gross. Gross had come from the Water Department, but after the City lost the federal grant that funded his office, City Hall moved him to a vacant position as assistant superintendent of WCI until somebody could find him a permanent job elsewhere. His uncle was a big Blandford donor. When Governor Rhodes appointed the superintendent to the Ohio Parole Board, Gross slid in as acting superintendent. In over two years, no one had gotten around to replacing him.

"Gross, this is the director," said Bruno.

"Good morning, sir."

"Anything to report?"

"Nothing much. Today, our count is down since some of the girls picked up by the cops in the raid on the Fancy Club got released."

"Anything new about the death?"

"No, sir. Everything is quiet."

"Listen up. The mayor says he wants us to put an end to anyone who might want to investigate her death. Do something to help. He also wants us to give him proof that we don't discriminate in hiring. Take a census of staff and provide me with proof we don't discriminate. Maybe some programs we are working on. Got it? I need your report by Monday at 1300 hours, listing race and all that stuff at WCI. We need to show them Columbus has nothing against those people."

"Were there hiring programs before I took over? I don't recall any, sir."

"How in the hell should I know?"

"Well, I will check. Another question, sir. Are we allowed to keep track of employees' race, sir?"

"Well, God damn it, Gross, if we don't keep track of race, how could we know we are not discriminating? 1300 hours next Monday."

"Yes, sir."

"Over and out."

CHAPTER 6

OVERNIGHT, HASKEL GROSS thought about options to carry out Puchik's instruction to end inquiries of Honor's death. He decided to do something he had not done before. As acting superintendent, he invited a *Columbus Dispatch* reporter to WCI for an exclusive off-the-record interview.

After touring the facility with the reporter and showing her how clean and scrubbed WCI was, how fit the staff was, and how well-dressed the inmates were, he brought her into the staff room for coffee. While they waited for their cups of java, he showed her his undelivered report on nondiscrimination in hiring.

After listening for a few minutes to his rambling about discrimination, the wise reporter placed her pen down and crossed her arms. He sensed it was time to discuss why he'd invited her, just as Molene Jones, an inmate there, brought their steaming pot. He began with a lament.

"You know that death here the other night was pretty sad. I wasn't in the building when they took her, but from what I heard a guard say, she OD'd. Drugs aren't usually that big a problem here at WCI; we try very hard to keep them out. But every so often, something happens. I know people tell you this often, but drugs are a big problem elsewhere. Our team and the OSU medical staff did their best, but nothing could have saved her. We're very sad and concerned about our community's drug problem. But we've got to move on. You know what I'm saying?

"Say, let me show you our new mini-library when you finish your coffee. It was a gift from some lawyers in town."

He continued to tour her until she thanked him and left.

CHAPTER 7

AT HIS DIRECTION, POLLY scheduled Mayor Blandford to be alone all afternoon to prepare Sunday's address at the Ohio AME Church Conference dinner. Today, he placed all the 3x5 cards he had been jotting notes on for the past few weeks into four piles: history, change, injustice, and freedom.

He had added a quick note of the WCI death to his list but did not expect to discuss it. But now, for some reason, he thought he might use it to kick off his remarks to the church elders, those who officiate at funerals of those dying from overdoses. What could he say to them that they don't already know?

Blandford shared a universal human desire; he longed to be remembered. A new freeway, a new subdivision, a new park, and even a new City Hall would fade quickly from the public's eye. He yearned to give a speech so masterful that schools would require children to quote it, like the words delivered on the bloody field, "Four score and seven years ago..." But unlike Lincoln's address, he hoped people would embrace his oration immediately.

How could he find words of unity on this contentious topic of the drug war? With one opening after another, he tried to pluck sprigs of universal truth. Again and again, he carefully selected prized word-flowers from his vocabulary garden to arrange a verbal bouquet describing his "war on drugs," hoping his arrangement might contribute to the national discourse on drugs and freedom. But he was getting nowhere.

When he finally looked up, it was dark outside. He rose to straighten his legs when he heard rustling in his outer office.

Raphael Horton was entering his inner office, wearing a dark city-issued uniform that contrasted with his silver-sprinkled black hair and his gold-rimmed glasses resting about halfway down his thick brown nose.

Horton was of the night people, the silent world of workers who clean banks, offices, and other places after the sun drops. Day people come to work rarely pausing to think how their discarded paper cups and crumbs on their carpet are removed overnight. For over 12 years, Raphael Horton had been a member in good standing after conceding defeat following 27 rejections in his struggle to find a white-collar job.

"Good evening, Skippy," said the mayor, returning to his seat.

"Evening, Mr. Mayor."

"I've been so busy today, and it got dark before I realized it. How is your day going?"

"One's pretty much like another, sir," Skippy said, limping along.

"I've been meaning to ask you, Skippy, how did you get that nickname?"

"Well, after I broke my leg at work, some guys there started calling me that, and it just stuck."

"Should I call you Skippy or what?"

"Whatever you choose, sir."

"Okay. Skippy, I want to ask your opinion. I'm trying to write a speech for a dinner Sunday night with AME church leaders about the drug crisis, and I'm pulling together a bunch of jumbled thoughts."

"Well, I don't know much about that kind of stuff. I suppose you have experts to help with that work," Horton said, thinking he may have to do a little shuckin' and jivin' to avoid going down the Hole.

"Yes, but I don't always trust them. I try to listen to lots of different viewpoints."

"Different doesn't always mean better, I wouldn't think," said Horton, looking toward the floor.

"Maybe not, but ivory-tower lectures aren't always as helpful as street talk."

"Can't say much about it, sir," he said as he emptied the mayor's trash can.

"I am trying to contrast freedom with drug addiction and encourage obedience to our drug laws," Mayor Blandford persisted. "I am trying to find a theme that everyone agrees with. What do you think of this statement, 'The price of freedom is obedience to law'? Does that sound right to you?"

"Well, I couldn't rightly say," Skippy mumbled while thinking, *Why ask me? Because I'm black? Because I'm a janitor? Or because I'm the only one around?* Against his better judgment, he put his toe in the water. "I suppose it depends on which law, doesn't it? I mean, didn't Reverend King resist some bad laws?"

"Wouldn't you agree that no one has freedom without order?"

"Perhaps, but order, like it was down South, meant no freedom anyway. I don't pay much attention to politics. I like poetry. Obedience makes me think of Langston Hughes' poem, *Ballad of the Landlord*. Have you read it?"

"No, I am not familiar with him. What's it about?"

"Well, Hughes was an American poet who was black. Before the war, he wrote a poem about a tenant who couldn't get his landlord to fix his place. The angry tenant threatened him when his landlord demanded rent but refused to make repairs. The landlord rushed to the police, crying that the tenant was trying to create disorder and overturn the country. Law and order favored landlords. On the landlord's statement, the police put the tenant in jail.

"The newspaper reported the arrest but not the landlord's refusal. For some, that may be law and order, but it wasn't freedom for the tenant."

Horton regretted his words. He had ventured from the world of night people and violated their creed to avoid controversy. "Well, it's just a little poem," he mumbled.

Mayor Blandford paused for a moment, absorbing it. "But that was before states had laws protecting civil rights and tenants. People don't think that way now, do they?"

Raphael quickly retreated. "Well, I guess not, sir. It was just the first thing that came to me," he said, nimbly slipping back into his night world.

"Skippy, you must be a reader."

"Well, I don't read as much as I did in college. I still like poetry and sometimes write a verse or two."

"College? What school did you go to?"

"I graduated from Wilberforce."

"I see. What did you study?"

"American literature, with a minor in American history."

The mayor paused, unsure of what to say next now that "Skippy" had suddenly risen in his eyes to "Rafael." The mayor, over the years, touted tales of those few people of color obtaining higher-paying jobs while overlooking many black men with one or two college degrees denied that opportunity.

Raphael wanted to tell him that the American Dream for many was no more than a white man's fantasy, like the mayor's notion of freedom in the context of drug laws. While he yearned to say more, Raphael retreated with, "Well, Mr. Mayor, good luck with your speech. I got to tend to my baskets."

He closed the door softly as the mayor rearranged his cards.

CHAPTER 8

TERRY AND THE MAYOR HOPPED into a plain, city-owned Ford Fairmont and drove toward St. Paul's AME church in the Near East Side. Forgetting their earlier conversation, Terry expected Blandford to say a quick hello and be off, allowing campaign staff to take it from there to show them his strong connection to the black community.

"Well, Mayor, are you ready to address those people?"

"Those people are our people, Terry."

"Not according to my polls. Am I correct that we'll leave after you say a few pleasantries, make a statement or two showing you believe in justice for all?"

"Well, actually, I intend to discuss with them our fine record and improvements to our prison system, particularly regarding drug control. Puchik provided me with some info about WCI improvements, which I think they will like hearing about, but of course, we cannot ignore problems like that death the other day I mentioned to you. Drugs will ruin us all."

Terry was not fond of speeches of substance, particularly to hostile audiences. They were both gratuitous and unnecessary. No matter what Blandford would say to them, he sensed pastors would give sermons urging followers not to vote for him. If the mayor blundered, it would only intensify "get out the vote" efforts. Besides, Terry found the food at these dinners scarcely savory for his discriminating buds.

Terry suddenly recalled the mayor telling him earlier that he wanted this to be an important speech.

"Bruno said that? When was the last time he toured either the men's workhouse or WCI? Mayor, let me suggest you not say anything too specific, particularly about WCI. Your audience might know more about what's going on there than Bruno. Of course, I defer to your wisdom, but this is not the time or place to reveal too much about WCI or drug control. The election is not far off, and we must avoid discussing problems."

"Yes, I'm aware. Take a right on Long Street."

The Ohio Conference selected St. Paul's as the host church for the dinner. It stands on the eastern side of the inner-city black community. The city separated it from its western members when it constructed I-71, which paved over many houses owned by blacks, gutting local culture. Publicly funded freeways and white flight had caused Columbus to see its bosom of urban homes dry up.

Middle-class blacks lost homes, and well-to-do whites scampered to the suburbs after selling their mini-mansions to landlords who sliced and diced them into multiple apartments. The Long Street Bridge across I-71 was eventually constructed, linking the church back to its western flock, but the tight connection between the church and its members was never the same. The freeway destroyed the community. Blandford was about to address many with deep resentments.

When he arrived, church members civilly greeted the mayor, women dressed in colorful outfits with hats and white gloves, men in black suits, while others wore monochrome outfits where shirts, ties, suits, and shoes were white, gold, maroon, or an occasional burnt orange. The mayor, dressed in his traditional gray suit, blue shirt, and nondescript tie, stood out in more ways than dermatologically, but he was comfortable both in his skin and clothing. On the other hand, Terry stood stiff—a white stranger in a strange land.

Local pastors respectfully greeted the mayor and introduced him to those from outside the county attending the conference. Congregants welcomed him politely without enthusiasm. He remained largely unknown, and his demeanor did not impress them that night, although it was not entirely his fault. Unwritten protocol prohibited preachers from talking to him about his election campaign or his discussing topics involving religion. With politics and religion off the table, they had little to say to each other than spewing very small talk.

They strolled downstairs into the social hall, where the Ladies' Auxiliary would later serve dinner. St Paul's elders boasted that they had paid the church mortgage and "stood pat" with the bank. He congratulated them.

After devouring fried chicken, mashed potatoes, and pecan pie, the pastors and others lit up cigarettes or pipes and sat back to listen. Pastor Jenkins, selected to introduce Mayor Blandford, began with a few short jokes and added thank-yous to the Ladies' Auxiliary for dinner and to the mayor for honoring the group with his presence. He gave a big welcome to those visitors from other congregations and bragged that his church had been organized in 1823 as the first black church in Columbus.

Once niceties were dispensed with, Pastor Jenkins got down to business. His voice dropped, and he paused, wiping from his face his broad smile. He was not about to let this opportunity pass to express to the mayor the voices of many congregants.

He noted that police arrested and incarcerated young black men at a much higher rate than young white men, and he despaired at a recent trend toward arresting more black women. Gently but clearly, he called out the cruel hypocrisy of black sisters going to jail and being shamed in the media for prostitution, while the media shielded white participants. He railed against costly bail bonds for those of no means and criticized other police-related actions. Continuing to press his concerns until he reached the outer edges of politeness, he then introduced

A. S. White

Blandford by monotonously reading the mayor's scaled-down biography provided to him.

Few want to address those who disagree with what they say or do. Blandford was not fully aware of their level of bitterness, nor had he paid attention to Jenkin's introduction. But it didn't matter to him. He was convinced that a "clearer message" was all that was needed to win them over.

Nodding his head and mouthing a pantomimed "thank you" through his well-practiced smile, the mayor approached the podium to subdued applause. After acknowledging church dignitaries and thanking both Jenkins for his kind introduction and the Ladies' Auxiliary for the food, he referred to two pastors by name, having just met them. (He'd developed this recall talent from years on the campaign trail.)

Blandford started slowly at first, using broad body movements, leaning this way to speak to one pastor and that way to address another. Just as he was about to go full bore into his prepared remarks, he sensed from some crossed arms and muffled comments that the crowd needed a little more warm-up. Heaping more praise on the chefs for the delicious pie might connect him with the group. Still not satisfied, he strayed into an anecdote he often used successfully at GOP fundraisers.

"Speaking tonight to a room full of ministers reminds me of the old story about a preacher who planned to play hooky one Sunday morning so he could golf. In preparing for his adventure, he complained to a few congregants on Friday and Saturday that he was not feeling well. Early Sunday morning, before any parishioner awoke, he left to play at a faraway golf course where no one would recognize him. He was enjoying his illicit getaway alone when God punished him. He blessed the preacher with a hole-in-one, who gushed with gratitude until the preacher realized...he couldn't tell anyone!"

The Matter of Honor

The mayor quietly chuckled into the microphone to indicate humor and awaited laughter to fill the vacuous silence. Some of his listeners did not know what a "hole-in-one" meant. Others took offense at his negative image of a member of the cloth speaking falsely to his flock. But the joke failed mainly because the audience resented golf-club discrimination. Somehow, in less than 100 words, the mayor had offended nearly everyone in the room. From the fiery eyes of those nearby, he sensed that his little joke had been, to use a politician's expression, "ill-advised." Experience begged him to heed Terry's earlier suggestion to say something light and quick and be gone, but he refused to quit after he had spent so much time preparing. Off-script again, this time into quicksand, he struggled to correct his previous error and turned serious, almost severe.

"I come tonight to assure you that my administration is deeply committed to improving the criminal justice system. As mayor, I have devoted a great deal of time and effort to building a powerful police force and highly trained prison staff to protect our lives and our property while prosecuting offenders fairly and rationally. For example, we've doubled the number of black police officers, held social awareness classes, and distributed materials provided by EEOC to our staff."

His delay after each announcement did not bring the applause he had hoped for. He tried some more. "We've trained our officers to protect communities, regardless of skin color." Ignoring what Raphael Horton had told him, he declared, "Our goal is to maintain law and order. At the same time, we work hard to improve our prisons. Though I have no control over criminal sentencing as mayor, I believe one of my highest obligations is to handle prisoners fairly for the short time they are in our custody. We don't believe in coddling prisoners but always shine our light toward justice." Again, silence. For no explainable reason, he continued to push it.

"Before I was mayor, I was a judge, where I learned the importance of law and order. I also learned that cities can now be liable for violating citizens' civil rights. One of my personal goals is to assure the citizens of Columbus, including those within your community, that the City of Columbus will stand tall among American cities in protecting law and order while defending the civil rights of its citizens arrested. Every day, I work to accomplish both goals. It is my sacred duty. Columbus is a model

American city, for blacks, whites, and everyone! This is what makes America great!" he shouted. Again, no rousing response.

"When I first campaigned for mayor..." he stopped suddenly when Terry ascended the head table to hand him a note just as he was about to launch his address for the ages. Terry had gone to the bathroom during Jenkin's introduction, avoiding touching anyone. The main headline of the new *Call and Post* issue about the death of a young black woman, Honor Wilson, caught his eye. He understood quickly why the mayor was facing such hostility. His note said, "Wrap it up. Black press using WCI death to attack you. Need to reevaluate."

After reading the note, the mayor reflected quickly before continuing, with the ad-libbing but on another topic. "During my first campaign for mayor, I pledged to myself and Almighty God that I would protect the rights of all the citizens of the City of Columbus. Tonight, before you and my maker, I renew that pledge. Thank you for inviting me, and may God grant you wisdom and good fortune during your conference. Welcome to Columbus," he said with arms raised and two fingers in a 'v for victory' position.

Amidst tepid applause, Terry hastened the mayor out the door and into his car. The pastors were somewhat surprised at his quick exit but assumed he needed to attend to other business, although it was Sunday night.

CHAPTER 9

AS THEY RETURNED TO CITY HALL, the mayor told Terry to arrange a meeting with Safety Director Puchik and WCI officials first thing Monday morning. Bringing lower-level officials to his office was not his style, but this time, he wanted to hear facts directly from those involved, anticipating a need to address the black press hyping this inmate's death. He wanted this story over once and for all. Since Gross had talked to the reporter, *The Dispatch* published no more stories about Honor.

Terry was less concerned with *The Call and Post* headline than the mayor's ratings. His analysis showed the story so far was not affecting the election; that was all that mattered to him. Without *The Dispatch* on the warpath, his advice would be to ignore *The Call and Post* and quietly ride it out.

The following day, around the conference table in a room off the mayor's private office, Safety Director Bruno Puchik was busy writing orders to his subordinates. To his left, Terry Prince was shaking his head at the mayor's new poll numbers plummeting since the WCI "incident." A young lawyer from the City Attorney's office was at the far end. Haskel Gross sat with no one to talk to. The mayor began.

"Well, Mr. Gross. Am I correct? Is your name Gross? Let's start with you. Pardon my French, but what the hell happened at WCI?"

"Mr. Mayor, yes, I'm Haskel Gross, acting superintendent. Nice to meet you. We are still checking things out, but I want you to know how bad our hard-working staff feels about the unfortunate events that night, despite all of our diligent efforts, we..."

"Save the speech for the press. Just tell me what happened."

"Yes, sir. On Sunday night a week ago, guards called the EMT squad to rush an inmate named Honor Wilson, who was awaiting trial on drug charges, to OSU Hospital. She died a few hours later. The coroner's office preliminary report said she died from cancer. I wasn't on duty then, but officers and inmates filled me in when I came to work. Both nurses and the doctor had seen her and found nothing unusual. Some say she might have overdosed. It was a bad scene, but there was nothing we could have done about it."

"So, you think we're covered? Some people are making a lot of noise about this. You know how important it is to my campaign to keep this matter quiet?" Turning to the others, he asked. "What do you think we should do?"

Puchik spoke up, knowing Haskel had no clue how to handle these matters. "If the autopsy says she died of natural causes, then I say we emphasize it. Certainly, it would defuse any claims of wrongdoing. If you want, I'll assign someone to investigate and report back."

"Mayor," said Terry Prince, "if she died of natural causes and nothing could have been done about it, then you might consider a photo op of you visiting her mother, who, according to *The Call and Post*, has been calling WCI. I can see TV cameras recording you comforting her, saying how sorry we are for her loss. It could be compelling. It should play well, and we may be able to use the clip later in a campaign ad."

"Mr. Mayor," said the young attorney at the end of the table, "on behalf of the City Attorney's office, I respectfully disagree with any of the aforementioned suggestions that you converse with the mother and/or with anyone else who might become a party to a lawsuit against the City. Words can be misunderstood. Apologies or expressions of sympathy can be misinterpreted as admissions of liability. It would be the advice of the Office of City

Attorney that you not publicly participate in this particular matter until we are confident that there will be no legal ramifications."

"Yes, but we would miss sending a strong message to the community," said Prince. "People want their mayor to care about others, including those we lock up at the Women's Bars and Grilled," chuckling at his attempt at humor.

"Well, let me think about it," Blandford said. "I don't imagine they will have a funeral until the coroner completes the final autopsy, so we have a little time. Bruno, we may need a short investigation to give us a clean bill of health, but let me think about how and who might conduct it. In the meantime, are there standards WCI follows?"

"Yes sir, there are," said Gross, delighted with being able to contribute to the conversation. "The State of Ohio, through the Bureau of Adult Detention, imposes standards, but frankly, Mr. Mayor, they are pretty minimal."

"I see. And does the Bureau conduct inspections?"

"Yes, we are inspected every two years."

"Did we pass our last one?"

"Of course we did. Every city in the state passed. As I said, the standards are pretty low."

"If we were inspected soon, would we pass again?"

"I'm sure we will."

"When are we due for inspection again?"

"Let's see; this is January... our last inspection was...why, come to think of it, we are due next month. I'm glad you reminded me. I'll tell my staff to get ready."

"Please call me as soon as you pass," Terry interrupted. "We may hold a news conference to make the announcement."

"Announcement?" asked Gross.

"Yes, a press conference announcing we passed inspection."

"I don't get it," said Gross. "You are going to create a news flash that WCI again passed a test every city in the state has passed for years?"

"You're right. You don't get it."

"After that, Terry," the mayor resumed, "as soon as this whole thing slips away, I'll think about talking to the mother." He rose. "Anything else? Thank you, gentlemen. That's all."

CHAPTER 10

LUTHER "LUCKY" RIVERS, MILLIE'S ex-husband, was doing a show at the Front Row Theater in Cleveland when Millie called with tragic news. Losing his favorite child was devastating. But as with most of his life, he lived it from a distance. He was relieved when Millie rejected his offer to come in early to help with the family. It would have meant being with his kids long enough for them to press him on why he hadn't seen or talked to them in months. He didn't need them to make him feel guilty.

After her call, he began beating himself up nightly on stage while singing the blues. Tears mixed with sweat when he sang the "Lean on Me" chorus and realized he was there, where he too needed somebody to lean on.

But no one could know how real and immediate his blues were. He did not immediately open his heart to the bartender who praised him. "Lucky, you never sounded so real." Later, he told the guys in the band that his eldest daughter had died and that he would be needing a little time off to go to the funeral. He could not admit that he hadn't visited her since she moved to Columbus. At the end of the last show, the band members, his family on the road, took up a collection and gave him $200. His voice cracked when he said, "I love you guys."

After finding his replacement for the band's gigs that weekend, Lucky began driving two hours southwest to Columbus the following morning. He expected to be alone there—his kids avoiding him, and his family from Tennessee absent.

The Matter of Honor

While driving I-71 south, he faced his self-created anguish. *It's too late; I'm too late. Someday*, he kept telling himself over the years, *I will leave the road and be the father I was meant to be*, but that day had come and gone. Honor had moved to Columbus many months before, and sometimes, like now, he was only a short drive away, yet he hadn't visited or called her or met his grandson. Soon, his visit would be to her dead body. What could he say now to her cold face? Would she hear his strained words about the many nights in cheap motels when he would open his wallet and lay her photograph by the side of his bed and dream about wonderful things they would do together? Would she hear his tales of daydreaming walks with her in Franklin Park or trips to the zoo? Would she taste the flavors of ice cream cones they never licked?

Over the years, he refused to let the reality of his absence obscure his fantasies of what he would do with her when he returned home. He always intended that on the first Someday in the month of Maybe, he would show her his garden of dreams where they would plant daisies together. Instead, he would soon plant her body in cold Ohio mud.

He pulled into a rest stop to dry his eyes. He tried to cheer himself up by recalling why they named her Honor. About when she was born, Lucky showed Millie the lyrics of Miles Davis' song "Four," where Davis described the four things you get out of life: Truth, Honor, Happiness, and Love. They were young, happy in love, and living their truth. By naming their daughter Honor, they hoped they would enjoy all that Miles told them life could offer. The song became a jazz standard, but their hopes disappeared like a faded dream.

Feeling refreshed after a long rest, he drove south, imagining Millie and their other children dancing in the cornfields along the way. He expected their rejections. He treated them no better than he treated Honor, his favorite. Still, he drove on; he had to.

Somehow, he convinced himself that they would grant him absolution after he pled for forgiveness. He knew he didn't deserve it and resolved to make it right by them. *I can change; I will change*, he kept telling himself between Mansfield and Columbus. But in his heart, he knew, as he felt the asphalt beneath his wheels, what the road to Hell was paved with.

Millie told him to meet her at the funeral home if he came to town by early afternoon. He arrived just as she'd finalized arrangements with the director for services she could not afford, even though Pastor Jenkins offered to let her use the church for free for her years of service.

Lucky paid little attention to the curved back of a woman in black standing next to a man also in black. He was about to leave when he heard a familiar voice say, "Lucky, is that you?" For years, her soft words in her low, liquid voice had awakened him in the morning and tucked him in at night. It had been his comfort food, warm and easy, sweet, and savory with a hint of a giggle. Today, it was cold and tasteless, flavored only with tear salt. Turning, he looked at her reddened eyes, runny nose, and ashen cheeks and opened his arms. She ran to him. "We've lost our little girl. She's gone. She's gone."

He said nothing while he lifted her to his heart and, in his rich baritone voice, quietly sang Nat Cole's "Too Young." It had been their song, their defiant statement of love. "They try to tell us we're too young to be in love." But, as the years tragically proved, they were right.

Her legs went limp, and her heart cried out for yesterday while he held Millie suspended in a moment past. For a brief second, they were kids and lovers again. In his arms, she gathered strength from the beauty of their past before returning to their ugly, awful reality. She gently pushed away as he glided her to a soft landing. Straightening herself, she introduced him to the funeral director.

"My deepest condolences," said the man in the well-worn black suit.

"Thank you," Lucky said. "I am Honor's father." They shook hands.

"My name is J. W. Ross. We just finalized the arrangements. The service will be at Millie's church, St Paul's. She has asked Pastor Jenkins to preside tomorrow at 11 a.m. Afterward, the body will be laid to rest in the Evergreen Cemetery."

The words "laid to rest" sank six feet into Lucky's heart. He choked while saying thank you.

Millie and Lucky walked from the funeral home to her car. "You're welcome to stay with us if you like," she offered.

"Thanks, but I found a place not far away," he lied. "Listen, I want to help out with the cost of the funeral, and the guys in the band chipped in too. Here is $250."

"Thanks. It will help a lot. Please come for dinner tonight and see the kids. I'll make barbequed shrimp, your favorite. See you at six," she said as she drove away.

Lucky made it to Resch's Bakery just before closing, where he got the last cake, a kid's chocolate and white round birthday cake, iced but without writing. It was the children's favorite, he recalled. As a stranger, he knocked at Millie's door on Sherman Avenue, not knowing what his welcome might be.

CHAPTER 11

BILLIE, LUCKY'S YOUNGEST daughter, opened the door.

"Hi, Daddy, come in. Dinner's almost ready," she said, turning her back and rushing inside, "Daddy's here, and he's got a box from Resch's."

He ventured in with a forced smile, placing the box on the small table beside the couch in the living room. As the kids came to the living room, he held out his arms as each red-eyed child, except Duke, dutifully approached him for a brief hug.

He wanted to console them but didn't know how, nor could they warm to his rare embraces. They all stood awkwardly in the hall until Millie came from the kitchen to give him a quick hug and announced, "Dinner will be in a few minutes."

They took their usual seats at the kitchen table, except Duke, the oldest, who moved over to let Lucky sit at the head of the table, where he sat years ago. Millie brought shrimp, rice, and vegetables on hot serving platters.

The conversation began with Miles, their second oldest boy, rambling on about seeing their family on the six o'clock news and how a newscaster said Honor died from a possible overdose, but an autopsy later said she hadn't taken drugs, and Mama was angry that the mayor had dissed Honor and the family, and she's been talking to lawyers and how *The Call and Post* ran stories about them, and after dinner, Pastor Jenkins was coming over to meet with them and how all his friends had been talking about him and his sister, and on and on.

Lucky nodded without saying much, trying to imagine what his children were going through. He marveled at Millie for keeping them together amidst this tumult. But what was most on his mind was this family meal, his chair among them, and a dinner made especially for him. He kept looking at them, as if he had never lived with them, which was almost true.

"I'm so proud of you kids," he suddenly announced.

"Pass the rice, please," said Duke.

"I hope we can find a way to get through this. It's the worst thing that has ever happened to us," said Lucky. "I feel especially bad that I haven't been here for you, and I know you won't believe how much I think about all of you and talk about you to everyone I know. My job takes me on the road, but I want you to know that you are on my mind wherever I go."

Duke suddenly left the table to go upstairs to the bathroom. Millie sat at the other end of the table, poking at her food, thinking dark thoughts during Lucky's apology, wondering if the kids would give him a pass. There was a long silence before Duke returned with the box Lucky had brought.

"Right, Dad. We are always on your mind. Huh? Look at this," he said, dropping the box on the table and revealing the undecorated birthday cake.

The family gasped.

"You don't even know, do you? You don't even know that today is Honor's birthday!" Duke screamed as he ran to his room.

CHAPTER 12

LUCKY LEFT BEFORE THE CAKE was cut and before Pastor Jenkins knocked on the door. Millie welcomed her minister into her living room, where they sat with an album containing pictures of Honor. Jenkins expressed the sympathy of congregation members before retrieving a notepad. As a spiritual and political leader, he brought fire and brimstone to the pulpit but was ice-cold when negotiating a new recreation center for his community. He was bitter to bigots but sweet to children.

Millie told him without his interrupting what little she knew of the circumstances of Honor's death. He tactfully reported to her that her daughter's arrest for seemingly no reason was not unusual, nor was hers the first inmate death he had encountered, although most others had died violently. But oddly, her death seemed more troubling to him and the community because it seemed that a failed system killed her rather than a random person. Then, Pastor Jenkins voice rose as he also made an announcement.

"Ms. Rivers, I bring news from the Black Ministers' Alliance. Today, we drafted a letter to the mayor demanding an investigation into the death of your daughter. More and more young people of color are dying while in the hands of law enforcement. It must stop. *The Call and Post* reported she received no medical care. Is that true?"

"She told me they wouldn't let her see the doctor for a while, and when they did, he didn't do anything to help her."

"They must be held accountable. Do you have a lawyer?

"I have asked her court-appointed lawyer, Mr. Alan Gold, to look into why she died."

"Will he bring justice to you and your family?"

"We pray he will, Pastor."

"Tomorrow, many of our sisters and brothers from the church will be with you, and the Ladies' Auxiliary will provide refreshments. We want you to know that you and your family are not alone.

"I will say a few words at the service. Now, let's sit a spell so you can tell me about what your daughter was like. Maybe your photo album can help us through this difficult conversation. She was your oldest, right? I remember I married her to a man from out of town. She seemed quiet but a child of God, no doubt. Didn't she move after the wedding?"

"Yes, to Chicago. His mother lived there, and they stayed there before she returned home after the divorce. Her baby, Winston Wilson, is now living with us. Her ex-husband, Reginald Wilson, Jr.—I call him Junior—lives in Chicago with his mother. I invited them to the funeral, but they probably won't come. Please don't mention him by name tomorrow."

"You have four other children, two boys and two girls. I remember seeing them in Sunday school."

"That's right. My oldest is Duke, who's now 16. Miles will be 15 in a few months, Ella is 13, and Billie is 10."

"All named Rivers?" he asked, writing quickly.

"Yes."

"Will your former husband attend?"

"Yes, as a matter of fact, Lucky came to dinner this evening, and he just left."

"Honor went to East High before she got married, didn't she?"

"Yes, that is where Duke goes now."

"Tell me more about what you know of her death. Take it slow. I know it's hard."

"I came home from Bible class that night. I remember because we studied the Psalm about giving justice to the poor. The kids told me that Honor had not come back from the store where she went for aspirin for her headache. I was a little worried she wasn't back but a little later, my neighbor, Ms. Ellie, knocked on my door to tell me that as she was coming home from her Bible class—we go to different churches—she walked by Benny's Quick Stop. There, she saw police taking Honor away in handcuffs. Well, Pastor, I almost passed out. How could a child of mine be arrested? She's never been in trouble in her life."

After wiping her eyes, she continued. "Honor called me later from jail, and we talked for a little while. I visited her the next day and tried to bring her a few things, but they wouldn't let me give them to her. She asked about Winston and told me how much she missed him. She said she was still having headaches, but they wouldn't let her see the doctor. She told them she was supposed to have a six-week checkup after the stillbirth. After weeks of complaining so much, she finally saw the jail doctor, but he didn't even look at her or take any tests.

"I only saw her a few times because their visiting hours don't match my work schedule. She looked worse each time I saw her. I complained to the guards that she looked terrible. They told me treatment was up to the doctor, but they wouldn't give me his name or phone number.

"One morning, I got a call from the mother of another inmate. She said Honor was very sick. I called the jail and asked them how she was doing. The guard told me that she was doing fine as far as she knew. Later that night, another guard called and told me my baby was dead. That's about all I know."

"We are saddened by her death but not surprised by the treatment she got," Pastor Jenkins said. "When I told the Black Ministers Alliance what I had learned from my sources, we all agreed that the day of her death would be a day to remember.

Many will not pay attention, and others will try to cover it up, but we will not forget. Let us know whatever your family needs. I also want to know how you and the kids are doing?"

"It's been hard, very hard. The good Lord dropped a heap of woes on me and my family over the years, but nothing like this. I don't know where to turn or who to ask. I'm lost, Pastor."

"You will find your way, Sister. Since you came to our church a few years back, I have found you are one of the strongest women in the auxiliary. You'll find your way; it just takes time. The Lord is watching. What about the kids?"

"They're doing as well as can be expected. Since Honor came home, it was amazing how quick she became part of our family again, like she was never gone. Oh, how I miss my Honor! She was my heart. Her death has probably hit Duke hardest, and I pray for him, Pastor. He has a temper."

"We're here for you. See you in the morning. May the good Lord bless you and your family," he said as he closed his notebook and walked to the door.

CHAPTER 13

Dawn was hours away when Reginald and his mother, Maureen, left her home in the Bronzeville area of Chicago to drive to Columbus for Honor's funeral. She waited until she warmed up before unbuttoning her fur coat. Her maroon Chrysler LeBaron, loaded with extras, made their seven-hour journey more comfortable but no less challenging.

They knew little about what had happened to Honor other than she died. Millie was brief, almost curt, when she made the obligatory call to Junior, giving him the grim news and inviting him to the funeral. Even through copper wire, he heard her contempt for his failure to support Honor and little Winston.

"Not so fast," Maureen said. "I want to get to the funeral alive."

"I know how to drive, Mom. Leave me alone."

"But it snowed last evening. The roads are slippery."

"I know what I'm doing, Mom."

"Well, I'm glad you finally know what you're doing."

They drove in silence for the next 30 minutes.

"I've never been to Columbus. Do most people live on farms?" she asked.

"If you had come to my wedding, you would know how big it is. It's the state capital. Ohio State University is huge, and there are many smaller schools there, like Columbus Technical Institute, where I went."

"You wouldn't have had to go there if you had kept up your grades at UIC. We both know it's a much better college, and you could've stayed in Chicago. When I was an editor at *Ebony*, we hired many UIC students as interns. You could have gone anywhere in the country if you had worked hard at the Chicago Lab High School. Maybe after college, you could have worked at Seaway, like your father. As bank VP, he would have found you a solid position. Your father, may he rest in peace, and I had great plans for you, Reggie."

"I know I am your great disappointment. But you didn't ask me what I wanted. I never wanted to sit at a bank desk and look important. Look, we're almost to Indianapolis, and we should get there by 10:30."

CHAPTER 14

EARLY AT HOME, MILLIE went from room to room, banging on bedroom doors and the door of their only bathroom, hurrying anyone who was slowing things down.

The boys were quiet as they donned their black suits (Duke wearing the newer suit, while his younger brother, Miles, wore Duke's hand-me-down from last year), clean white shirts, and polished shoes. Duke stood before the mirror, primping his Afro.

"I've never been to a funeral," said Miles. "Have you?"

"Yeah. They ain't pretty. Last year, I went to Ahmed's after he was beat to death by some fat white kid and his buddies. Cops didn't do nothin', never even put someone on the case. Later, somebody told me a lieutenant said, 'Good, one less spook in town' and made it a cold case. His funeral was rough."

"Will they really put Honor in a box?" asked Miles.

"That's how they do it."

"And they'll shut the box and put it in the ground somewhere?"

"That's what they do."

"And then what happens?"

"Pastor Jenkins will say words, and we all go home."

Miles shook his head. "That don't make sense."

Although Millie's kids seldom got new clothes, Ella,13, got newer clothes because Honor had been much larger. Billie, younger than Ella, learned to take a strong interest in Ella's clothing choices, knowing she would be wearing them next.

Today, each wore a black skirt with a sweater. Ella wore boots that zipped up the side, while Billie wore her school shoes. Millie would not allow them to wear makeup in church, so Ella fixed her straightened hair while Billie played with a doll Honor had given her. They had already moved Honor's clothes and Winston's baby things out of their room.

"Do you think Winston will remember his mom?" Billie asked.

"I don't think so. I once heard someone say kids most remember the smell of folks who die. What do you remember about her?"

"I remember how she would stop whatever she was doing and sit and play with me. I can still remember how she helped me with my homework before she went to Chicago. She always made me feel like she wanted me to learn, so I tried harder. She listened like she really cared."

"What I remember most," said Ella, "is how hard she worked taking care of Winston even when she was so tired. I think she could have been someone important someday—not a star or stuff like that— but someone that everybody knew cared about others. I want to be like her."

"Yeah, me too."

In her room, Millie changed Winston's diaper and dressed him, adjusting his top while sensing him staring into her tearful eyes. Despite what *The Dispatch* said, she could not tell him that his mother was a fine woman who had great dreams for him. He was too young to understand. Honor had sworn to herself and Millie to devote her life to his success. Millie often wondered why Honor did not have dreams of success for herself as well.

Winston touched Millie's heart. She saw a determination in his eyes that she did not see in her own kids. She knew he would be special. He even began sporting a swagger while toddling. She lifted him to her mouth and whispered in his little ear, "You have become a part of our family now, Winston, and I'm gonna help you someway be the man your mama dreamed of. That's a promise, Lil Man!" After putting a little suit on him, she took him back into her arms and squeezed him with all her heart.

CHAPTER 15

THE RIVERS FAMILY DROVE a few blocks north of their home to the church nearby. As she got older, Millie understood more the fragility of family and how precious moments together—in happiness or tragedy—were.

Approaching the church steps, she cautioned her brood to be on their best behavior. Never wanting to be in the limelight, she hurried them inside, politely avoiding long visits with congregants already there to express their sorrow.

She saw Lucky was already seated in the second row on the right, while to her surprise, Junior and his mother, Maureen, were on the left. Alan Gold sat on the aisle in a back row near a young black man she did not recognize, wearing sunglasses and keeping his coat collar high, and a young black woman with a pen and steno notebook was seated nearby.

J.R. Ross had placed Honor's open coffin below the altar. When Millie saw the coffin, her knees buckled, but Duke and Miles grabbed her elbows and gently guided her to her pew. The crowd settled in their places as quiet organ music wafted above them. Pastor Jeremiah Jenkins rose after Miles and Ella read hymns and the choir sang,

"Can I hear Amen?" he wailed in his husky voice without a microphone.

A feeble "Amen" came from the funeral assembly.

"In the name of Jesus, can I hear AMEN?" Jenkins exhorted his lackadaisical flock.

"AMEN!" they called enthusiastically.

"Praise God. Thank you, my brothers and sisters. We've come together to pay our respects to sister Honor Wilson, who died so young, leaving behind her parents, brothers, and sisters and her young baby. Like you, I asked myself, why did she die? What is to become of her child? What caused her death? What does her death mean to our people?

"I talked to her mother, Millie Rivers, and she told me her family's woes. I spoke with some people in our community, and they shouted their outrage. I spoke to God, and he told me to look to the Good Book.

"A few months ago, Honor returned from Chicago to Columbus and her mother and family. She came to start a new life. God transplanted her here like a beautiful flower eager to bloom in our soil. While recovering from the loss of her stillborn baby, she still found the strength to take care of both her living child and Millie's children and also to apply for jobs. What a woman.

"Then, the police took her prisoner. Her life was cut short while in the hands of city officials at the Women's Correctional Institution. Today, our hearts are filled with sadness for her family's suffering, her little boy, Winston, who will never know his mama, and for the gloom we feel, knowing another sister has been taken from us. We find comfort in knowing that Honor is with sweet Jesus in heaven.

"Life is fragile. So are words. A few months ago, she returned to us from Chicago to bloom here in Columbus. Now, instead, what we have is gloom. Bloom—gloom, a change in only one letter, tells us the difference between a world with Honor and one without.

"Now, some of us are angry and demand retaliation. Young folk talk of revolution. Some of us just sit back and say it is the usual way black folk die; ain't nothing we can do about it. Her death confuses us. We can't understand God's will. We don't know what our city is doing. How do we make sense that she was taken to jail healthy and in a few weeks, died there? Who is responsible? Who will guide us through these senseless times?

"When I looked at the Good Book, where God told me to look, I found Paul and Silas, who, like Honor, went to jail. Luke tells us in Acts 16 that the Lord ordered Paul, during his journeys spreading The Word, to remove an evil spirit from a fortune-teller. After he removed the spirit, she could no longer prophesize. People who made money off the soothsayer took Paul and Silas to a magistrate. They accused them of being Jewish, having manners different from Romans, and having evil ways. They said the two brought confusion because they were different. And the crowd rose up together, the Good Book says, and the magistrate ordered Paul and Silas to be beaten with rods.

"What can we say about those accusers? What filled their hearts? And what about the magistrate? What was he doing when he ordered them beaten?

"I'll tell you what he was doing. He was doing prejudice, ugly prejudice. Prejudice like we see today. Look around you. You know what I'm talking about. Prejudice is the soup of the devil. Yes, it is. Beelzebub begins by taking a hock of poisonous ignorance; then, he scalds it in despair and flavors it with fistfuls of hate. When folks eat it, they stuff themselves with hate. Like the devil, they become hate-filled. Like the devil, they become evil. Yes, they become just like the devil. My brothers and sisters, we've got to fight the devil!" he shouted.

"That's right," shouted a parishioner.

"We've got to fight the devil!"

"Amen, brother," shouted another.

"We've got to spit out his poison soup! Instead, we must drink from the cup of love. We've got to love ourselves, and we've got to give grace to others. And even when we fight, we must do what Paul did while imprisoned. When the jailer asked forgiveness for putting Paul and Silas in the stocks, the Good Book says Paul showed him love and baptized the jailer that very night.

"In the morning, when the magistrate learned Paul was a Roman, he ordered the jailer to release them. But Paul refused to leave his cell. In the name of the Almighty, he said, 'No, that won't do.' He made that magistrate come down and release him himself. Yes, he did! He made him spit out the bitter soup of hatred in front of everyone. He made the magistrate taste his own prejudice. Only then did Paul and Silas walk away from jail to spread the word of God to others. Paul made that politician fess up to his bigotry and his sins. He made 'em fess up. Hallelujah!

"My brothers and sisters, we got to follow Paul and make the city fess up for Honor and all the other young black men and women they wronged. Like the old spiritual says, 'We got to keep our eye on the prize and hold on!' We ask the good Lord to help us hold on to the prize, as we say Amen!"

Pastor Jenkins then looked to the back of the room directly into the eyes of Alan amid the Amens and Hallelujahs from those assembled.

The choir began singing, "Hold on, Hold on, Keep your eye on the prize, hold on."

The congregation sang the chorus, "Hold on, Hold on," as pallbearers carried the casket out to the hearse. Honor's family followed behind. Mourners stepped from the dim church into the cold daylight. They walked a little straighter, their heads slightly higher, looking ahead toward a new horizon. While Millie remained silent, the Pastor's message touched her very core, as it had others.

After they interred Honor, cold and hungry congregants returned to the church, where a hot and sumptuous repast prepared by the Ladies' Auxiliary was waiting. Lucky said goodbye to his family at the cemetery and drove back to his band.

Standing by the entrance door, Millie and most of her family thanked everyone for coming. Ella sat with Winston near the kitchen, unbuttoning his snowsuit. Soon, well-wishers crowded in, filling the room with lively conversation. Millie and her family later took seats near Ella.

The president of the Ladies' Auxiliary stopped by to comfort Millie and to let her know who had made which dishes. Millie listened carefully so she would know whom to thank later. Then Honor's high school friends came by, many with young children in their arms. Alan Gold paid his respects, after which Millie introduced him to congregants who knew Honor.

Ms. Ellie, Millie's neighbor who had told her of Honor's arrest, stopped by.

"Millie, my Bible study group at Trinity Baptist is praying for you and your family. One lady in our study group said her husband was arrested and nearly died at the men's workhouse because they wouldn't give him his blood pressure medicine. I declare I don't know how they live with themselves. Have you learned anything more about what happened to Honor?"

"Not yet, Ms. Ellie. Do you see the white man talking to folks over there? He was Honor's court-appointed attorney and is looking into it for us."

"As the Good Book says, 'Remember those in prison as if you were with them.' We will not forget."

"Thank you, Ms. Ellie. Believe me, neither will I, and I will keep asking until I find out what happened to her."

Maureen and Junior stopped by. "Thank you for inviting us, Millie. Our deepest sympathies to you and your family. We are filled with grief, aren't we, Reginald?"

"Yeah, Mom."

"Thank you for coming, Maureen. Was the trip hard?" Millie asked, looking toward the guests behind them.

"Not bad. Reggie did the driving. Would you like to hold Winston, Reggie? May we, Millie? How is he doing? Oh, he is so precious."

"Well, if you want to. He is doing fine with us."

Maureen crossed over to Ella, who had just retrieved a bottle for the baby.

"May I feed him?" asked Maureen, taking the chair beside her. Ella handed the bottle to her. She was thrilled. Reggie touched his son's cheek before going to the dessert table.

CHAPTER 16

AFTER LEAVING THE CHURCH, Reggie and his mother began driving back to Chicago. Millie had been slightly less than polite when speaking to Junior, her contempt for him not lost on Maureen.

Millie always rued the night Honor went to that party off Ohio State's campus and came home gushing over a guy she met with hazel eyes and curly hair. His nickname was Junior, and he danced well and had nice threads. Honor had had a few dates before with a guy who became a disk jockey, but Millie could tell that the days of the DJ were over.

Neither mother approved of the marriage. Maureen did not favor her only son marrying beneath him. After all, she was a Bronzeville woman, a light-skinned member of the colored aristocracy of black Chicago. She earned that position when she married Reginald Wilson Sr., vice president of Seaway Bank. They then assumed the mantle by purchasing a home in Hyde Park. They cemented their place among the elite 400 when, after years of dedication, their only living child was accepted as a student at the University of Chicago Lab. Reginald deserved better than marrying some dark-skinned girl from Columbus.

As they drove, Maureen mused aloud, "Isn't Winston cute? I loved holding him—such a darling. I love his name as well. I'm so happy we chose it. Your father would've approved of a name fit for what we thought would be his station in life.

"Columbus seems like a nice little place, but I would have thought Reverend Jenkins—was that his name?—well, whatever-could have presented his eulogy in a more refined manner. But perhaps that is their way in places like that. We would never hear Scripture described so crudely at Olivet Baptist. I suppose he is all they can attract to this remote location," Maureen said, lifting her chin.

"I don't know what you mean," Reggie said, looking toward Chi-Town. "I felt something when he spoke. I mean, everyone else seemed moved by his words."

"Well, yes, but his manner of speech sounded ignorant to me. Our people don't need leaders who talk crudely. He should encourage his congregants—particularly the young—to speak clearly, use proper grammar, and convey an aura of education. Like you were taught at the Lab."

"Yes, perhaps it would be nice, Mother, but I don't think talking like a professor is what his people want."

"Well, perhaps, Reggie, but how can they improve themselves if they aren't hearing men of words?"

"But folks don't listen to men of words who talk the talk but don't walk the walk."

"I think they need better people to show them the way."

"Like you, Mother? Are you going to show them the way? Are you gonna save anyone in Columbus? Say, turn up the radio. Isn't that the new Stevie Wonder song?"

They listened to Stevie sing about a nasty boy wishing back to the days when he was sent to the office for smokin' cigarettes and writin' on school walls.

Reggie thought of his past and smiled. Maureen thought of her grandson's future and sighed.

CHAPTER 17

HONOR'S DEATH DELAYED GOLD'S interviews at WCI with his other court-appointed clients. On Monday afternoon, he drove to the south end of town to discuss their cases with them. He gave his list of inmates to the guard at the desk, went to the attorney conference room, and took a seat. When he finished with one inmate, the guard replaced her with the next one on his list. As he reviewed their charges and arrests, he also asked if any knew anything about Honor's death. Although most said no, two mentioned a tall, black inmate who might have been her friend. They told him her first name was Johni. That's all they knew.

After the interviews, on a whim, he asked the guard at the front desk if she knew a tall inmate named Johni.

"Oh, you mean Johnetta LaGreaux. She's the only one I know they call Johni."

"Yes, she must be the one. Let me speak with her, please."

Johni took a seat in the attorney conference room with her arms crossed. Her makeup, or what little she was allowed in prison, highlighted a woman of exotic beauty, despite a scar on her right cheek given to her by her last pimp before she turned independent. She sat back, mute, arms crossed, long legs extended, and looked away from him.

"Hello, Ms. LaGreaux. I'm attorney Alan Gold. Millie Rivers, Honor Wilson's mother, has asked me to help her find out why her daughter died here. You recall Honor, don't you? I heard you might know something about her death."

"Who is you? And what you want from me?"

"Honor's mother just wants some answers. I am trying to help her, Ms. LaGreaux. May I call you Johni?"

"Sure. Why she got a white lawyer?"

"I was Honor's court-appointed lawyer in the criminal case. Guess I'm the only lawyer she could get so far. The authorities are kind of tight-lipped about her death, other than to say what I already know, that the coroner said she died from cancer."

"How did you find me?"

"Other inmates told me you two were tight. Word travels fast, if you know what I mean."

"Well, I ain't no doctor. I can't tell you why she died."

"No, I know that. I'm trying to learn more about how she was treated, what conditions were like, etc. Look, she came here apparently healthy and died within a few weeks. That's not right. Maybe jail officials could have helped. What do you think?"

Johni stared at the wall for a moment. "What's your name again?"

"Gold, Alan Gold."

"Come see me next week. I gotta check out a few things."

"Fair enough. Please put me on your visitors' list. The next guard may not allow a conference like this."

The following day, Gold called Millie.

"I wanted to report back. It may not be much, but I might have found somebody inmates told me about with information concerning your daughter's death. So, I met her yesterday when I was at WCI, but she clammed up. Told me to contact her next week. I'm not sure she has anything relevant to say, but I just wanted to let you know."

"Don't worry about Johni. Someone called last night, checking you out for her. She didn't know whether you were a cop or something else. Folks from all over have been calling me since Honor died. Some have kin in WCI, and some have been there themselves. I told her you were with me. She'll talk to you now, but I don't know what she'll say."

When Johni met Gold the following week, things were different. She sat forward in her chair, looking directly into his face. After providing some basic info, she answered Gold's personal questions about herself. Cops had killed her younger sister as she happened into a raid in progress. Then, a candy man gave Johni drugs until she was addicted before forcing her into prostitution. She was 15 at the time.

Even though her grades were good, she dropped out of school as a junior to take to the streets to support her mother, who'd become disabled from severe hypertension, and her habit. After the pimp carved a mark on her face, Johni left him and began working the streets herself. Occasionally, she would wind up in WCI. Despite the difficulty, her mother would still make exhausting trips to see Johni at WCI.

As Johni explained to Gold, "As a working girl, visits here is like part of the cost of doing b'ness. Me? I sell and service. Now, sometimes, while I'm servicing a john, cops interfere with my b'ness relations, if you can dig. They put bracelets on my beautiful wrists but never on the john. What did I do that he didn't? It don't take no genius to know that ain't fair.

"So, they take me here once in a while. Judges usually give me a break, guards leave me alone, and, whoosh, I'm out in a few weeks. This time, the damn judge gave me six months. My mom watches my stuff while I'm gone, and soon I'll be back in b'ness. It ain't right and it's hard, but it's all I know. But this place needs to change. It may look white and smell bleachy clean, but it's a nasty place."

Gold then gently moved the conversation toward Honor. Despite her tall, tough body, Johni's voice quivered.

"I called her BabyCakes from the first day we was here. I was working in the back of the Fancy Club when cops busted the place and brought me here. Can't say why I sat down next to her. We still had shackles on. She looked so helpless, like a big little child.

Didn't know how to act. She must have been really scared. Usually, I don't pay others no mind, but she was different—big but scrawny. You know what I'm saying? I liked her as soon as we talked.

"She wasn't no troublemaker; she was a trouble-finder. She found trouble from the first. They gave her a top bunk in the dorm, but she was too big and achy to climb. I mean, I ain't no scientist, but getting her up to a top bunk was like messin' with gravity, if you know what I mean. I tried to get them motherfuckers to give her a bottom bunk, but they just kept sayin 'Rules is Rules,' like Jesus told them she got to be closer to heaven.

"Then she found trouble with her crazy bunkmate sleepin' in the bottom bunk. Fabiola started seeing funny things and acting all weird on her. Why they stuck BabyCakes with her I don't know, but she was a real trip."

"What was Honor's health like?"

"She told me she was healing after a stillbirth when she got arrested. She moved slow and said how tired she was all the time. She got worse. I watched her start to lose weight and turn pale. She got mad after telling them pitiful nurses she was supposed to have a six-week checkup, and they called her a liar. Her eyes started to bulge. I didn't see her for a day or two before the squad took her away from the Hole, but Puddin did."

"Who's Puddin?"

"Don't know her real name. I s'pose I could find out. She was in the Hole with BabyCakes."

"What's the Hole?"

"That's where they put you either 'cause they want to punish you or 'cause they want to treat you."

"I don't understand. Why would they use the same place for punishment they use as an infirmary?"

"Mr. Gold, you won't understand lots of things around here, but it's what we live with."

The guard announced, "Time's up. LaGreaux. Let's go."

Gold shook his head as he walked through the WCI parking lot. *I've been coming here at least once or twice a month for years, yet I knew nothing about the Hole. What else don't I know?*

CHAPTER 18

PROUD OF ACCOMPLISHING both assignments, Haskel Gross marched to the superintendent's office to submit his minority employment report and to boast of his briefing with *The Dispatch* reporter. He had cleverly but subtly urged the reporter to move on from Honor Wilson's death, suggesting an overdose probably caused it. He was nearly gleeful relating a callback from the reporter, who said another reporter would add a quick note about Honor as part of an in-depth story on drugs in central Ohio. He clicked his heels as he announced that the reporter covering WCI told him she was done with Honor.

Puchik looked up for a second, nodded, and swept his hand across the air dismissing Haskel before returning to a book he was reading on the military invasion of Midway. *I never get any credit*, Haskel complained to himself, returning to WCI without a gold star on his forehead.

Today, Haskel's agenda was selecting an applicant for the vacant lieutenant position. No woman had ever been appointed before, and two were front runners. Sgt. Betty Lynks, a 10-year guard, had scored well on her application, enjoyed a fine reputation, and had proven herself in emergencies during several difficult episodes. Sgt. Viola Mitchell was a five-year veteran whose application and experience were middling, but she was hard-working and dedicated.

Haskel couldn't care less who won. Promotions were about him, not them. They both wanted the job, but Mitchell wanted it more. Lynks was a stuck-up white bitch. She kept to herself, and he knew by her eyes she was always thinking about something else or someone other than him. He detested her kind of woman—hard to please, stuck up, self-contained. *Fuck her, she's too much trouble.*

On the other hand, Mitchell viewed herself as a rising black star who would do what she had to do to get ahead, he thought. Besides, he could tell she had a thing for him. The way she said "yes sir" and "no sir" satisfied his ego, even though he wasn't quite sure they were always on the same page.

He scheduled interviews the following day between 3:30 and 4:30 p.m. He would start with Lynks and see if the bitch would give. If not, he would end the interview and move on to Mitchell. He interrupted his game-planning long enough to write brief notes to both informing them of their interviews. He looked forward to seeing them groveling beneath his feet.

Tomorrow, he would either have his way with at least one of them or appoint no one. *The lieutenant position has been vacant for more than a month, and if these two don't come around, it can stay vacant till I find someone who will. There is always someone who knows what it takes and will play along to get along.* He leaned back in his chair like a wizened old philosopher. He could hardly wait.

The next day, he heard a knock on his metal door.

"Come in," said Haskel Gross in a very businesslike manner. He was seated behind his desk wearing a new shirt flavored with too much after-shave. He had played this role before. He remained cool and in charge on the outside, while inside, he was on fire.

Sgt. Lynks pushed open the door to Gross's office, pausing for a second before taking her first step. She guided her left leg smoothly with a casualness not typical in those seeking promotions. She gazed about the room like a potential homebuyer inspecting a den, overlooking anyone sitting in it. She's already playing hard to get, *This is my show, damn it, and the bitch was already trying to take over.* She ambled forward until she stood in front of his desk, arms at her side, and waited. Looking down at him, she said, "Hello, Mr. Gross. Thank you for this interview."

Gross looked up at her face, unable to pierce through her cold blue eyes. She usually called him Haskel, but today, she was formal, using just the right words for an interviewee. Was she doing it to mock him? He blurted out before he could stop himself, "Thank you for coming. I appreciate it."

She sat down and glanced at him with her eyebrow raised as if to say, "Your response was barely adequate. Try to improve if you know how."

The play was going badly for him. He was not quite sure what was happening nor how to take back the lead. He felt like an actor who forgot his lines and could not fake a familiar scene.

"I see that you have applied for the vacant lieutenant's position." He waited for her reply, expecting her to grovel, according to his script. Instead, she tossed him another silent, frigid stare from her chiseled face, taunting him, 'Not good enough, Haskel. Keep talking.' He cleared his throat. "Your test results, as you know, place you in the top three. Let's discuss about what this promotion would mean to you and what you would give for it." As soon as he said it, he realized how clumsy it sounded. She confirmed his ineptness by raising that one eyebrow again. Another long silence.

"What I mean is, why do you think I should appoint you to this position?"

"Well, Mr. Gross, I do my best. My record speaks for itself. You've seen my work. You know I can do the job."

He sensed she was talking down to him again, but he was powerless to retake the narrative she was controlling, mainly through silence. He decided there was no chance in hell she would bow to his wishes, and he'd best go no further. After a few more failed attempts, he ceased trying,

THE MATTER OF HONOR

"I'll let you know soon. Thank you for stopping by."

She rose, popped him another pose before exiting, and nodded in a way that told him she knew what he was up to, and if he were to try anything, she would file the biggest harassment lawsuit the city had ever seen.

CHAPTER 19

"Hello, anyone here?" Sgt. Mitchell asked as she stuck her head in his office door. "I am here for an interview... I'm not sure I have the time right...for lieutenant...were you expecting me now?... I'm not good at remembering appointments... I hope I'm not interrupting anything... If you're busy, I can... Oh, I forgot my notebook. Anyway, well, whatever," she said while still leaning through the door but not stepping inside.

Haskel raised his eyes from the papers on his desk to see a short, slightly plump black woman popping her head into his office. He hid a smile as he directed her in, thinking, *This is more like it. She won't act like a stuck-up bitch the way Lynks did. I've got this one. Another fish in the stream.* He was neither aware nor concerned with her struggles to succeed at WCI.

She'd left Weirton, West Virginia, where she was born on July 1, 1947, the day the city was created from one of the largest unincorporated areas in America. As a steel town, Weirton rode up and down on the roller-coaster of steel prices. Her daddy started at the mill right out of high school. Her mom packed his lunch every day in a black dome lunchbox with a thermos of hot coffee. Viola was home from fifth grade the day two white men from the plant came to tell her mother that daddy died on the factory floor. Mama got a little money from worker's compensation but had to find a job. By the time Viola was 12, she cleaned house and cooked dinners for the two of them. After her mother died, and with no kin left in Weirton, Mitchell moved, becoming another from West Virginia who learned the four Rs: readin, 'ritin, 'rithmetic, and road to Columbus.

She stayed at first at the YWCA downtown on 4th Street until she found a job in the south end at Buckeye Steel Castings. Making steel castings was dirty work, but the pay was better than most jobs. She joined the Second Baptist Church, the oldest black Baptist church in Columbus, and soon became a Sunday regular, sitting at the far end of the fourth pew.

Some days after work, she would go to the main library and read before going to her small apartment. While reading *The Columbus Dispatch* one day, she came across a want ad for a job as a guard at WCI. Her score was second highest on the entrance exam, and she happily quit Buckeye Steel despite a pay cut. She proudly donned a WCI uniform, vowing never to return to factory work. A few years later, she applied for a sergeant's position. She failed to make the top three on her first try, was not selected on her second attempt, and was finally promoted two years ago. Unmarried, her life was the job, the library, and church.

"Come in, Sgt. Mitchell. Sit down. Make yourself comfortable. How ya been?" he said while thumbing through his papers.

"Real good. Yes, sir, I've been working on my..."

"You must have really studied for the test. You made the top three on your first try."

"Well, yes, I worked very hard. I try."

"I can tell. You want this promotion, don't you?"

"Yes sir, I do. To me, it means... 'Course there are a lot of qualified people besides me... I just think I could... But I ain't got the education of some... Still, I think I could do a good job as lieutenant."

"Well, my appointment recommendation goes to the Safety Director, and he always appoints my choice. So, this time we have together is important."

"Yes, I know how important this is."

"Great. We got that straight. Now, tell me why you think I should pick you."

"Well, sir, I've got a really good record... Don't hardly miss any work... I've been blessed with good health... I think I work well with the people at WCI... no incidents on my watch, except for that woman a year ago who got looney in the dorm room, but I didn't know until later what she had done and reported it as soon as I knew. I mean, who woulda know'd she would try to off herself? And I work very hard."

"Your supervisors are pleased with you?"

"Yes, sir, I think they're satisfied with my work. No demerits or discipline."

"You know, it's important to please your supervisors."

"Oh, I know. People got to be happy up and down the line."

"Sometimes, you gotta go the extra mile for your boss."

"Yes, sir. You said it true. You got to keep your boss happy."

"Because if the boss ain't happy, ain't no one happy," he said, his heartbeat starting to quicken. "Like me. I'm your boss."

"Yes, I suppose you... Course I think of the lieutenant as my... but I guess you're right. You're my boss too."

"Well, what would you do to keep me happy?"

"I'd certainly do whatever I could to keep you satisfied. I mean... I hope you're already pleased... I must've satisfied someone, or I wouldn't be a sergeant."

"Whatever you could. That's right, that's right. Whatever you could. Now, you see, I've got some special needs to make me happy, if you understand what I mean."

"Oh, you mean like special assignments? I like work that's out of the ordinary... Something new is a challenge... Of course, I like my work... I'd be glad to help."

"Well, some of my needs are kinda personal. You dig?"

"I suppose we all bring ourselves to the job, and it's just how things are. I understand."

"Do you want it?"

"I do, sir. I worked hard to get where I got."

The Matter of Honor

"How bad do you want it?" he said, breathing harder.

"I really want it... It would mean a lot to me to... I'd be proud to be lieutenant and bend over backward to satisfy you that you made the right decision."

"Really?" That image got him more excited. The moment had arrived.

"Well, I'm gonna take you up on that. You bend over, and I'll get ready," he said with a giggle, as he turned around to unzip his pants. *This is gonna be sweet. I spotted her from afar. I guess I know women pretty well.* When he turned to mount the conquest he had so carefully arranged, he found Mitchell standing upright, fully dressed, staring at his middle, the whites of her eyes jumping off her dark face.

Before abruptly leaving, she said, "Mr. Gross, you ain't right."

"Bitch. You just lost your chance," he said to the wall as he turned around and zipped up.

CHAPTER 20

THE DEATH OF HONOR, WHICH seemed to be the only reason for the poll results showed that the mayor had slipped 13 percent in black wards and 4 percent in white ones. They persuaded Terry Prince to arrange a press conference for Blandford to talk about this unfortunate matter and put it to sleep. Before the conference, Terry called Mr. Foxx, the owner and publisher of *The Columbus Dispatch* and the largest radio and TV stations in town, to arrange his cooperation in the press conference to end coverage of the death of Honor.

To Terry, press conferences were not meant to be confrontations between political leaders and reporters seeking truth. Far from it. They were opportunities for candidates to manipulate stories for political gain. Truth might occur, but the goal was gain. To achieve his goal, Terry usually skipped reporters and communicated directly with news media owners. Mr. Foxx, a big supporter of the mayor, obliged him.

In this case, Terry was sure he could bring around those reporters who might be straying from supporting Blandford by serving up his tried-and-true recipe for "Turn-Around Masserole." He often cooked it when incidents like this threatened his candidates. His recipe went something like this:

Start with a sincere dollop of, "We will conduct a thorough investigation to get to the bottom of this" into a mixing media bowl. Add a handful of "We will appoint a commission soon to evaluate our procedures." Pour it into a larger bowl of "What took place seems incomprehensible" while flavoring in a pinch of "We really care!" Then, let the whole thing cool for a long time—a very long time. Serve the mixture tepid on a bed of sincerity much, much later but only if anyone really hungers for it. Actually, it's best when not served at all, letting it decompose until no one remembers what the dish was, or why it was made at all.

The mayor's speech, as he planned to write it, would provide the media with two talking points: Wilson died of a fast-growing cancer to which, unfortunately, she would have succumbed anyway, even if the finest doctors had been at her bedside; and second, a mild suggestion (certainly not an accusation!) that she could have been on drugs. The first point would diminish the outrage, regardless of what those WCI jokers had done, while the second (if done delicately) would lead folks in another direction toward a serious, although unrelated, problem.

All the while, he would present the mayor as a leader (without actual involvement) in WCI activities, a man in charge (but not responsible), a commander who cared about his people (even when results were inevitable), an empathetic public servant heartbroken by this senseless tragedy (beyond his or anyone's control), and a stern (but compassionate) admiral dedicated to keeping the crew in line on the tightly run ship called *The Great City of Columbus*. If misdeeds occurred, an unlikely event because he always hired only the finest people, he would take decisive (although undefined) action.

His speech would be sincere, emotional—but not tear-jerking—and forthright, without disclosing details or suggesting explanations or solutions. The mayor would conclude sympathetically but without either offering an apology or offending anyone. It would be magical.

After starting a draft for the mayor to mouth, Terry was pleased with his outline. He laid odds that Blandford's numbers would rise within three weeks. Terry thrived on damage control. Over the years, he had honed his skills in creating diffusion, obfuscation, and flummoxation to such perfection that he was confident he could handle any "irregularity" without allowing his politician to admit anything, even if caught holding the bloody murder weapon. His art was as old as democracy and as nuanced as human emotions.

He often boasted of his body of work among politicians across the country. Over the years, his words had emerged from the dishes he cooked up for his many political talking heads who won over electorates again and again. Ah, he could almost smell his latest Turn-Around Masserole cooking on Blandford's hot seat.

Working through the night, editing and re-editing the mayor's speech, Terry reduced it to about 1,500 words, around 10 minutes—long enough to hint significance (containing four quotable soundbites to feed his media pigeons) but not so general as to require more details.

As was his custom, he did not share his masterpiece with City Hall members who might try to edit or take credit for it. Because of his generous use of vague generalities, it required no fact-checking. As a *coup de grace*, he would alert the press that due to the "ongoing nature of the investigation," the mayor, remaining above the fray, would be unable to answer questions. Through Terry, the mayor would perform the highest form of what Muhammad Ali called, "bobbing and weaving." Nobody would lay a glove on his man Blandford.

Terry sighed in relief when Polly told him about the mayor's hectic schedule this coming week. It meant that he probably would not have time to preview Terry's speech. He usually was not so lucky. Previous politicians had not always appreciated his creations. They'd edit and thereby mutilate what he'd created. He considered his speeches works of art not to be trifled with, especially by those giving them. A politician should neither write his own speeches nor express his true thoughts. He recalled the mayor's fiasco at that black church the other night trying to go it alone. *Amateurs.*

As the press conference was about to begin, Terry rushed the mayor toward the brightly lit podium in his conference room filled with carefully selected reporters, saying, "Mr. Mayor, your speech is waiting on the lectern, triple-spaced as you prefer. It is short, only about ten minutes. Your address will be very moving if delivered slowly and with sincerity that only a person with your skills can demonstrate. Please remember to raise your voice at the end and say, 'and may God bless this wonderful city.' I will then jump in and inform the press we can take no questions, and we will leave quickly to attend the opening of that new park on the west side."

With that, Terry gently nudged the mayor toward the lectern raised slightly higher than the TV cameras to catch him looking his best and enable him to speak down to those reporters Terry invited, including those whom Mr. Foxx had instructed.

Blandford and Prince had worked together long enough for the mayor to sense the timbre of Terry's work without reading much past the first several sentences. By then, he was in character, emoting as Terry intended and transforming Terry's words into a moving and heartfelt valediction.

That day, Mayor Blandford was at his best—beginning in a businesslike tone, gaining composure while finding motivation. Pausing between phrases, he acted as if the pain of Honor's death prevented him from continuing. But the real reason for the delays was to allow him to digest the sentence he was about to say. While he spoke, a cub reporter from one of the TV stations wiped her eyes.

The cameras showed him overwhelmed yet standing tall describing the havoc drugs were causing in Columbus. At the same time, he called for (nay, he demanded) a review of WCI procedures by the State Bureau of Inspections. "We must get to the bottom of this!" he declared. "Either Columbus is complying with state requirements or not." Near the end, he raised his voice, punched out short, staccato sentences (Terry's hallmark), and concluded in a grand crescendo of 'and may God bless this wonderful city!' As planned, Terry quickly jumped in and triumphantly guided him away from the howling reporters before one could get off a single question.

In the car headed for the west side, Mayor Blandford thanked Terry for making the conference so exhilarating. Pleased but cautious, Terry replied, "Thank you, Mayor, but I don't think this Honor thing is over yet."

CHAPTER 21

ON AN INSIDE PAGE OF THE next Sunday *Columbus Dispatch*, the headline read, "Mayor demands action at WCI in death of drug suspect," followed by, "Mayor wants answers—calls for investigation." It described the mayor's announcement as "swift and decisive" and briefly mentioned Honor Wilson, describing her as a suspected drug addict who had died from incurable cancer. The preliminary autopsy reported the cause of her death was from natural causes. Later paragraphs described the mayor's efforts since taking office to generally upgrade WCI, including items previously shown to a reporter by Haskel Gross.

It was a different story in the black community. Although not invited, a reporter for *The Call and Post* gathered enough conference information from those who attended to write an article. *The Call and Post* headline, printed in extra-large bold letters, read, "MAYOR HIDING A SISTER'S DEATH!" The subhead continued, "CALLS FOR INVESTIGATION, COMMISSION, AND OTHER DELAYS." The article slammed him for not explaining Honor's death, suggesting the city had caused it, and that he was now covering it up. "Acting Superintendent Gross (Blandford failed to appoint a permanent superintendent) refused to be interviewed except to deny that he was guilty of any crime."

Unlike the *Columbus Dispatch*, *The Call and Post* was owned by a Cleveland family with no stake in Columbus politics and little financial interest in the election outcome. They knew their readers were deeply concerned about police and jail reform.

Reporting on jails and prisons was second only to accounts of murders and robberies at *The Call and Post*.

The following Sunday, ministers in many black churches bewailed the plight of incarcerated black prisoners like Honor Wilson. Blacks, they lamented, were much more likely to be jailed for the same crime and sentenced for longer terms than whites of the same age and gender. They called on Jesus of the poor and oppressed to save them.

Some shouted for sit-ins and demonstrations, following cries for justice for Honor Wilson. Concerned citizens and organizations throughout the community weighed in, demanding justice in flyers stapled to wooden telephone poles. Activists called on national black leaders urging them to come to Columbus and lead a march. The uproar caused other pastors concerned about riots to meet to find ways to cap this blowout of outrage.

It didn't matter to activists that few, if any, of them had known Honor or the particulars of her death. The issue had become bigger than Honor, WCI, or even Columbus. It was the start of a genuine movement.

When his Masserole turned into a devil's stew, Terry Prince opted for a new recipe. He hunted for a scapegoat to roast. There is still plenty of time until November, he kept reassuring himself.

Police and others working in the black community warned City Hall of unrest from this incident despite *The Dispatch* article. Unsure about what to do, council members fell back on the mayor to lead them out of this quagmire. Reacting to police brutality, job loss, and poverty, black communities throughout the country had become tinderboxes of hostility and sources of new voters wanting to oust those in office. Politicians were worried. If Republican council members defended the administration and if WCI officials were later found to have committed errors or worse, they might face defeat in the November elections. Democrats sensed this issue could defeat the mayor and provide a rallying cry for their candidates to retake City Hall. Along party lines, politicians chose their fates.

CHAPTER 22

IN HIS OFFICE THAT EVENING before dinner, Gold watched the mayor's press conference on Foxx TV. Despite the autopsy showing that Honor had been drug-free, the mayor so fused Honor's death with drug addiction that Gold could not tell where one started and the other ended,

"Why the deception? Why don't you tell the truth?" he screamed at the TV.

He wanted to work that night, but after watching the mayor skew the news of Honor's death toward drugs, he couldn't concentrate. He lay down on his leather couch for a few minutes "to rest my eyes," as his father used to say. His dreams brought him to his father, butchering alone in the back of the large grocery store in Philadelphia where he'd worked, listening to a radio, a loner with few friends and no hobbies. After dinner, Mr. Gold would read the newspaper for 30 minutes, watch television for two hours, and go to bed after the 11 o'clock weather report. On Saturday mornings, he went to the synagogue, where he sat in the same seat as the week before. His life was as routine as that of a railroad engineer's—until his wife divorced him, perhaps to break the monotony of her life.

Alan's mother had converted from Catholicism to Judaism and raised him, an only child, in the Jewish faith and tradition. His father was heartbroken when, after Alan started Miami University of Ohio, she served him papers, renounced Judaism, and returned to her roots as an observant Catholic. But he did nothing, just carried on as if nothing happened. Alan could not understand why his father chose to do nothing. He dreamt his father replied to his inquiry, "What can I do? If she wants to go, how can I stop her?" But Alan knew the worst choice for his father was to do nothing. In opting for ambivalence, he'd lost his self-respect and his son's esteem.

Alan could still recall in college the irony of his father wrapped in a prayer shawl in synagogue on Saturdays, while on Sundays, his mother would kneel at mass. In time, his now-deceased parents faded separately into his background, leaving no trail but away. He was lucky that he never had to choose between them.

Despite convincing himself that he had rejected his father's ambivalence, Alan had never married, run for any club office, or taken a public stand. His political party was independent, his religious preference unaffiliated, and he had no favorite sports team. When he occasionally dared to raise in poker, everyone in his game knew he would only do it when holding at least three of a kind. His life glided along rudderless. He chose not to choose. Any independent thoughts that arose, he quickly suppressed. Even in his practice, he avoided offering opinions to clients other than explaining what the law required.

Only once did he deviate in a significant way. He almost cast his fate to the winds, when just out of Antioch Law School and working at the Public Defender's office, he met Daphne. She was still living in the 1950s, wearing black leotards, thin shoes like ballet slippers, high-collared tops, and a black beret sitting rakishly above her closely cropped hair. She was of Bergman, Brando, and Montgomery Clift; she was "On the Road" going nowhere, scouting to find a daisy land where a breeze began. He often still dreamed of their nights in bed together; he still saw her eyes, wild and exciting; still heard her voice scream in ecstasy, "Razz my berries!"

She was delightfully and unpredictably crazy. Daphne once quit her job at a record shop to go to San Francisco for a month to show solidarity with Lawrence Ferlinghetti during his obscenity trial for publishing Allen Ginsberg's poem "Howl," a poem she never read.

Living with her gave him a ticket to ride in her bizarre world. She was always at the forefront of joining, starting, or resurrecting something but rarely there at the finish. Maybe he was more fascinated with Daphne's world than her mind, but she enriched the other side of his brain, an exciting yin to his dull yang. It wasn't long before he found her caprices brought him more yin than he could stand. She was a brightly colored hyacinth in his gray world, but her whims quickly got old. It wasn't very smart of him to expect practicality from an artist.

One day, she was gone, taking her prized poster of the movie *Rebel Without a Cause* with her. Daphne was as close as he had gotten to commitment. After that, he returned to his sleepy hollow.

But the matter of Honor had awakened him. Other attorneys' rejections of Honor's case made his blood boil. Didn't her death deserve at least some inquiry? He decided to dig a little, maybe find something interesting to tempt the trial experts and try again. But he pledged to himself to go no further. From experience, Gold knew the lawyer's adage: "The best case is often the one you refuse." Stories he heard over the years of attorneys still kicking themselves for not rejecting cases earlier increased his trepidation. This case was too big for him. He would not know how to handle, settle, or try it. Its preparation costs could break him. But then again, what if he won? He would be an acclaimed legal genius.

Stop it! he told himself. But he could not. An enticing lure to sit among elite lawyers, to be a man among men, was seeping into him. It's the lure felt by every young athlete hoping for a pro team draft, every rising actor dreaming of stardom, every starting entrepreneur person awaiting a seat at The Big Table. Foolish, unrealistic, and impractical? Sure, but the lure can be more beguiling than cocaine. For Gold, who was neither young nor rising, accepting this case would be even more absurd. His internal conflicts were interrupted by a phone call from Millie.

She too had been feeling a lure but different from Gold's, though no less demanding. She wanted to show the world that her daughter had not been an addict and her family was good and decent. During the repast, she had watched from afar as Gold spoke with various church members. His broad smile and deep eyes displayed a sincere interest in what each person was saying, a quiet confidence reflecting genuine concern. His eyebrows tightened in a way that said he cared. He seemed like one who could tell the world calmly and convincingly what she wanted to scream to the high heavens.

"Hello, Mr. Gold. This is Millie. Sorry to call you after hours. I just got off work. I never thanked you for coming to the funeral. It meant a lot to us."

"Hi, Ms. Rivers. Thank you. It meant a lot to me as well. I was amazed at how the pastor and your friends treated Honor's death as if it was their child who had died. You're lucky to be part of that congregation. After the funeral, I talked with folks who said they knew people who did time at WCI. Honor's death to them sounded like stories of others they knew who died in prison. Several told me of their own family members' mistreatment in jail. I had no idea it happened so often."

"Have you learned anything more about Honor?"

"Not much. I talked with Johni, but she didn't get to say all she wanted. The guard made her return to her bunk before she was done. We'll talk again. She did mention someone named 'Puddin' who was with Honor when they were in the Hole together. Know anything about her? I need to find her."

"No, I never heard the name. Holy Jesus! What did they do to my child? Why would they put Honor in a hole?"

"It's not a hole in the floor; it's just the term they use to describe part of the prison where they keep inmates in cells. Johni said they put Honor in the Hole because she was sick, and put Puddin there to punish her. "

"What? In the same place? That doesn't make sense."

"Yeah, Johni said there are a lot more things there that don't make sense. I'll keep you posted if I find out more. And please let me know if you hear anything about Puddin."

The next morning, Gold stopped at a gas station for a fill-up and his usual cup of coffee. Some regulars there were yakking about followers of Jim Jones, who died in Jonestown months before. They were shocked to hear that nearly a thousand Americans had died in Guyana after their religious leader told them to drink poison.

"You know, I'm beginning to think that we've become like those Kool-Aid drinkers, dumb followers willing to believe anything a leader says," one patron remarked.

"If just one of them had stood up and said 'No, this is crazy,' he could've saved nearly a thousand people," said another. Others nodded in agreement.

"Yep, it only takes one if he's the right one."

Gold paid his bill but said nothing. *Could anyone in Jonestown have refused their leader? Who would have been the right one to stand up? How would that person know they were the right one?*

As he walked into his office, Frannie told him Millie had called. "Ms. LaGreaux, the mother of an inmate, called her. She said she was passing a message from her daughter Johni who wanted you to know that she had arranged for you to meet Puddin at Stone's Grill on Fourth Street on Thursday night at six. She didn't say how she pulled it off while still at WCI. Just be there," she said.

CHAPTER 23

STONE'S BAR AND GRILL WAS downtown at a corner close to where, decades earlier, the city's Central Market once flourished. The Market had been one central building plus two surrounding streets full of vendors selling every fresh food item a family might need. After Greyhound replaced the market building with a bus station and supermarkets emerged, customers stopped coming to buy eggs, cheese, and produce. The neighborhood lost many of its businesses and residents. Stone's was about all that was left, except for Dick's Fish Market and the Queen Bee restaurant.

In this skinny bar, lonely customers found solace in semi-darkness. Unwelcomed elsewhere—wounded Vietnam vets, released mental patients, and a few former inmates breaking probation or parole—sat alone with others pouring down a few. Tacky smoke, like low-hanging clouds, floated in the upper regions of its windowless space.

Gold hesitated after his first steps into the dankness. His ears filled with honky-tonk music whining from a jukebox next to the bar, and his nose itched from the smell of cheap liquor and tobacco smoke. All eyes turned toward the man at the door wearing a suit. All talk stopped.

Usually, those wearing ties were cops, parole officers, or others coming to thin the herd. Suddenly, a rush of patrons ran to the john or hid their faces. After his eyes adjusted and the crowd calmed down, Gold spotted what appeared to be a young girl sitting alone in a corner booth, the smoke from her cigarette adding to the haze. Gold walked over.

"Ms. Gates?"

"Maybe. Who are you?"

"Alan Gold. Johni asked me to meet you here. I am the attorney for Honor Wilson's mother."

"The dead girl? Yeah, she got shit on."

"Here's my card. I told her mother I would try to find out what happened to her daughter. May I join you?"

She exhaled a thick puff toward him and nodded.

He scooted into the well-worn Naugahyde booth while asking her, "So,...What can you tell me?"

"I didn't know her 'cept being across the cells from her in the Hole. She was one sick chick. Moaning and all. Not eating. Them motherfuckers just let her die. I told 'em someday they gonna answer for their sins. Now, I ain't no preacher. And I never know'd a god I liked, but I know what's right. And lettin' her die wasn't right."

"What happened to your arm?" he asked, pointing to a white cast going up to her elbow.

"Got into a little dispute."

"Yeah? What was the fight all about?"

"It was a matter of honor."

"Yeah, it always is. What happened?"

"When I was in WCI, some bitch called me a white nigga. I mean, I had to protect my rep. In there, if you got no rep, they'll eat you alive."

"So, what did you do?"

"Took care of business. I whooped the shit out of her. Her nose was bloody, and one of her eyes was puffy when they pulled me off. She was some fat-assed nigger who now knows better than to call me a name. When I cooled down, they put me in the Hole, but I found I couldn't move my fingers. So, they took me to the hospital and fixed my arm. After I came back from the hospital, they sent me back to the Hole, but they let her fat-ass outta jail.

Ain't that a shit? They got a funny way of doing things around there," she said, shaking her head.

"OK. So, you took care of your rep, broke your arm, and had surgery. When did they send you back to Cell Block?"

"Oh, maybe January. Ain't nobody keeping time for me in there."

"When did you first see Honor?"

"After surgery and back in the Hole. They brung her in one day. She was hurtin' real bad."

"Did you talk to her?"

"A little, but I usually keep to myself. Sgt. Mitchell dragged her in, moaning. She hit the sack right away. Later, we shot the shit a spell, even though I don't usually talk much when I'm inside. I asked her why they put her in the Hole, and she told me she was having headaches and pains down below and stuff like that. Said she had a dead baby. She was a puppy; I could tell. Well, her pain got worse, and she began to stink and filthify the place. Pretty soon, the Hole smelled like an outhouse."

"I kept calling them motherfuckin' guards to help her, but no one came. Finally, when Moley Poley—that's what I calls her—brought us dinner, she takes one look in Honor's cell and gives out a holler for the guards. I guess Honor shit her pants or somethin'. And there was blood too. The girl could hardly sit up, but those goddamn guards made her clean up her own shit. That bitch couldn't walk straight, and later, they make her clean out her cell and the other ones as well, except mine. I'm telling you, there are some mean motherfuckers working there. If she hadn't leaned on the mop, she would've dropped her ass to the ground.

"But she didn't complain. I ain't sure she could've; she was so weak. Well, she did the best she could before dropping back to her bed. I kept saying to them, 'You're killing her! Ain't you got no decency? Y'all are gonna pay for this.' One motherfuckin' guard comes back later and throws a bucket of ice water on me. Someday I'll get that bitch too."

"Then what happened?"

"Later, they took her out. But in a few days, I'll be damned if they didn't bring her back. And this time, she was in even worse shape. I ain't never going to forget her bulging eyes. They was gonna pop out of her head, I swear. She began that moan like she'd done before. Then I heard her screaming. I called the guards again. Do you think they helped? Shit! Those motherfuckers just let her scream.

"After a spell, she falls off her bed to the floor and starts pulling out her hair by the handful and starts making a gurgling sound. But then she goes quiet. I start yellin' 'She's dying, she's dying.' A guard came in with Sgt. Mitchell. Sarge takes one look and calls the squad. That's when they took her away. I told those motherfuckin guards that they was goin to pay for this. They shouldn't be allowed to get away with it. Hell, next time it could be me."

"Well, Puddin, you'll get your chance to make them pay."

"What do you mean?"

"It means you are going to tell what you saw to a jury."

"Oh no, I ain't into that shit. I got enough to do to take care of number one, and I don't help nobody, and nobody ever helps me. Besides," she said as her voice cracked, "who'd ever believe me?"

"Puddin, tonight you made me a believer of you and in you. Let me buy you a beer."

CHAPTER 24

GOLD RETURNED TO THE office thinking, *What would happen if a network of inmates and ex-inmates of WCI gathered inside information about what happened to Honor and also collected before trial intel on what WCI officials were planning? How much of an edge would that give Millie's trial attorney? Maybe the network could find witnesses, perhaps even some with greater credibility than inmates, to describe conditions at WCI.*

But he was no fool. He knew that most jurors regarded arrested lawbreakers as untrustworthy, never considering that many other lawbreakers deemed trustworthy were never arrested. In his few trials of court-appointed defendants, he often wanted to ask jurors if they ever wondered if police arrests were selective. He was sure they never stopped to consider that if police chose to raid OSU student dorms and fraternity houses instead of Benny's Quick Stop or The Fancy House, white college students would be inmates charged with the crimes instead of Benny and Honor.

Who might jurors believe if Honor sued the city? He couldn't count on WCI employees to provide straight answers, so he began tracing her steps from when the police picked her up. She was arrested, taken to WCI, and then arraigned. Arraigned? He immediately called the Public Defender's Office, looking for the attorney who represented her at Honor's arraignment.

"Hello, this is Anne Jennifer. Can I help you?"

"Hello, Anne. My name is Alan Gold, attorney. I was appointed to represent Honor Wilson, who was charged with drug trafficking a few months ago. You represented her at her arraignment. Does any of this ring a bell?

"Wilson, Wilson... was she a large black woman, a first-timer?"

"Yes, I think so. Do you remember anything about her?

"Well, I recall her asking me a bond question that I'm still thinking about because I couldn't give her a straight answer. She asked me why the judge was giving low bonds to those who had money to flee anywhere but gave high bonds to those who couldn't even afford a bus ticket to Dayton. She stumped me. Why are you asking about her?"

"Well, she isn't going anywhere now. She died at WCI, and I am trying to find out why. Did she say anything about her medical condition?"

"No kidding? My God, that is so sad. Now that you mention it, I recall her telling me she wasn't feeling well. Maybe something about a miscarriage and a six-week checkup. When I told her to tell the medical staff at WCI, she said she did, but they didn't believe her. I may not have it exactly right, but that's the best I recall. So many defendants each day, it's hard to keep track. I think she got hit with a $30,000 bond. That was probably more than the net worth of her entire family, I'll bet. Don't know why the judge set them so high that day, but I keep thinking about her question."

"I understand. Thanks."

Gold hung up, feeling deeply curious about the possibilities of this case. From very different people, he was hearing the same story. He decided to go back to see Johni.

This time, Gold reserved the attorney conference room at WCI for privacy when speaking with Johni. She came in looking pale and lifeless, with no expression on her face. When he told her what Puddin had said about Honor in the Hole, he saw a tear float across her scar.

"This is such a sorry place. They didn't have to do that to her. She didn't do nothing to deserve what she got."

"Johni, I want you to start from when you met Honor and take me through your last meeting. To save time, I have brought a tape recorder. I'll write notes later so that you can talk faster. I know this is painful, but I must learn everything I can about her. Take your time. Start when you first met her on the bench in the holding room."

Johnny looked down with her eyes closed, trying to compose herself before she began.

"'First time?' I asked her. She looked down. I saw her shaking. 'Well, BabyCakes,' I says, 'mind yourself and stay out the way. Don't talk about yourself. In here, what you say can hurt you.' Then what she said next told me she didn't know shit about this place. She asked me, 'Can you tell me how I can make the lady up at the counter understand I didn't do anything, and I need to go home to my baby boy?' I tried not to laugh. I goes, 'I hear you, girl, but they don't, and they won't.' I told her she would get to make a call after she was processed, but she kept talking about that lady at the counter.

"I finally had to lay it to her straight. I goes, 'I got double bad news for you. First, the guard at the counter is no lady and can't do shit to get you out. And number two, it's Friday night. You ain't going to see a judge till Monday morning." She asked me why she had to wait, and I told her judges don't think speedy justice means they got to work weekends. She didn't get it. She was bawling when they called me for my strip and dip, when they look us over for hidden stuff.

"Now, I don't recall every time I seen her, and I ain't sure when or where. For a time, we saw each other near every day. But there were some times I couldn't forget even if I tried, like the next day in the dining hall when she was sitting with her head on the table. She couldn't go to her dorm right then 'cause some sisters were mopping floors there. I asked her if she wanted breakfast. She said she wasn't hungry, but she was sleepy and just laid her head back down. She told me she hadn't been to her bunk in dorm B, and as soon as I heard 28B, I said, 'Get ready to climb, BabyCakes. You gots an upper bunk. The As are the lower bunks.

"That's when she told me about her stillborn and how she didn't think she could climb up to bed. She said she was to see a doctor in the next week or so, and she asked me if they would give her a lower bunk and drive her to see the doctor. I nearly fell off my chair. I tried to stay easy and says, 'You can ask 'em, but I don't think they'll give a shit. They got them rules. And rules, BabyCakes, is rules. They'll go, 'If we give you a lower bunk, they's all be wantin' one.' You might want to try to ask a nurse about seeing Dr. V, the WCI doc, but shit, that ain't likely either. You just may be fucked.' I says. She put her head back on the table and I went for oatmeal.

"We went to court together on Monday for our bond hearings. Before that, I warned her that Monday would be a "hurry-up and wait" day. They got us up before daylight, ran us through the showers, and gave us breakfast before they put us in chains and bused us to court. We stayed in a holding pen in the basement of the courthouse. Guards took a few of us at a time up to the courtroom where a judge set bonds. She wasn't in my group, but I know that neither of us made bond 'cause we later found each other back at WCI.

"Then, she told me she had started going to pill-calls with Nurse Kratz."

"What are pill-calls?" Gold asked.

"Pill-call is when you wait in line to see the nurse. She may give you a pill if you're sick. Or if she says okay, she'll send you to wait in line on Fridays to see Dr. V. That's a sick-call. You can't go to sick-call without first going to pill-call.

"Anyways, BabyCakes found trouble again after she told the nurse about her dead baby and her six-week checkup. Nurse Kratz, that bitch, said she must be lying because she'd called some nurse-friend of hers up on the new baby floor who couldn't find Honor's name on their list. She wouldn't believe her when Honor said she lost the baby in the ER, not up there. But Kratz wouldn't believe her. She just didn't get how things work around here. She told me she felt like the walls were shakin' and the roof was comin' down. Couldn't stand girls' screaming after 'lights out'. Said her head was hurtin real bad. Most of all, she told me she didn't care no more and wasn't sure how much longer she could hang on."

"Did you believe her?"

"Mister, if you could've seen her bulging eyes, you woulda known she was for real. I've known some who lost hope. It's real heavy when someone talks like that, you best believe. I says to her, 'Now you listen to me, BabyCakes. This is how it goes down. You lose hope; you lose life. Don't you be talking that way. Hell, you ain't been in here that long. Find hope wherever you can.' I told her to try going to pill-call in the evening with Nurse Hill. She might do better than Kratz.

"I think it was then we became tight. I never gave another inmate no never-mind before, but that girl got to me. She was something' special.

"A few days later, we began hangin' out. Later, she told me Nurse Hill, during a pill-call, put her in the Hole when she passed out and fell. Sgt. Mitchell had to drag her to the Hole 'cause she was so weak. Hill scheduled her for a sick-call, but before she saw Dr. V, they took her from the Hole and put her back in the dorm.

"Honor told me her sick-call visit was a real fuck-up. Kratz told Dr. V BabyCakes was a liar, so he sent her on her way without even looking her over or getting her to a real doctor who'd know what to do. Not even a quick once over. He gave her a suppository. Yeah, like that's gonna help! But I didn't need no Dr. Welby to tell me that bitch was sick. She wouldn't eat and had to hold my arm when we walked, on account of she got dizzy. And she was always having terrible headaches. Still, those fucking guards wouldn't even give her a bottom bunk."

"You mentioned her bunkmate. What was her name?"

"Fabiola. Yeah, that's another reason I felt tight with BabyCakes. I saw her once in the mess hall listening to Fabiola blabbering. Fab was talkin' some strange shit. She said Jesus was talking to her through electro-magnetic vibrations comin' from the metal bunks or some shit like that. Said she was carrying his child and he had just anointed her to tell the world about him. Jesus told her he was about to give her the gift of prophecy, but she didn't want it. He said it would be a blessing, but she thought it would be a curse.

"Me? I can't do crazy, but BabyCakes, even hurtin' as bad as she was, listened to all her shit, never saying nothin' bad to Fabiola. After she finished her Jesus stuff, BabyCakes looked her in the eye, put her hands on her head, and told her to pray for guidance. Now lemme ask you, why should a person as good as that be treated the way she was?"

"What happened to Fabiola?"

"A guard caught her later with a shank trying to off herself, still talking 'bout her blessing and curse. I heard they put her in a straight-jacket and took her to a funny farm."

"For how long?"

"Can't say, but she ain't gettin' out any time soon. She crazy."

"What will they do with her there?"

"Just keep her away from shanks and feed her sleepy-time meds for a long time. They think crazy heals itself."

"Too bad."

"I never saw BabyCakes again. I heard they put her back in the Hole, and then the squad took her to the hospital to die. When I heard she was taken away, I felt like I did when the cops killed my sister, and there was nothing I could do about it. Watching her go down while she was in this fuckin' place makes me want to do something'. I don't know what, just do something'. But shit, all I ever do in here is my time, and then get the hell out."

"Johni, suppose I told you that you could do something more than your time, that you don't have to sit back and take all this shit without a fight. Would you do it?"

"Like what?"

"Like helping the family put the screws to them, like finding witnesses and telling me or some other attorney what's happening here at WCI. It's a lot to ask, but would you? I am trying to find another attorney to take this case—so far, without luck. I can't handle this case myself, but her family needs help. I haven't decided what to do. Your decision might help me make mine. I can see you shaking your head, but look, helping her attorney won't bring Honor back. It won't bring back your sister either, but just maybe, it might make you feel like you did something to help. What would you say?"

"I don't know nothin' about that kinda shit. I ain't even got a GED, and I'd probably fuck it up. Never done nothing important like that."

"You got something better than an education, Johni. You have location and motivation. You are in the right place at the right time, and you want to do it for yourself and others. That's all we need. The rest you can be shown. What could you do that would be more important?"

"Well, would you be there for me? You seem like you give a damn. Maybe I'd do it for you."

"Not for me, Johni, for Honor and for you. Thanks. I'll get back to you."

CHAPTER 25

WITH WHAT HE LEARNED, Gold was sure he could now persuade a trial attorney to accept the case and be done with it. When he returned to the office after his interview with Johni, he called every trial attorney he knew. To his dismay, the results were the same as before.

One attorney laid it out for him: "Al, don't you think I would take the case if I could? My office can only accept a few cases a year. Sometimes, we spend tens of thousands of dollars and hundreds of hours preparing to try one case. Why should we choose this one? Think about it. Liability is questionable, the law is uncertain, damages are speculative, and jury sympathy would be low. And we'd have to spend a fortune on experts. We'd rather spend that time and money looking for a case where a driver with a million-dollar insurance policy runs a stop sign, leaving a sweet, white, church lady paraplegic. I'm sorry. The problem is your case lacks fundamentals. But I'll tell you what. If you ever find a church lady case like the one we're looking for, give me a call. Then, we'll do business."

Gold listened silently. He could not argue with success. Financially, his attorney friend was right. The white church lady's case would be far more profitable with less effort. The words of his colleague did not sound like prejudice or politics. But instead of describing his office as an example of professionalism, he had likened it to an MBA business model.

Despite advice from nearly every colleague he talked to advising him to drop the case, Gold pressed on. He had no choice now. After the press conference and its consequences, he was at the corner of "Do or Die." He recalled a suggestion given to him at a recent cocktail party he attended to try calling Ohio State University Medical Center. With its effort to start a new cancer center, maybe they now have someone with experience. On a whim, he dialed OSU Medical Center. As he did so, he said under his breath, "This is a waste of time."

"Ohio State Medical Center. May I help you?"

"Yes, I'm looking for a doctor, a cancer doctor, who treats choriocarcinoma."

"What is that?"

"I think it has to do with cancer in pregnant women."

"Hold on please...I'll transfer you to the OB/GYN department. Please ask to speak with an oncologist there."

Alan's heart pumped faster.

"Gynecology. May I help you?"

"Yes, may I speak with an oncologist in your department?"

"Is this about a patient?"

"No, I'm trying to find a doctor who has treated choriocarcinoma."

"Well, the doctors are very busy now, but let me find one who has a moment to talk."

Gold could not believe he had made it this far, but after waiting several minutes, he started to return the receiver to its cradle, sure that his journey had led up a blind alley. Having attended seminars where med-mal attorneys bragged about how much time they spent updating their Rolodexes of doctors willing to testify, Alan was sure his direct approach would only lead to humiliating defeat. Then he heard, "This is Dr. Faraday. How may I help you?"

"Yes, Doctor. I hope you can. Do you know a physician who has successfully treated choriocarcinoma patients? Have you?"

"No, I'm only a resident. I have not encountered any patients which choriocarcinoma."

"I see. Have any of the doctors in the department?"

"I can't say. I recently started rotation to this area."

"Are any other doctors available, perhaps?"

"Not at the moment. They are all treating patients, but I'll check around for someone to return your call."

Color drained from Alan's face. He held no hope that anyone would return his call but dared not to close the door. "Thank you. Let me give you my numbers, both in the office and at home."

When he hung up, he looked around his somewhat faded office and thought about how little he had accomplished during his years of practice. Now he was about to travel on a fool's journey. His recent moment in the media sun had resulted only in his receiving a red face and severe sunburn.

As he drove home that night, Gold was haunted by what more there could be to Honor's death than what the mayor said in his press conference. Could he prove anything? Could he do something never done before in Columbus—make the city pay for the mistreatment of an inmate? Conversations with Johni and Puddin pushed his crazy idea…a community of inmates helping him win. Crazy, yes…but what if?

The next afternoon, he called Millie after she returned from work.

"I spoke with Puddin. She was near Honor in the Hole when the emergency squad took Honor to the hospital. She told me the staff did nothing to help her as she suffered. Johni saw her getting worse as well. Johni described an infirmary with no medical care. I'm smelling a cover-up, but I could be wrong. Also, my very quick legal research shows the law is changing toward making cities pay when they are responsible. Not much to go on, but it's a start. It's never been done before, making Columbus pay for the mistreatment of an inmate."

"Maybe this case might be a first?" Millie asked.

"Maybe."

"Maybe this case will show America that this city can't get away with lying about my daughter taking drugs as an excuse for what it did wrong?"

"Maybe."

"Maybe the lawyer, in that case, will have to use new ways to win."

"Maybe."

"Maybe the lawyer, in that case, will be Alan Gold?"

"Maybe."

"For real? You'll take the case? Oh, Mr. Gold, thank you."

"Hold on, Ms. Rivers. I haven't won anything. I will investigate the case. I may have to file a lawsuit to get the necessary information unless the city tells us the whole story. But if I find nothing, I'll dismiss the case."

"Don't you worry, Mr. Gold, you're gonna find something. We're gonna tell all of them that she was no addict and what things were like when she was there. Our reputation will be saved. I just know it."

"Please bring your family to my office Saturday to sign a retainer agreement. I forgot to mention, I found another new law in Ohio allowing most family members to make wrongful death claims. So, anybody closely related to Honor can claim for their loss. You can sign the agreement on behalf of the kids, but I still want to talk to them personally."

"Lucky, Honor's father, is out of town. I'll call him tonight. Thank you again, Mr. Gold."

CHAPTER 26

MILLIE WATCHED HER children's faces as they marched into Gold's office. She sensed unity in her family. Honor's death and this possible lawsuit were the biggest events that had ever happened to them, and she needed them to stand together. Gold told her that the media might try to badger them or worse, but to her, the people in her community were of greater concern. After health and safety, nothing was more important than respect. No one dared call a child of hers a drug addict and expect to get away with it. That's all she wanted to prove.

The Rivers family overflowed Gold's small waiting room. The boys stood until Frannie ushered them into the conference room. Gold entered a few minutes later, yellow pad in hand, along with a typed letter of agreement for Millie's signature on behalf of all of them. He nodded to her, seated at the head of the other end of the table. To his left, a young girl was holding an infant in her lap, contently drinking milk from a bottle.

"This must be Winston, right?" he asked. They nodded. Suddenly research, legal theories, trial techniques—all were transformed from a lawsuit into a human reason for taking the case. At the same time, Gold drew back, afraid that he might let this case turn personal, causing him to lose his professionalism and objectivity.

He cleared his throat. "First, I want to review our agenda. Let's start with my representation agreement. If we win by suit or settlement, then my fee will be one-third of what we recover, plus expenses. If I quit, or we lose, you would owe only the expenses, which I will advance for you, like tests, transcripts, and expert fees. Because you are minors, your mother can retain me on your behalf, but still, I want you kids to know what's going on and be comfortable in our arrangement."

"Can I ask you something? Why you gonna take our case?" said the young man with the giant Afro who had not taken his eyes off Alan.

"I'm sorry, I didn't catch your name. I'm Alan Gold. What is yours?"

"Duke Rivers."

No one had asked Gold that question before. How could he explain why he would take a flyer like this? He was committing to a case that could last for years. He had a little stash in savings he would need to draw from or get a loan. A couple of bad decisions during the course of this case could deplete his savings entirely. Nor had he illusions about the worth of the case, but still, he was attracted to it like a moth to a flame.

Why should he take this case? He was not about to tell the young man that he could sum up his life as a lawyer in a single word: mediocre. Nor could he describe his desire to be recognized for doing something real in his life of pretense. The case seemed so odd. An apparently healthy young woman goes to prison for a short time and dies there. Nobody seems to be at fault, a brainteaser of all brain teasers, but he was keenly aware that this was not a mind game. This case was real and meaningful, but perhaps impossible to prove.

Gold replied simply, "It might be worthwhile."

After Millie signed, Gold asked Millie and the kids to tell him about Honor and what little they knew about the night she was arrested, how she went to Bennie's for aspirin and never returned.

Honor left high school pregnant to marry Reginald Wilson, Jr. She had met him at a party on the OSU campus and fallen in love. Later, they moved to Chicago, his hometown. She worked nights, kept a neat apartment, studied for her GED, and took good care of her son Winston. His mother paid for things when Junior lost one job after another. While in the early stages of her second pregnancy, she divorced Junior, and each moved back to the homes of their mothers.

Gold listened as never before to a client's description. He began to acquire a new sense of perception, seeing the world as a trial lawyer does, evaluating every fact and person in terms of how jurors would view them. How would they treat the mayor, a famous politician? What would they make of the autopsy? Would they be offended by Duke's hair?

Mixed into the margins of Gold's notes were descriptions of what jurors might see as Honor's strength and perseverance. Jurors might find how each setback of hers could have taken her down, yet she kept fighting. When she moved to Columbus, pregnant and unemployed, she not only filed for welfare for Winston and her, but she also applied to over ten employers for jobs (even before she was able to work full-time), while taking care of Millie's kids, as well as Winston. To them, she had become their second mother.

Gold also noted what other jurors might conclude as her weaknesses. She was a foolish woman who made bad choices: quitting school, getting pregnant the first time, marrying a good-for-nothing, and getting pregnant again when her marriage was on the rocks. Arriving in Columbus broke, she began looking for a handout to cover the consequences of her poor judgments. Jurors might tag her a "welfare mom."

As Millie and her kids shared their memories of Honor, Gold also noted family traits that might impress jurors: Millie's industriousness, for example. Would jurors view Honor as a woman about to develop into a hard-working mother like Millie, who worked her way up to supervisor, or someone destined to have more welfare babies? What he saw in them gave him hope.

He pressed on, looking for more ways to prove his case. Gold began mapping out a strategy to focus damages on Winston and describe Honor's welfare applications as a passing stage in her recovery before joining the workforce. And he would use any wrongdoing by defendants to energize juror outrage. Good strategy, except that he still had no proof that anyone had violated her constitutional rights or even had been negligent. The game plan seemed sound, but victory was nowhere in sight. Still, he could not fly from the heat of the flame.

Another thing he noted. The family appeared to be "normal," whatever that meant. Jurors would be hard-pressed to find fault in the Wilson kids. Admirable plaintiffs were nearly as indispensable for courtroom success as winning facts—at least one favorable thing, only one so far.

CHAPTER 27

GOLD BEGAN ORGANIZING the case. He laid out an extensive to-do list: obtain a loan, transfer savings, hire a law clerk, rearrange his calendar, and set limitations for accepting new clients. He listed witnesses he needed to find and interview, legal issues to research, documents to prepare (e.g., complaint and discovery requests), etc., etc., etc. He then prioritized his list and scheduled what he would do when. His list, which ran over a page and a half, seemed overwhelming. *All this for a case I'll probably dismiss anyway*, he mused.

Regardless of the law, the *sine qua non* was to find an expert doctor to testify that the city had failed to provide Honor the care that would have prevented her death. Otherwise, the court would dismiss the case. From his limited information so far, that expert did not exist. Yet, Honor had seemed to be in good health when she went into WCI and died at OSU Hospital a few weeks later. Not much to go on.

The next day, he completed some of his financial to-dos, rescheduled several cases, and placed want ads for a law clerk with both Capital and Ohio State University Law schools. Within days, he was interviewing law student applicants. Not knowing what he wanted in a law clerk, he told students what he knew about the case and listened to their ideas, trying to imagine what it would be like working intently with that young person for six months or longer. He narrowed his search to juniors with nothing on their plate other than completing law school, who had aced constitutional law, and whose strengths were research and detail, not necessarily trial technique.

After interviewing more than a dozen candidates, he selected Frank Pearl, a junior who had transferred from Wisconsin to American University before coming to OSU Law School. Having wealthy parents, Frank didn't even ask about his salary. Gold was impressed when discussing the case with him that he didn't get bogged down in details. He jumped immediately to the meat of the matter. Frank started the following Monday. Because Gold had no space for him in his small office suite, Frank worked at the county law library.

On Monday afternoon, Gold met Frank at the library. They commandeered a conference room, where they first outlined goals and objectives. Gold gave Frank a copy of the file that Frannie prepared, including a copy of the coroner's report and a few cases he had saved while scanning the legal horizon.

Gold began by briefly repeating in greater detail what he knew: Recently divorced, Honor Wilson was recovering from a stillbirth when arrested and taken to WCI to await trial. A few weeks after detention, she was rushed to OSU Hospital ER, where she died of choriocarcinoma, leaving a small child. Her parents and four siblings also survived her.

"Was her choriocarcinoma treatable?" asked Frank in his quiet but firm voice, lisping slightly.

"Don't know yet. I am looking for a doctor now, and I have read that it might be treatable."

"If her death was not preventable, do we still have a case?"

Gold was stunned at how Frank had reduced his mighty crusade into one short question to which he had no positive answer.

"Probably not, but we must assume for the moment that had she been treated, she would have lived."

Looking through his thick tortoiseshell glasses and tightening his eyebrows slightly, Frank, without saying a word, questioned why Gold was pursuing so weak a case. Gold was pleased with his choice of law clerks, even though Frank's initial assessment only increased his anxiety.

"We have to start somewhere, Frank. If trials were easy, there would be no need for lawyers. It sounds daunting, but proving injustice often begins with a smell test. This one does not smell right. Is that enough to accept a case? Probably not, but I did it anyway. So, let's get started. You will focus on the law, even though we don't know yet what issues we'll face."

"And you need to include the city because the doctors and nurses don't have sufficient insurance?" asked Frank.

"Don't know yet what their coverage limits are. Of course, the more pockets there are, the greater the chances of settling. But there is a bigger reason. Our client, Ms. Rivers, insists that the mayor apologize and declare personally that her daughter was not a drug addict. I know they don't teach this in law school, but this is life."

"Was she?"

"Don't know. Never met her. All I know is that her toxicology report says she was clean, except for marijuana. I need your research to give me answers to lots of legal questions. Take some notes," he said as he paced the small room. "If Honor died because WCI didn't provide her medical care, can we sue the city for failing to care for its prisoner? But should she be classified as a prisoner when she was not serving a sentence? Are non-convicted prisoners' rights to medical care different from those of convicts? Are medical standards of care the same in prisons as in medical providers' offices and hospitals?"

Frank was writing furiously, trying to catch questions as they dropped from Gold's mouth.

After Gold finished his litany, he paused before concluding with, "I'll have more questions for you, but those will get you started. Try answering each question in a separate memo, attaching copies of relevant cases that both support and contradict our position. Frannie will type up your work but write clearly so she won't make mistakes. Number your memos and, as you go along, refer to as many prior memos as possible, so we can relate each memo to others. Don't be afraid to ask the librarian for help. Call me when you have questions. We'll review your progress next week. Good luck.

* * *

On Friday, Gold filed papers in probate court closing the estate of a bitter old lady who left $75,000 for the perpetual care of her living Chihuahua, Fadoodles. While waiting for the clerk to stamp his papers, he couldn't help contrasting his two clients—one who paid for the best care for her orphaned dog, while the other could not pay to bury her daughter.

He then went up to the law library to see how Frank was doing. The first question Gold asked was, if the city had done something wrong, was it liable? Gold learned years ago the answer was no, but based on newer cases, Frank gave him a qualified yes. Gold had read back in law school the *Monroe* case, where the United States Supreme Court decided that "cities" were not "persons" within the meaning of the famous federal civil rights law written when Lincoln was president, now referred to simply as '1983'. While a "city" was not a "person," its employees were. This meant municipalities could either defend their employees when they were sued or hang them out to dry, leaving plaintiffs uncertain about whether they would have a defendant who could pay.

But decisions from federal courts had gotten more favorable to plaintiffs. Frank reported that the Supreme Court overruled *Monroe* in a case called *Monell vs. Department of Social Services*. In the 1970s, New York City refused pregnant employees paid medical leave when they gave birth but did pay when they were ill. Jane Monell sued the school system to revoke its maternity leave policy and award her back pay. The U.S. Supreme Court agreed with her. A city could be a 'person' liable when the damaging acts of city employees were done to carry out 'official' municipal policy," said Frank.

"Oh, great!" Gold sighed in exasperation. "You are telling me we'll have to prove not only did city employees do something wrong, but they did it to carry out 'official municipal policy.' How in the hell can we do that, Frank? Are we supposed to come up with an order from the superintendent saying, 'Let inmates die'?"

Frank had no answer: the decision was too recent for him to find lower court case examples, other than Monell, which fleshed out one practical meaning of "official municipal policy", but that only related to pay.

"Okay, Frank. More questions. What is an 'official policy?' What facts will prove those city officials carried out official policy? Must that policy, as it was carried out, be the sole cause of her death, or is it enough to prove it was the primary cause or one of many causes? ..."

Nothing.

Alan Gold left the library confused but challenged. This first briefing told him generally that the law was moving in his favor but only marginally. The change would mean nothing without evidence of a municipal policy violating Honor's civil rights. *Monell*, over time, might create giant waves in municipal law. He wondered if he would end up a great surfer riding them or a fallen beach bum without a board.

The next meeting was only a little more productive.

"Okay, Frank, I've read your memos, spoken with the family, and interviewed a few inmates. We can't do much more to find out what happened without filing suit. My letters to the superintendent and safety director have been ignored. There is nothing more I can learn without filing a complaint, demanding documents, and deposing witnesses. If we find no liability, we'll dismiss and go home. I am preparing my first draft. Tell me who we should sue and for what."

Frank pored through his copious notes. "Well, sir, assuming those working for the city did something wrong, I see various scenarios. We could simply sue the nurses for negligence and the doctor for malpractice, but we may not be able to get around their governmental immunity defense. Suing the city itself, as you guessed, is much more complicated. State law won't be of much help, but maybe we could use 42 U.S.C.1983. It reads briefly, 'Every person who, under color of any statute... subjects ... any citizen of the United States ... to the deprivation of any rights, privileges, or immunities secured by the Constitution and laws, shall be liable to the party injured ...' This short statute has been changing civil rights law across the country. Isn't this what her case is about?"

Gold nodded in agreement, admiring Frank's ability to simplify complex issues. "Okay, we'll use 1983 to sue Columbus for the deprivation of Honor's constitutional rights and file in either state or federal court," said Gold. "So far, so good. The next question is, what constitutional right was Honor deprived of?"

"I would say our best argument, Mr. Gold, would be that she was deprived of protection against cruel and unusual punishment under the Eighth Amendment. I found a great case in which the U.S. Supreme Court recently ruled a prisoner can sue her jailer for lack of medical care while incarcerated. Justice Marshall was again the author. He said the law required a plaintiff to prove her jailer showed 'deliberate indifference to serious medical needs.' That would include intentionally denying or delaying access to medical care or intentionally interfering with prescribed treatment.

Frank continued, "I couldn't find any cases deciding whether Marshall's decision in the Gamble case would also apply to prisoners awaiting trial, nor examples of 'deliberate indifference'. I guess this recent decision, like Monell, has few interpretations yet. In this case, Texas refused to provide medical care to a prisoner named Gamble who got hurt carrying a bale of cotton. Because jailers and nurses act as city officials and can be liable under federal law, I think we'll need to sue all those individuals involved."

"My God, Frank. We could list defendants, starting with guards and going all the way up to the mayor himself. The trial could turn into a three-ring circus, and I guess that's good in one way, but bad in another. We will have more pockets available, but more defendants could mean more defense attorneys to make things go wrong."

"Frank, I want you to look for some complaints used by other counsel we can use in drafting ours. We won't know if we have a case until we get documents and witnesses, but we won't get them without starting a lawsuit. So, take a look."

"I figured you would ask me for them, so I already checked for other complaints. So far, no luck, sir."

"Did you also check who could be plaintiffs? Probably not. Ohio just passed a new law allowing any next of kin who suffered from a wrongful death the right to sue. Check out language we should use in the complaint for their claims while I will start drafting it."

"Will do, Mr. Gold. Seems like this case is ahead of its time in a lot of ways. New decisions, new laws, new everything."

"Well, the decisions may be new, but the issues are as old as *Crime and Punishment*."

Gold recognized from Frank's research another legal hurdle to overcome. How could he ever prove "deliberate indifference," or "intentionally denying" medical care? Frank will have to examine each relevant word and its implication for their case.

Over the next few days, Gold drafted a complaint to start the lawsuit. Like an artist starting with a blank canvas, he dabbed a fact here, lightly filled in there with words from decisions Frank found. He added contrast with dark allegations that defendants showed "deliberate indifference by intentionally denying" Honor needed medical care while they were carrying out "official municipal policy." He touched up his sketch as best he could but still had difficulty seeing his final work. Eventually, the complaint began to take on form, shape, and color. When he finished, he could only say it looked good on paper.

After reworking the complaint further, Gold asked Millie to come to the office to review it. He didn't know it, but she was having second thoughts about filing. Some in her church had warned her that filing a lawsuit meant accepting white judges, mainly white juries, and most importantly, white justice. They said white justice for a black woman is no justice. How many centuries of oppression would it take, they asked, before black folks learned that white courts suppress them?

Not only would she lose in court, but her loss would once again provide white folks an example of uppity blacks trying to use their judicial system to get rich, instead of trying to earn an honest living. Did she realize what she was doing, taking on the entire white establishment? No ofay judge would let her beat a white mayor, a white doctor, and all the other pale faces. They warned her, "Before this is over, they'll get you, one way or the other."

Her son Duke also attacked her. "How can you trust a honky lawyer?" he asked. "Ain't we learned yet when push comes to shove, whitey pushes, and we get shoved? I'm telling you, Mama, he will tuck and run before this is over."

Her family's lack of confidence in Gold made her doubt her choice, but she had no one else. Pastor Jenkins, and others, on the other hand, urged her to use the system, to trust that people of good will would come to her aid.

Millie looked at Gold as her only choice, when doing nothing was not an option. She could not explain her trust in Gold, a connection as undefinable as a love affair, where two people understand each other before they talk, not romance, but a sense that his intentions were genuine, and he knew her needs.

After Gold reviewed with her what he wrote and why, she approved the complaint, despite her misgivings and inability to grasp the legal jargon dripping from the pages.

Before Millie could serve as plaintiff for her family, Gold needed probate court authorization for her to act for the estate of Honor and the minor beneficiaries. He filed papers to open Honor's estate with Millie as administrator, to create a guardianship for Winston, and to authorize her to sue as guardian and on behalf of her kids, all of whom were minors. Lucky waived his interest. Without objection, the Court granted Gold's motions. Millie would sue on behalf of her children, her grandchild, and herself.

CHAPTER 28

ALAN GOLD STEPPED OUT of his comfort zone when he decided to hold a press conference announcing the filing of his complaint. He had his office cleaned, his suit pressed, and he even bought a new tie, blue with a bright red stripe. Never had he tried to display himself as a big-league trial attorney.

Others warned him how disastrous press conferences could be, but he thought that he needed to keep the death of Honor before the public or lose momentum. He told himself it was necessary to tell the people in the county, including potential jurors and his opponents, that this might be a big case, deserving a significant award. He was laying it all on the line even without a clue how he was going to prove wrongdoing. He could not help it. He had to put the cart before the horse, or both would go away. He hoped to find out why she died, even while his inner self warned him that hope is not a plan.

If he failed, he pictured himself forever known as the fool of the bar, another naive Don Quixote knocked on his ass by his own lance.

To his surprise, Millie agreed to a press conference. She didn't seem concerned about defeat. She only wanted a stage where she could declare her innocent daughter was not an addict and that her family deserved respect. To her, that message was all that mattered. He didn't know how to prepare her for a press conference; he had never conducted one. And it showed. He had scheduled it too late in the afternoon for TV stations to run it at six in his office, which was not large enough for the cameras and equipment.

The first to arrive was a WBNS-TV cameraman who, after surveying Gold's cramped library, set up his camera and a light on a tripod before stepping out for a smoke. His reporter followed. Later came reporters from *The Columbus Dispatch*, *The Citizen Journal*, *The Call and Post*, and other outlets. The Foxx family owned WBNS radio and TV, as well as *The Dispatch* and *The Citizen Journal*. Chesterton Foxx supported Blandford for reelection, having spent years cultivating him into a "reliable" public servant. He sent his team of reporters there with instructions.

Alan and Millie sat behind a table in his small, newly created library in front of law books hastily borrowed from the county law library, a crude effort to show Gold as a learned and successful attorney. His efforts were quickly upended. The cameramen made the room appear cramped and cluttered while their zooms caught them repeatedly in unflattering shots. Gold wore a white shirt, too bright when seen on the tube. After tapping a microphone and taking a deep breath, Gold began,

"Thank you for coming today. I am reporting to the people of Franklin County a wrong of enormous consequences. Honor Wilson died at the Columbus Women's Correctional Institution from the deliberate indifference of city officials. Her death was needless and preventable. We intend to hold Mayor Blandford, Safety Director Puchik, Acting Superintendent Gross, Dr. Villanueva, and nurses Kratz and Hall accountable. Each, in his or her own way, helped cause Ms. Wilson's death.

"We will be filing suit under state and federal laws. We are confident a jury will hold both them and the city itself responsible for her needless death. Seated next to me is Millie Rivers, mother of Honor Wilson, who now must care for her grandchild. Honor's baby, Winston, will never know his mother. Ms. Rivers would like to make a statement now."

The Matter of Honor

Millie was staring at a tiny crack on the table when Gold spoke, musing about how proud Honor would have been yesterday when Winston said his first word. Startled when she heard her name, she looked directly into bright lights deliberately set to make her squint. In a moment, her eyes adjusted to the light, and she opened them wide, showing two dark eyes surrounded by white floating on a caramel face. The cameramen caught her gawp. They knew how happy Mr. Foxx would be with their handiwork. A picture was still worth a thousand words.

Millie began hesitantly, her voice quivering.

"My family and I are grieving the death of my oldest daughter. Putting her in jail was wrong. She never got into trouble before and was never arrested. And she didn't take drugs. She died in prison because we didn't have money to get her out on bond. When they put her in prison, she was full of life. Now, she is dead because no one paid attention to her.

"Not long ago, my daughter and grandson came from Chicago to live with me and start a new life here. After she moved in, she not only took care of her son Winston but when I was at work, she tended to my other children too—all while she was recuperating from losing a baby at birth. Why did she die? What did she do at the prison to deserve death? Honor was my pride and joy. All I have now are memories of why I was so proud of her and her infant son. Winston is without his mother, and our family is hurting.

"I want to warn every mother. You may think that this could not happen to you or your child, but be aware! Honor could have been your daughter," she said, wiping her eyes. "I have to go to work now."

Gold covered Millie's hand with his own and gave it a gentle squeeze. "Thank you, Ms. Rivers," Gold said. "We'll take a few questions before she leaves."

A voice from the crowd shouted, "The coroner's report says she died of natural causes due to choriocarcinoma, metastatic to the brain. How could authorities be held responsible if she died of natural causes?"

"We will prove that the city improperly cared for Honor and improperly trained its employees. The details will come out at trial."

Another asked, "Did the authorities know of her condition?"

"She reported serious pain and symptoms many times to the medical professionals in prison but her cries for help were ignored. Until it was too late."

Yet another added "Wasn't she going to die regardless?"

"I don't want to go into trial matters, except to say we intend to prove every element of our case, including damages."

The *Dispatch* reporter chimed in, as if on cue, "Didn't the city report they suspected a drug overdose?"

"Yes, without any basis and due to racist stereotypes. That report was wrong."

"But she was charged with a felony drug crime, wasn't she?"

"She was not guilty of those charges."

"What was she addicted to?"

"As Ms. Rivers just said, Honor did not take drugs."

"Do you think if she was taking cocaine, it could have affected her brain tumor?"

"That would be pure speculation. She did not take cocaine."

"Then, are you saying her drug of choice was opiates?"

"No, we are saying and keep saying she did not take drugs. This concludes our conference. Thank you for coming."

The media quickly turned off their bright lights and left. One Foxx reporter mumbled to another, "I think the boss will be pleased." Millie said goodbye to Gold, while Frannie was escorting the press out of the building. When Frannie returned to her desk, she could hear Alan in his office pounding the wall.

An hour later, Millie called him from work, thanking him for giving her the chance to say her piece on television. She said she was pleased with all that had happened and hoped it would be on the 6 o'clock news, but if not, she would see it before she went to bed. Gold remained quiet, fearing her gratitude would turn to anger once she saw it on the tube.

At 11 p.m., the story was hardly a headline, just a brief two-sentence blurb right before sports reporting a mother was suing the city for her daughter's death. The newscaster reported the city's claim she may have died from an overdose while the screen showed close-up footage of a black woman with crazed eyes sitting in a cramped office next to Gold. The story omitted everything Millie had said.

Millie was shocked how the entire press conference had been recreated by television people. She never thought about news-makers manipulating facts. She had been burned this time, but it only made her more determined to get her message across.

Several days later, Gold filed the complaint. With it, he attached "Interrogatories"—questions to be answered in writing under oath (such as identifying all prisoners and all employees at WCI when Honor was there—and "Requests for Documents," such as WCI regulations and Honor's records. A few reporters he called came to record his filing at the clerk of courts where he educated them about the suit (negligence, malpractice, and violation of her federal civil right to be free from cruel and unusual punishment). He also described to them the plaintiffs and explained Ohio's new wrongful death statute and sundry other details. He waited to see what they would do with his lengthy explanation.

A close-up of the first and last page of the complaint was shown on the 6 o'clock news of a non-Foxx station, as the last story before the weather report. It showed the names of the parties and the demand for money. The local section of *The Columbus Dispatch* read, "INMATE'S FAMILY SEEKS MONEY

FROM CITY" while the front page of *The Call and Post* read, "BLACK FAMILY SEEKS JUSTICE FOR DEATH AT JAIL."

A few days after his news conference, Gold was in his office studying one of Frank's many memoranda when Frannie asked if she should put through a call from Cynthia Carlton, Gold's only millionaire client. He had dodged her earlier calls but knew he would have to face her sometime.

"Good morning, Ms. Carlton. I was about to call you."

"My father is starting again, Mr. Gold. He just won't leave me alone. Why do these things always happen to me? Yesterday, he donated my mother's emerald brooch to the art museum after hiring his golfing buddy, a jeweler, to appraise it for three times its value. He is going to claim a gigantic tax deduction, and I am going to lose my brooch. My mother promised it to me before she died. It belonged to her aunt, who died before I was born. I haven't seen the brooch, but I hear it is beautiful. Mr. Gold, we've got to put a stop to this, or he'll steal everything I've got.

"I am so sorry to hear this. Did your mother include the brooch in her will?"

"Well, no, but she once told me that when she died, whatever jewelry I wanted was mine. Let me just say, she would have wanted me to have it. You'll get it back for me, won't you, Mr. Gold?"

"That might be a tall order, Ms. Carlton. As I understand the situation, in your mother's will, she left everything to your father except two houses and a car, plus the money she put in trust for you. If she didn't include the brooch in her will, then I think a court would almost certainly find it belongs to your father."

"Speaking of court, did the judge approve our objection to the trial continuance my father asked for?" she whined.

"That's what I was going to call you about. I've given considerable thought to finding a way to oppose his motion without getting on the wrong side of the judge. On the one hand, your father requested a 60-day continuance to recover from his heart surgery, while on the other, we would argue that the delay might interfere with a cruise you're planning. Frankly, objecting would not, in my opinion, be in your best interest."

"So, you didn't file it? Was it really because of your opinion and my best interest, or because you didn't have time?" she said in her typical snide way while lingering on some words.

"I don't know what you mean."

"Oh, come on now, Alan. I watch TV. I saw you trying to get money for that other woman because her druggie daughter died. Let me just say that you seem to have more time to form an opinion of her best interest than you have for mine."

"Cynthia, I can assure you that I take whatever time and offer whatever opinion is needed for each of my clients."

"Well, I am not so sure. How come you didn't put me on TV like you did her? Maybe you didn't think the TV stations would cover my case, like hers, huh? Well, let me tell you, I know Militia Foxx. We were classmates at Columbus School for Girls. Unlike that woman you were with, I would have spoken up. I would tell everybody what my father is doing to me, instead of looking all crazy like she did. I'm starting to feel like you care more about her and her case than you do about me and mine."

In a calming voice, Gold said, "I hope you know that I devote myself to all my cases and all my clients. I have worked hard on your case and will continue to do so. We will be prepared when your case comes to trial."

"Will we? Have you scheduled the deposition of Uncle Biff? I told you that he once called my father a greedy bastard. Don't you think, if you really took the time for my case, you would have deposed him already? Don't you think, in your opinion, that a jury would like to know what his own brother thinks of him?

Cynthia cleared her throat. "I'll be frank, Alan. I need an attorney for me, not one who goes looking to protect the rights of low-lifes. Let me just say that you seem to be forgetting about where you get your bread-and-butter and what's important." She raised her voice, "I need to know right now, Alan Gold. Are you going to be my attorney or hers?"

He paused, wanting to tell her that he restricted other cases in his portfolio to afford her case the time he would need. He wanted to tell her for the fifth time that deposing her uncle— even if he would admit saying it, which he would never do— would be a costly waste of time. The judge would not admit it into the record.

There was so much he wanted to say, but he knew it was over. Like lovers about to end it, he sensed when she first said hello that she was saying goodbye. After watching 30 seconds of altered TV, she had made up her mind. At the same time, he recognized a kernel of truth in what she said. He had been overlooking what was important, but this moment, this confrontation, brought it to a head—and might bring his practice to its knees. He took a big breath and let out a sigh.

"I remain attorney for all of my clients and will continue to serve them unless they choose otherwise."

"Have it your way. I'll just find another lawyer who will know who I am. Goodbye, Gold."

Alan returned to his memorandum. After a few minutes of silence, Frannie tiptoed into his office and quietly placed a pink inter-office memo slip in his in-basket that read, "Sorry. I never liked her anyway."

CHAPTER 29

LIKE MOST JUDGES IN THE county, Rumsfeld's office scheduled preliminary pretrial conferences a few weeks after cases were filed to allow the judge to review with counsel anticipated issues and to help parties settle their differences. At the conferences, judges also set deadlines to complete discovery and to file certain motions like those to dismiss cases. Judges schedule them for 8:30 a.m., a half-hour before they don their robes to take the bench.

When Gold arrived at the new Hall of Justice for his conference, he noticed how it had aged since he attended its opening a dozen years earlier, when he heard politicians announce the dawn of a new era, a time of justice for all. Now, he saw graffiti adorning its elevator walls. As he got off on the seventh floor, Gold wondered whether he would be treated fairly because he had not donated to Judge Rumsfeld's campaign. He knew that defense lawyers made enormous contributions to judges' campaigns, possibly from insurance companies that viewed donations as paying premiums for a later benefit. Gold donated to no campaigns and no candidates.

"Good morning. I'm here for the pretrial conference with Judge Rumsfeld in the Rivers vs. the City of Columbus case. My name is Alan Gold."

"Yeah, I know who you are. Take your seat in the conference room. The judge isn't here yet," said the once-muscular man, looking at Gold as he would a suspect.

"I don't believe we've met. Am I famous or something?" Gold asked with a sheepish laugh.

"Saw you on TV a while back, pumping this case for that Negro family."

"Oh, ugh. I wasn't ... did you? ... What did you think of it?"

"Frankly, I didn't care for it. When I was on the force, we arrested girls and took them to WCI all the time. We did our job, and the staff there did theirs. Never thought it would lead to inmate lawsuits. Cases like this hurt the reputation of law enforcement. I may not wear a badge anymore, but I worry about our boys in blue just trying to their jobs."

"I'm sorry. I didn't catch your name."

"Walton, Ben Walton. I've been Judge Rumsfeld's bailiff since he took the bench."

"Well, Mr. Walton, I'm not sure what their jobs were when you were a cop, but while they were supposed to be doing whatever they do, Honor died."

"Yeah, well, we all gotta go sometime. Take a seat. The judge will be here soon."

Gold walked into the small conference room to the head of the table where he expected the judge would sit. After his experience with Rumsfeld's bailiff, Gold needed to compose himself. Ben's negativity could be a bellwether, a bad omen.

Later, Walton walked opposing counsel into the small conference room. Introductions began, followed by small talk. The others knew each other; none had met Alan. Weather, traffic, lawyer gossip, and sports filled the stifling air as they waited for the judge. Someone glanced at the clock, well past 9:00 a.m.

The lawyers grew annoyed with the delay. Each was thinking, *What would the judge do to me if I were as late as he is?*

Judge Rumsfeld arrived at 9:23 a.m. He took a seat at the head of the conference table and peered through his bloodshot eyes at those around him while he opened the file, looking only at the tab.

"Rivers v. the City of Columbus. Well, boys, why are we here?" he said in his gravelly voice, acknowledging he was unprepared.

"Well, sir, we are here for the preliminary pretrial you scheduled," Ed Auber, Assistant City Attorney, began. "I represent the city, as you know. Frederick Livingston represents nurses Kratz and Hill, and Gordon Chase at the end of the table represents Dr. Villanueva. Mr. Gold, seated across from us, filed a complaint on behalf of the family of one Honor Wilson, once an inmate at WCI, alleging some general malpractice, nonspecific violations of civil rights, and other vague claims allegedly linked to her unfortunate and unavoidable death while in the custody of the city."

"Any pending motions?"

"Not at this time, Your Honor. We expect to file motions soon to end this case. We do not believe it is possible that the plaintiffs can win," said Auber.

"Mr. Gold?"

Alan cleared his throat. All eyes were on him. "Your Honor, we have only begun discovery, but we expect the evidence to show Honor Wilson, the deceased, was in the workhouse only because she had no funds to post bail. She was convicted of absolutely nothing, and her gross mistreatment while incarcerated at WCI caused her death."

"Do you have an expert, Mr. Gold?" growled the judge.

"Not yet, Your Honor. We will retain one before discovery is completed."

"Better get one soon. Ben will set the trial date. I will review motions when they are filed. Anything else? If not, good day, gentlemen." Judge Rumsfeld went straight to the coffee pot for some wake-up juice.

Alan gathered his files into his briefcase. He saw the backs of defense counsel huddling. Gordon whispered to Auber, "Has the

City decided yet whether it will defend or dump on its medical staff?"

"Not yet," said Ed. "All in good time."

"Give us a call as soon as you can, Ed. Holding hands works a lot better than pointing fingers."

CHAPTER 30

WVKO, A BLACK-ORIENTED radio station in town, had an assortment of disk jockeys who not only introduced songs but also provided community talk, weather reports, announcements of jazz groups coming to town, news snippets with a bit of commentary, and selected topics on musicians. Those who withstood low pay and long hours sometimes became local cult personalities. Of all WVKO disk jockeys, none was more popular than Sweet Willie Moss. His youthful enthusiasm made him an instant attraction, while his home-grown background gave him authenticity. And his smooth voice made him a natural for radio.

At East High school, he had dated Honor Wilson, but nothing much came of it. They would sometimes get together after they graduated. But any hope of a lasting relationship ended once she met Junior at a party off OSU's campus. She was smitten by the man from afar. Willie completed broadcasting school and interned at WVKO. A year later, he became a DJ there. He heard that Honor had returned from Chicago, but he never got around to giving her a call.

He came to Honor's funeral with his jacket collar up to avoid being noticed. After Pastor Jenkin's eulogy, he quickly left, profoundly affected. Although his job as a DJ was to wax on the falsetto of Eddie Kendricks from the Temptations, after her funeral, he needed to talk about Honor. He wondered if her death affected his listeners as much as it did him. Moss asked around about what happened to her and picked up bits and pieces about others who had been mistreated while in WCI.

A. S. WHITE

He began his show one day with a casual comment about her funeral. Later, he said something about her arrest, and near the end of the show, he made a few comments about her incarceration. The station received outpourings of calls and letters from those claiming they or those they knew too had faced false arrests, outrageous bonds, poor medical care while incarcerated, and issues he hadn't mentioned.

Moss, whose soft radio voice and gentle personality confirmed his nickname "Sweet Willie," became angrier as he reviewed each day's responses. Nearly every aspect of what he described as leading to Honor's death was met with both calls and letters from listeners reporting similar experiences. How could this have happened in the city he loved?

He continued the conversation, replacing his gab about the divorce of Ike and Tina Turner with the marriage of bail-bond agents to judges. As his ratings jumped, his station manager urged him to keep talking.

On one show, he interviewed the reporter from *The Call and Post* covering Honor's death and the upcoming trial. He asked if listeners agreed with James Baldwin ("And the police are simply the hired enemies of this population [blacks]. They are present to keep the Negro in his place and to protect white business interests, and they have no other function"), or whether Richard Wright was correct, ("Men simply copied the realities of their hearts when they built prisons"). Later, he used his conversation with the reporter to start another on the value of prison itself, quoting Malcolm X ("The prison systems in this country actually are exploitative and they are not in any way rehabilitative.").

Moss also shared his microphone with victims of police abuse who told of their experiences. Listeners responded to his quote of Elijah Muhammad warning that a white man "doesn't care anything about the innocent, no more than he cares for the guilty. His only evil intention is to get rid of the Negro in any way he possibly can." Listeners stood in line at the station downtown to tell Willie their stories.

To his manager's surprise, listeners wanted Willie to take time away from R&B gossip and talk about incarceration. As Sweet Willie's ratings rose, his manager told him to transform his show "Stack of Shellac" from playing Stevie Wonder to wondering why so many abuses occurred at WCI; from Motown to Mayor Blandford's staff running from accusations regarding public safety; from "Where is the Love?" to Where is the Justice?

A few listeners dropped out, but most could hardly wait for his next program. Sweet Willie himself morphed from a bubble-gum DJ to a serious critic of criminal justice. His sweet voice became ever more strident. He started wearing a T-shirt showing a black fist and reading all he could about incarceration.

Much of what Sweet Willie said put him at odds with the older Pastor Jenkins, who advocated working in a conciliatory manner with those holding power. The black community was united yet divided, united in their anger and distrust of the mayor and city leaders but divided on what to do about it. It didn't matter that Gold had not proven anyone at fault in Honor Wilson's case. The issue of prison mistreatment had taken on a life of its own.

Owners of WVKO were delighted with Willie's recent ratings, never mind his program content. They pushed his show whenever they could, especially after Sweet Willie turned bitter and his latest numbers spiked even among white listeners, increasing by seven percent.

His opportunistic station manager found another way to boost Willie's ratings. He convinced the principal of East High to provide its auditorium as a forum for a community debate, to be aired exclusively on WVKO, on the topic "Criminal Injustice—How to Fix It."

A. S. White

The debate was to feature Pastor Jenkins and Sweet Willie Moss, and as an added attraction, the manager lined up Archie Griffin of OSU football fame to be moderator. The hour-long event would be divided into four 10-minute parts with commercial breaks before, after, and between. WVKO hired additional staff to sell ads. The manager had a sign (with the WVKO letters boldly displayed) erected on the front lawn of East High two weeks before the debate. Black barbershop and beauty salon owners agreed the upcoming debate was the leading topic of conversation in their shops.

Before the debate, Pastor Jenkins aroused positive support from his parishioners with a Sunday sermon advocating social justice by working with city officials. Sweet Willie, on the other hand, advocated confrontation. To add spice to the debate heating up, Willie enticed listeners to attend the debate and hear him drop a bombshell announcement.

Since the mayor's press conference, none of the Foxx-owned media outlets mentioned either the upcoming debate or any developments following Honor's death. It was as if her death had never happened, wasn't newsworthy, or the problem (whatever it was) had been fixed. Terry Prince was sure he would later get a bonus for his work convincing the Foxx family to bury the story.

The auditorium was packed 25 minutes before the debate, although those attending were not as sharply divided as WVKO had portrayed in its many teaser ads. Pastor Jenkins was old enough to be Sweet Willie's father, and Sweet Willie did not attend Sunday services regularly. WVKO hyped their minor differences to increase listener interest. Few came that night to learn. Some came to support one or the other debaters, while most came because it was a happening they wouldn't miss. And everyone wanted to know what Sweet Willie's bombshell was.

Millie did not want to sit in a special front-row seat, preferring to be away from the spotlight. But as is often the case, events overtake preferences.

Every sound from the audience reverberated off the auditorium's high ceiling. The cacophony turned into a roar of approval when the town's football darling, Archie Griffin, wearing gray slacks and a scarlet shirt with the OSU logo, walked across the stage to start the evening. As fit as a running back in season, he walked to the podium and adjusted the microphone.

"Tonight, I have the pleasure of moderating a discussion between two very fine men, both of whom care deeply about our city but who have strong differences on how to deal with the current situation. The death of Honor Wilson is a mystery to us all. We are being tested in how we respond. Tonight, we will hear different ideas on what we should do. Before I introduce our speakers, I ask you to really listen to these people. You really can learn so much by simply listening. It's an increasingly lost skill in our hyper-connected, multi-tasking society. And that makes listening all the more important."

His words gently quieted the crowd, and they relaxed. He introduced Pastor Jenkins, who, by agreement, spoke first. Skillful in crowd control, the man of the cloth eased the noise level down another notch with a few thank-you's and some pleasantries. When the time was right, he got down to business.

"Friends, just the other day, with sorrow in my soul and rage in my heart, I officiated at the funeral of Honor Wilson. She was a young sister in the prime of her life who went to Paradise, leaving her baby son to be cared for by her mother, Millie Rivers, who is here tonight. Please join me at this time to express our sorrow (*Applause*).

"Honor had been arrested a few weeks earlier, but without money to post a bond, she, like so many others, rotted in jail awaiting trial. She walked in alive and healthy, and a few weeks later, they carried her to a hospital to die. They say she died of cancer. They say her death was nothing but a natural occurrence. They say her death could not have been avoided.

"But that's not what I say. Her death was not the will of God. I say she died at the hands of men in power, white men in power. The White House has asked law enforcement around the country to pay less attention to cocaine and marijuana crimes and focus on others, but still they continue to prosecute drug cases above all others. We need change.

"Few of our people are judges or lawyers, but we can be proud that one of our brothers, who is here today, sits on the City Council. Another was recently elected to the school board. Ladies' and gentlemen, I see a new dawn awakening, when we'll look to our first black mayor holding the reins of power and taking control of WCI. Cleveland saw it a dozen years ago and it will come here too. That dawn is 'a-comin'.

"We suspect great mistakes were made, unforgivable judgments were executed, tragic errors occurred. We must find out what happened and work with those in power to correct any errors and ensure they never happen again. We need an investigation. But most of all, we must work together to resolve our differences and build a multi-racial community. My friends, there is no other way."

Polite applause followed. Archie then introduced Sweet Willie, who got straight to the point.

"Let's talk about those white men in power Pastor Jenkins spoke about. They're using their powers in a new way, a mean way, an evil way. They're locking up more of our brothers and sisters as they arrest more poor people, not only here but everywhere across the country. I warn you, the power to lock up, even for a little while, is the power to destroy. Jail destroys jobs and families. It takes away income. It ruins relationships forever. Most important, it destroys self-worth. If we don't stop the incarceration of our brothers and sisters, it will destroy us. And they use their power to keep us down. ('Yes, they do, yes they do!'). They use their power to repress us in jobs ('Amen'), in schools ('It's a fact'), and especially in law enforcement ('Lord, have mercy!'). Incarceration has become the most significant tragedy our people have faced since slavery.

"I declare the present mayor incapable of running the police force. His cops are arresting too many of our people, putting them in jail. He doesn't know how to operate a jail when young people like Honor Wilson die there.

"For too long, our elders have urged caution, advised us to work with white folk, telling us hope is on the way. They forget Dr. King's words from the Birmingham jail, warning us that the Negro's great stumbling block in his stride toward freedom is not the white Citizen's Councilor or the Ku Klux Klanner, but the white moderate, who is more devoted to "order" than to justice.

"They ignore Malcolm X 's words speaking about white folks, that he never saw a sincere white man, that he only uses black folks for his own benefit, that he cares more about a little dent in his white Chevy than he does about a big police crack in a black man's head.

"We have a right to know what happened to Honor. We cannot trust what City Hall tells us, and we must find out for ourselves what happened.

"Tonight, I am announcing for all to hear. Starting next Monday, I will begin broadcasting my WVKO program, "Stack of Shellac," from our WVKO sound truck in the parking lot across from WCI. I will interview anyone leaving or coming to WCI who is willing to share their experience, particularly anyone who can tell us what happened to Honor Wilson. Please listen to my show for complete details. Maybe you will be listening at the very moment someone tells us what really happened to Honor." Everyone cheered and made a note to listen to his broadcast.

A. S. White

As the crowd left the school, its roar of support could be heard in Bexley, the wealthy town east of the railroad tracks separating it from Columbus. *The Call and Post*'s reporter, whom Sweet Willie had interviewed, filled her notebook and even took photos of the historic moment.

Terry Prince's only black staffer, who had been detailed to cover the debate, left without talking to anyone and reported to her boss from a nearby phone booth. Mr. Prince was not pleased.

CHAPTER 31

TO GOLD'S REQUESTS FOR documents, defendants provided copies of the following:

- Honor's 3x5 medical records,
- her arrest sheet,
- her intake sheet,
- a summary from someone named Bobbin,
- WCI regulations,
- medical staff rules,
- all pill-call and sick-call sheets for the days she was incarcerated, etc.
- 196 names of prisoners and employees who had been at WCI while Honor was there.

Because his requests were not adequately designed, defendants had cleverly provided data without direction. As a neophyte to complex litigation, Gold was staggered by how much he received yet what little he could make of it. He found little connection between any person and Honor, except obvious ones, like nursing staff and the medical cards they wrote or inmate summaries signed by an employee named Bobbin, but little else. Because sleeping quarters were dorm-style, WCI responded to his question that it couldn't tell him on any given day which prisoner slept in which bunk nor which guards patrolled which dorm, leaving him unable to tie anyone to Honor or her death.

He looked again, hoping for a way out of his wilderness. How could he find out who knew what? He could not depose 196 guards and inmates. Besides, many inmates had been released or were leaving soon. Except for what he'd learned from Johni and Puddin, he had no clue which inmate or guard had even met Honor, or had helpful information. What to do?

Frank reviewed what they received in finer detail. Later, he came to Gold's office.

"I think I found some things that might be of help. I reviewed all the pill-call and sick-call sheets. Honor's name first appeared as the last person on a pill-call sheet four days after she arrived. After that, she stood in pill-call a total of 23 times, mostly with Nurse Kratz. The day after her 19th pill-call, I found her name on the sick-call list for the first and only time. We don't know how they ran pill-call, but we have names of inmates standing in front and behind her who might have heard what was said."

"Can you imagine, Frank, what it must have been like for her to complain to a nurse 19 times before getting a chance to see a doctor?"

"Not really. My only major medical event was when they took out my tonsils."

Gold started taking depositions of those who had stood near Honor in pill-calls or sick-call, and anyone mentioned by Johni or Puddin. He didn't know how else to begin. He started with low-ranking employees and moved up to named defendants in charge. He made the tactical decision not to depose either Johni or Puddin to protect them. He planned to list every prisoner and guard as a potential witness, confusing the city until trial. The danger in not deposing those helpful, he knew, was that they might not show up for the trial, and he would be embarrassed at trial without them. But the danger in exposing them was that they might clam up. He chose to protect them from intimidation.

Gold's first set of depositions included Sgt. Mitchell (a guard mentioned by Puddin), a few random guards, Ms. Bobbin (the inmate summaries author), and a few inmates listed before and after Honor in pill-call lines. At Gold's request, Gross requisitioned the WCI staff breakroom for these depositions. On the first scheduled date, defense lawyers with their files and yellow pads sat on one side of a table, while Gold sat on the other with his. The court reporter was stationed at the head of the table to hear and see the mouths of Gold on one side and each deponent on the other.

Sgt. Viola Mitchell, wearing a WCI uniform for her deposition, looked wide-eyed around the breakroom as if she had never been in it. She haltingly sat next to the court reporter, jerking toward whatever direction she heard a voice, like a trapped animal. Out of the corner of his eye, Gold saw Auber, attorney for the city, nod when Mitchell looked at him. From that little gesture, Gold assumed Auber had instructed her before the deposition. After being sworn in, she continued squirming while awaiting Gold's questions. He debated whether to leave her in her agitated state or to try to calm her down. He chose the latter and slowly asked her preliminaries (name, address, date of birth, education, years of employment at WCI, etc.) before gently guiding her toward her recollections of Honor Wilson.

Before answering nearly every question, Mitchell hesitated. She repeatedly asked him for clarification of simple questions, then changed responses to previous answers. She thought she might have met Honor soon after she was booked, but she wasn't sure. She did not remember where Honor bunked nor who her bunkmate was. She didn't know anyone with whom Honor became friends. Perhaps Mitchell was on duty the evening Nurse Hill reported instructing Mitchell to take Honor to the Hole. The inmate might have been weak, but maybe not. She's not a doctor. Sgt. Lynks told her she'd let Honor out of the Hole, so maybe she wasn't sick at all.

When Gold tried to engage Mitchell in direct eye contact, she turned toward Ed Auber. She thought she recalled seeing Honor in the Hole after Nurse Kratz placed her there. Or, was that the second time she was in the Hole? She couldn't remember. She may have called the emergency squad to take Honor to the hospital. No, she couldn't remember another time she'd called the squad for an ill patient, but there might have been. It's so busy every day. She just could not recall much of anything about anybody.

Did she tell the squad that Honor might have overdosed? She wasn't sure, but it was possible. Because she didn't recall telling the squad of a possible OD, she could not explain why she said it. She did not know for sure if Honor was a drug abuser. She might have been. Mitchell sighed. She just could not recall; there being so many inmates who come and go. They all start to look alike. Her deposition lasted for hours without Gold getting anything but frustrated. Her answers were vague, contradictory, and meaningless.

As he did at the end of each deposition, he gave her his business card, encouraging her to contact him for any reason. Each time he gave a card to a city employee, Auber objected and instructed the deposed city employee not to communicate with Gold but to call the City Attorney's office first.

As she rose, Gold studied her face, particularly her eyes. Mitchell did not wear the satisfied look of a witness who had bested him, nor did she show regret that she could not provide more information. Her face was blank. As she left, he wondered what she was feeling.

He then deposed several other guards and inmates, all shots in the dark. He stopped most of them soon after hearing them testify that they did not recall Honor at all. One guard did remember being with Mitchell when the squad came but not much else, and she did not hear Mitchell speak to the squad. Guards repeated the same lines, like: "things were pretty hectic that day," or "I do not have good powers of recall," or "there are so many inmates, I can't be sure." or "I would only be guessing."

No inmate that day recalled being either at pill-call or sick-call line when Honor stood there, despite their names on the list.

CHAPTER 32

HIS LAST DEPOSITION FOR the day was Theresa Bobbin. Gold didn't know much about Bobbin, except for her having written Honor's inmate summary. Apparently, she was a social worker at WCI who wrote descriptions of inmates for the benefit of the guards. He assumed she might provide counseling as well. *More precious time and money I'm about to waste,* he thought.

Bobbin, a short, broad, black figure in a dark blue suit jacket, strode in, but unlike other city employees, she did not look toward Auber. Theresa carried a lot of weight from her waist down, as if a chocolate Pillsbury Doughboy had been squeezed at the top and bulged below. As he began asking her questions, Gold was encouraged by her businesslike attitude.

He asked her what she could remember about Honor, expecting another non-answer.

"I first met Ms. Wilson in my office. We talked for nearly an hour a few days after she was booked. It was from that interview that I compiled my summary."

For the first time, Gold heard a witness speak with certainty. He sat up in his chair and leaned forward.

"How did she appear to you?"

"Frightened and confused. She couldn't understand why she had been arrested."

"Did she talk about her health?"

"Yes, she did. She told me she was very tired and had headaches and pain in her genital area. She told me that she had suffered a stillbirth, and she informed Nurse Kratz that she was scheduled to see a doctor for a six-week checkup."

"Did she tell you Nurse Kratz's reaction?" asked Gold, leaning forward.

"She told me that Nurse Kratz didn't believe her, called her a liar."

"Did you discuss with Nurse Kratz what Honor said?"

"No, I did not. Nurse Kratz, years ago, made it very clear to me and others that no one was to interfere with the operations of the medical staff."

Ed Auber set down his pen and crossed his arms. He leaned back, his eyebrows raised.

"Did Ms. Wilson talk about anything else?" Gold pressed further.

"Yes, she complained that they wouldn't let her have a lower bunk. She said she was not feeling well. As I recall, she was a large woman. She said she was having difficulty climbing to the upper bunk. She complained to me later that she could not get a lower bunk even when her bunkmate, Fabiola Rodriguez, was removed."

"Fabiola. Oh, yes, do you know what happened to her?"

"Not entirely. I also had an initial interview with her after she was processed. While I cannot divulge the details of our conversation, I came away thinking she was losing her grip on reality. A week or two later, I saw Sgt. Lynks and another guard drag Fabiola soaking wet down the hall to the Hole, and I asked the sergeant why.

"She said Ms. Rodriguez had violated her direct order to take a shower. Fabiola refused, explaining that Jesus had just anointed her and given her grace. She could not take a shower without washing away her anointment. Sgt. Lynks ordered guards to carry her into the shower, where they doused her. Fabiola later attempted suicide and was removed to a mental institution. Unfortunately, many inmates at WCI have untreated mental illnesses."

Gold took a break from the deposition. After composing himself, he asked,

"Did Honor ever get a lower bunk?"

"Not to my knowledge. After Fabiola was removed from WCI, I asked Mr. Gross, the acting superintendent, if Ms. Wilson could take Ms. Rodrigues's lower bunk for medical reasons. After checking with medical staff, he informed me that WCI does not cater to liars."

When Gold completed the deposition of Bobbin, he felt limp, as though her words had drained from him his youthful belief in justice and human dignity. He wanted to beg Bobbin, like when cheating was uncovered in the 1919 World Series and a reporter begged Shoeless Joe Jackson, to "Say it ain't so, Joe." But Alan knew that it was. Good for his case, bad for his city.

CHAPTER 33

TRUE TO HIS WORD AND HYPE, Sweet Willie set up the WVKO sound truck, newly named Sweet Willie's "Moss Mobile," across from WCI. Cars honked as they drove by. A cop drove up to the truck to caution him before he started broadcasting to keep the noise down despite WCI's location in an industrial area near a noisy freeway.

It was an odd event—part carnival, part drama, and part serious radio conversation. Nearly a hundred fans stood around the truck for the opening, not sure whether they should cheer, grieve, or party. Sweet Willie would mention something on air, and in an instant, listeners would flood the station's phone lines with personal incidents of police brutality, false arrests, unfair bonds, and other events that might have caused them or someone in their family a loss of job, custody of their kids, or bankruptcy. Many reported inhumane treatments at WCI, which had increased since Gross took over.

After the tumult subsided, Willie maintained the Moss Mobile for weeks without having uncovered Honor's story, even with a large sign above the truck asking prisoners and guards for information. He instructed several fans to stand in WCI's parking lot and encourage guards and former prisoners or their families to talk to him, even if he would have to pay them.

After interviewing many former prisoners looking for easy money who had nothing to say, he spoke to Tonya Gates, a former WCI inmate. She could not stop complaining about her own maladies she accused WCI of ignoring. Eventually, Willie was able to focus her attention on Honor Wilson. When she confirmed that she once stood next to Honor in pill-call when Honor's complaints were ignored by Kratz, Willie jumped on it, announcing on the air his success in proving Honor died from WCI's failure to treat her.

The station manager saw it as a perfect opportunity to shut down the Moss Mobile. It had enjoyed a good run, drawn attention to WVKO, and, most importantly, sold lots and lots of ads. After exploiting the revelation of Tonya Gates for a few days, he instructed Sweet Willie to declare success and end the vigil but not the conversation. Sweet Willie's show continued to monitor the matter of Honor and provide blow-by-blow descriptions of anything he found. He followed each revelation with opinions from listeners who called to join the conversation. Never had a case in Columbus received so much local media attention, despite the station's small and narrowly focused market.

CHAPTER 34

JOHNI PACED THE FLOORS OF WCI, seeing BabyCakes everywhere. The death of Honor overwhelmed her. She had snooped for Gold, and talked to guards and Nurse Hill. But she was unable to speak to Gross or other high-ups, who suddenly turned tight-lipped. Johni knew they were hiding something. One evening after dinner when things quieted down, she cozied up to Sgt. Mitchell brooding in a hallway.

"Wassup, Sarge?"

"Pretty quiet around here tonight."

"I know what you mean, after the death and all. Seems like nothing can be as bad as that."

"Yep, it was one hell of a mess."

"Sad to see a sister go down, ain't it?"

"You said it, girl. So sad," Mitchell said, looking down and nodding.

"Is you the one who called the squad? That must have been tough."

"Yeah, but it got worse. Say, did you know the Wilson girl?"

"Oh, a little. We talked now and then. Why?" asked Johni.

"Was she doing stuff?"

"Stuff... You mean drugs?"

"Yeah. Was she doing stuff?"

"No way. That newbie was straight. Why?"

"Damn that Haskel!" Sgt. Mitchell said as she started walking down the hall, mumbling to herself.

CHAPTER 35

THE MORNING WAS FRIGID. Gray clouds swirled, warning of impending storms. Twigs crackled under his feet as Duke walked down Broad Street toward East High School, once a public school of the rich and famous, like writer James Thurber, footballer Chick Harley, and both football great and actor Bernie Casey. Those names meant nothing to the teen, and neither did the school's past or future. From his past, he wanted Honor to return. For his future, he wanted a well-paying job. From the present, he wanted nothing more than peace of mind.

He continued to conceal his grief under a black hat with a wide brim. He wore it as his unspoken statement of mourning, but with his bell-bottomed pants and his platform shoes, not everyone read him the same way. Walking up East's grand front steps, he could feel the eyes of other students looking at him. This was his first day back since the press conference, and he had taken a few days off. They'd probably seen his mother on TV earlier and maybe the photo in *The Call and Post* of the family leaving the funeral.

His head was down when he walked the noisy hall toward his locker. Wherever he went, silence surrounded him, like he was in a moving tomb. The sound of talk ahead of him hushed as he walked by and resumed after he passed, leaving him in a vacuum of silence. When he got to his locker, he worked the Masterlock combination to open it and put his hat and coat in.

He was selecting books and things to take from his locker, when Fat Jimmy and two of his gang approached, stopping across the hall from him. Fat Jimmy was a big kid who enjoyed making trouble. He heard their voices from outside his head, as well as his mama's from inside warning him to avoid people like Fat Jimmy. Soon she was drowned out by the blurred voices of Jimmy and his gang. To Duke, it sounded like they were talking about him.

He made a snap decision. If they dissed only him, he pledged to Mama to remain silent, but if they went after Honor or his family, he promised nothing. Mama always said family meant everything. He feigned looking at his assignment book when Jimmy walked up with a big smile on his face, like he were about to pull a practical joke.

"Saw your people on TV. Your family hired a white lawyer, huh? You turned your back on our brothers?"

Duke ignored him.

"Your family think they gonna be driving a big white Cadillac soon?"

"Shut the fuck up, asshole," Duke blurted out.

"Ooo, big man, huh?" Jimmy pushed Duke against the locker. "Your mama thinks she's gonna make a mint off your dope-head sister?"

Duke exploded. He turned so fast Jimmy didn't see his fist until it smashed his nose. Both hands of Duke pumped all his outrage into Jimmy's fat belly. *Thmp, Thmp, Thmp!* Jimmy doubled over in pain, but his two comrades quickly pounced on Duke. One grabbed his wrists while the other stepped behind him and smacked the back of his legs with a bat. Duke dropped to the floor with a thud. Fat Jimmy delivered a sharp kick to his gut before falling on him with a flurry of punches to the face. Duke could not protect himself.

"Hey, what's going on there?" a teacher yelled.

Fat Jimmy's thugs took off, leaving Duke on the floor beneath Jimmy. By the time two teachers pulled Jimmy off, both students were bloody blobs. When the teachers asked kids standing nearby what happened, no one reported seeing or hearing anything. The teachers dragged both kids to the principal's office.

When Millie got home from work, little Winston was taking a nap, and Ella and Billie were cooking mac-and-cheese and collard greens with bacon. Millie insisted on their eating dinner as a family. She had refused second-shift work to be with them for dinner, even when it meant not being there in the morning when they left for school. As each child got older, they were assigned dinner chores. After her divorce, Millie continued this nightly ritual, despite the difficulties it caused. Nor did the tradition stop when Honor moved in. If anything, family dinners became more important to her. It created order, and with it, a sense of family. Millie might tolerate sloppy rooms, but she would not stand for refusing to help prepare dinner or sitting at the crowded table with the family.

"Everything okay?"

The girls smiled and nodded.

"Where's Duke? He's supposed to pull the kitchen table from the wall and set it."

The girls looked at each other. "He ran upstairs just as soon as he came home today," said Ella.

As she stirred the mac and cheese, Billie asked her older sister, "Did your teacher tell you what school you'll be going to next year when the bussing starts?"

"No, we'll find out this summer," answered Ella.

"Everybody at school is talking about it. Will white kids come here? Or are we going there or what?"

"I just hope nobody starts to fight. I see a lot of fuss on TV from white parents, and I wonder what their kids think?"

"Do you think you could have a white friend?"

"Not sure. How about you?"

"I ain't never had a white friend and never been in a white house. What do you think they're like?"

"Don't know. I wonder if their parents are like our mama or like some mean old folks I see on TV. I'm scared about next year."

"Me too."

Millie hung up her coat in the closet at the base of the stairs. "Duke, Dinnertime!"

"I'm not hungry, Mama."

"Well, come join us anyway. You know the rules."

"Hmmm, I'm not well. Can I skip dinner?"

"You got a disease? Are your legs broken? What's the matter with you?" After a long pause, she said in a firm voice, "Duke, come to dinner now. Don't make me come get you!" she said, walking into the kitchen.

Duke walked down the steps, sat in his corner seat, and faced the wall with his fedora covering his face. Miles had pulled out the table and arranged the chairs.

"Duke, take off that hat. We're going to eat dinner as soon as you set the table. Duke, do you hear me?"

He slowly removed the fedora. There was a familial gasp as his puffy eye, split cheek, and bloody lip came into view. He looked like he just lost to Roberto Duran.

"Oh, my God! What happened to you, child?" shrieked Millie.

"Nothin'."

"That swelled eye isn't nothin'."

"Yeah, well, I got in a fight at school."

Millie glared at her son for a moment, as a tear floated down her cheek. "You know what I told you about violence."

"But Mama, Fat Jimmy said we was trying to get rich, and Honor was a dope-head. I got to him first, but his two buddies knocked me down, and then he beat me. I would've beat him bad, except one kid had a bat. Both of us got suspended. The principal says you got to come to school and talk to him tomorrow, else I can't come back."

"Duke, didn't I tell you violence only begets violence? Next time you see Jimmy, will you turn violent again? And the time after? When will it stop?"

"But he was dissing my sister and my family. I tried to be cool, but I couldn't let him mouth off like that. I couldn't let Fat Jimmy trash-talk our family like he was doing. My rep was on the line. Didn't you also say we got to protect our family's rep?"

The family was quiet for a moment. No one knew what to say, unable to reconcile Mama's words with Duke's.

"I'm sorry, Mama. All's I know is when someone goes on about my family, I lose it. Besides, if I don't stop Fat Jimmy, who will?"

"You'll lose more than your temper if you keep this up. Sit over here and let me take care of that eye." She turned to Ella. "Help Miles set the table so we can eat."

After a nearly silent dinner, Millie helped clean up and feed little Winston, who started crying when he awoke, before going to her room to put Winston down for the night. She'd have to see the principal and take more time off work, which meant less money and more problems with her boss. Unlike other supervisors at the home who had annual salaries, Millie was paid hourly as a nurse aide's supervisor.

The lawsuit already impacted her family more than she had imagined. She prayed for guidance before she helped get the younger kids ready for bed.

CHAPTER 36

POLLY GIBSON SENSED TROUBLE when three council members demanded to see the mayor immediately. The mayor instructed her to have Terry Prince there with him, and Blandford also told her to invite Assistant City Attorney Ed Auber, leader of the defense team in Gold's suit. The mayor and the City Attorney, who selected Auber, were elected Republicans, and they worked well together.

"Oh, Christ," responded Terry to her call. "Those spineless ferrets need petting already? They don't know a crisis from a problem. OK, dear Polly, I will come and hold their hands."

Terry arrived a few minutes early, but the mayor was late returning from another meeting. Ed came next, briefcase in hand containing Gold's complaint, the autopsy report, and his trusty yellow pad. He left other important documents in his office. Allowing a politician access to confidential trial documents is the same as delivering them express mail to your opponent and the press.

"Afternoon, Miss Polly. I haven't seen you in a month of Sundays. How's the family?"

"Good afternoon, Mr. Auber. It has been a while, and we're doing just fine. And you?"

"You know. New day, but the same old stuff. I don't suppose today will be any different."

"Probably not. Can I get you some coffee? You like yours with double sugar, if I recall."

"Oh, you're good, Polly. You never forget a thing. Coffee sounds great. I hope it will steady my nerves for this meeting."

"I doubt it, but you can try. Judging from the tone of Councilman Baer, this will not be a serenity session. Tell me if the coffee works or if you need more."

"Will do. So, Mr. Prince, what have you been up to?" asked Ed, turning to Terry.

"Oh, just trying to get the mayor re-elected and keep him out of trouble. This workhouse crap is not helpful."

"Understood. As usual, I don't get to pick my cases."

"Hello, Gorgeous," Lex Baer called out, leading two other councilmen into the mayor's outer office. He had met Polly many times but could not recall her name. Lex was sporting a red sport coat, bright blue tie, white pants, and white shoes, even in winter. In his mouth was his ever-present Churchill cigar, and he chewed until it resembled rotten seaweed. Then he would turn it around and chew the other end, displaying the moist, masticated mess.

"Hello, Mr. Baer. How are you today?" she asked him, continuing her typing as she spoke.

"Why, if I were any better, Darlin', I'd sell peanuts to those watching. Yes, indeedy. Say, is your good-looking boss here?"

"The mayor is running a little late and will be here shortly. He asked me to apologize for his delay."

"Well, normally, I would be offended by being stood up, but when an apology is sugarcoated with the sweetness I can see dripping from your luscious lips, I'll accept it," Lex said, bending over her desk and looking at her through his black, horned-rimmed glasses.

Polly gave him a half-smile and kept typing.

Lex and the other council members sat down together. The room turned quiet. Ed and Terry tacitly agreed to leave Lex alone, and neither harbored any intentions of encouraging more of Mr. Baer's banalities. Lex, uncomfortable in silence, chatted with his fellow council members.

Mayor Blandford opened his private office door, having entered from his separate back entrance, stepped forward, and broadly swept his arm toward his office to welcome his guests. They chose their seats at the mayor's conference table. Terry grabbed one immediately to the right of the mayor's chair while Ed sat next to Terry. The council members sat on the opposite side of the table, with Lex sitting next to the mayor.

"That Jimmy Carter has got himself into some deep shit," Lex commented. "Have you seen gas prices lately? Looks like they're going to be higher than a drunken sailor. And if they are, we will wring his neck next year."

"Can the President control oil prices?" asked Ed Auber.

"Son, I say, son, in politics, if folks believe he can, then he can. And we'll hold him accountable when he can't."

"Well, Lex, I don't suppose you came here to talk about the effect of global oil prices in next year's election. What's on your mind?" asked the mayor.

"Mr. Mayor, we have our own little bucket of shit to deal with. I want to be as straight-talking as I can. Me and these guys are looking to be reelected in November, and we hear the jigs are startin to get upset about some girl who died in jail. We don't need any of that shit before the elections. We're here to ask you what you're doing about it. We need to get the issue off the table now."

The mayor hesitated and Ed and Terry reflexively sat back from the table.

"Well, Lex, thank you for your concern. I plan to send Safety Director Puchik next week to City Council to update you when we have more information, but I'll be glad to tell you, as chairman of the Safety Committee, what I know now, based on staff reports. The preliminary autopsy reported she died of choriocarcinoma, a form of cancer that spread to her brain, but there has been talk she used drugs. Staff reported that nothing could be done to save her. My safety director, as well as the acting superintendent of WCI, assure me staff followed all procedures. Nevertheless, the family filed a lawsuit, and investigations are ongoing. The decedent's 18-month-old child lives with his grandmother near East High School."

"Much appreciated, Mr. Mayor, but it doesn't really answer my question. Is this girl's death going to be a campaign issue in November? I hear the Dems are complaining we can't run a lemonade stand, let alone a city. This issue only makes things worse. We don't intend to get stuck in a tar baby, and we need to know what will happen. Did you say a lawsuit? Shit! That's all we need—a goddamn spectacle court trial. It's not coming before November, I hope?"

"I asked Ed from the City Attorney's office, sitting across from you, to be here to answer your questions."

"Mr. Baer, I believe the trial is a long way off," Auber said.

"Ed, can't you file something to make this thing go away?" asked Lex.

"Yes, sir. We plan to file a motion for summary judgment as soon as it is possible." Ed replied.

"And this nigger-loving lawyer representing the family. I hear he's a Jew. Is he any good?"

"Well, sir, I haven't tried any cases with him, and lawyers in our office don't know much about him. No one remembers his winning any big cases. But of course, it may be a matter of luck. I mean he is not one of those lawyers out there advertising since the Supreme Court made that legal," said Ed.

"And who's the judge?" asked Lex.

"Stuart Rumsfeld."

"Hot damn! Tell me, Ed. Has Stuart shown up to court lately three sheets to the wind? He owes me big time for his job. Tell you what, Ed. Call me as soon as you file the motion, whatever you call it. I'll handle the rest. We'll get this monkey and her family off our backs. Thank you, Mr. Mayor," said Lex, turning his cigar around to chew the other end.

No one asked Lex the big question. No one wanted to know.

CHAPTER 37

AFTER HER SHIFT WAS OVER, Sgt. Mitchell wandered nervously into the near-empty staff breakroom. As she hoped, she found Theresa Bobbin, the social worker, sitting alone at a small corner table.

"Good afternoon, Theresa."

"Good afternoon, Sergeant. Haven't seen you in a while. How are you doing?"

"It's been a spell, hasn't it?" she said, dropping into a chair across from Bobbin. "Actually, I'm having a few problems. Let me ask you something. Are you a shrink? I swear I need one."

"Well, no, but I'm a listener. Come from a family of listeners. My father worked at the Salesian Center, near the library. For years, he listened to troubled youth and brought home many stories. Maybe that's why I went into social work. Anyway, what's on your mind?"

"I'm feeling tight, edgy. Can't sleep. Can't eat."

"How come, Sergeant?"

"Call me Viola. I haven't been well for a week or longer."

"Do you think it's something at home, Viola?"

"No, I live alone. Got no complaints and don't want none."

"How's your health?"

"Well, I've lost 10 pounds and haven't slept in a week. So, I guess I'm losing both weight and sleep."

"Things okay here?"

"Yeah, I guess they're all right—same old ups and downs. Always something going on. Never dull working here. Yeah, always something... Say, you heard about that girl who died?"

156

"Who hasn't? Did you give a deposition?"

"Well, yeah, I was the officer in charge when they took her away. Hey, Molene, please bring me some coffee. Yep, I watched the squad take her away."

"Was it hard for you?"

"It wasn't easy. I've seen 'em take people away before, an OD now and then, bad infections sometimes, but this one looked mighty sick, mighty sick. Can't get her face out of my head," she said, turning away.

"Did you know Honor?"

"No, except for a conversation or two. Otherwise, nothin'."

"Her face is stuck in your head, huh?"

"Yeah, she was in my dreams last night—same dream as before. I'm standing in front of some man holding a big book, and she is sitting next to him. They are talking, but I can't catch what they are saying."

"Did the man talk to you?"

"I'm not sure. I think he asked me something, but I can't recall my answer. Ain't that something? Don't know what he was asking. Can't recall my answer or what they was talking about. What a stupid dream."

"Do you think it might be trying to explain what's bothering you?" asked Bobbin.

"Maybe, but she was nothing to me."

"Did anything happen that night?"

"No, nothing really. After calling the squad, I called Mr. Gross and told him about her."

"What did he say?"

Molene put her steaming cup of coffee in her favorite mug, three sugars, like always on the table. "Thanks, Mo. He said she may have been OD'ing. Told me to tell it to the squad."

"Was she?"

"I never saw nothin'. She looked clean to me. When they took her, it didn't look like no OD I'd ever seen, but I ain't sure. You understand what I'm saying? The thing is, they told me, 'cause of what I said, the hospital didn't do nothing to help her, waiting to find out what she took. They called here to find out, and she died while they waited."

"How do you feel about that?"

"Well, I didn't kill her, if that's what you're saying. Look, I did what I was told. What if I didn't say what Mr. Gross told me? He would've fired me. Now, listen here, I ain't going back to Weirton to work in no factory. Got me a good job, and I ain't gonna lose it over some druggie."

"Do you think this is what's bothering you?"

"I ain't sure. But supposing it was and supposing you was a shrink, what would you say to me?"

Before responding, Theresa surveyed Viola's reddened eyes, surrounded by tensed facial muscles, and felt her panting from across the table. "Well, as I said, I'm not a shrink, I'm a listener. And from what I'm hearing, I think your dream is talking to you, telling you to pay attention. It seems to me you won't find peace until you resolve what's bothering you, and you can't do that until you do what you think is right."

"Yeah, Theresa, but how do I know what's right?"

"Oh, don't worry about that. You'll know right when it feels right."

"Still not sure what to do. But thanks for your advice. I feel better already. You could be a shrink, Theresa, and a damned good one."

* * *

Johni learned of Gold's lawsuit from the TV on the rec room wall. She wanted to give him what little information she had accumulated but couldn't call him on the WCI phone, which was monitored, so she waited for her mother to visit from her four-room house in Urbancrest, Ohio, a small village of less than a thousand primarily black folks just south of town.

THE MATTER OF HONOR

When her mom came, Johni casually waited until the guard looked the other way and gave her mom a scrap of paper containing Gold's telephone number wrapped and taped around a tiny stick she stuck through a hole in the Plexiglas. She asked her mother to call Gold and tell him what she was about to explain. Johni expected guards would halt Gold's visits with her because she was not his client. She appointed her mother the new go-between.

When Johni explained who Honor Wilson and Alan Gold were and what she had learned about her death, her mother lowered her eyebrows, leaned forward, and whispered, "We ain't gonna get into trouble, are we?" Johni smiled, "If we do, Mama, it'll be good trouble." Their eyes met like two telephone cords suddenly connected, rushing talk through them. "Well," the mother said, sitting back in her chair, smiling, "it's been a while since I know'd good trouble. Don't you worry. I'll make the calls."

CHAPTER 38

GOLD'S SECOND ROUND OF depositions did not go well. No one dared to get involved. Many tips he'd received from Johni through her mother did not pan out once inmates and guards were put under oath. Alan diagnosed their fidgeting when testifying as symptomatic of the amnesia epidemic he was encountering. Despite what they boldly had told Johni or others earlier, as soon as they were sworn in, guards and inmates suddenly lost their memories. Jobs and freedom meant more to them than Honor. Alan was starting to panic.

His third round of depositions was of the medical staff plus Acting Superintendent Haskel Gross. They admitted Honor had come to them (they could not deny the pill-call and sick-call lists) but recalled few specifics about her. They did not deny what was written on the medical cards. Dr. V testified he must have treated Honor because her name was on the sick-call sheet but could not recall much more. Nurse Hill said she referred Honor to see Dr. V after she complained of something or other...whatever the sick-call sheet said she complained of, but she could recall nothing more.

Nurse Kratz was the most specific, saying that she had checked with Grant Hospital when Honor told her she had a stillbirth, only to find that Honor had not been on the OB-GYN floor at all. All three stressed that they had treated Honor as they would any other inmate, consistent with WCI rules. It was simply an unavoidable tragedy. Gold could not help but be impressed with how well Auber had coached them. Nearly all testified that they knew nothing about Honor unless their knowledge had been undeniably recorded. Bobbin was the lone exception. Gold found her testimony helpful but not decisive.

As Gold started his deposition of Haskel Gross, the acting superintendent seemed more bored than nervous. When Gold brought up the medical treatment Honor had received, Gross cut him short. "Listen, let me try to get you to understand so we can get through this faster. I run my shop, and Dr. V runs his. He doesn't tell me how to run WCI, and I don't tell him how to practice medicine." To nearly every question Gold posed regarding Honor's treatment, he repeated a similar response.

Amnesia plagued Gross as it had others. He did not recall denying her a lower bunk, but if it occurred, he would have been obliged to follow the information provided by Nurse Kratz. He would not question the procedure she used to determine if Honor had a stillborn. That fell into Dr. V's bailiwick. Whenever backed into a corner, he re-stated his "shops" mantra.

When asked to explain how the Hole could be used both for punishment and medical treatment, his only response was that it had been done that way long before he came to WCI. He could not speculate on whether inmates might resist asking for medical treatment, knowing they could end up behind bars in the Hole. That was a medical question, he declared, and did not belong in his shop. No, he never asked other medical professionals to review medical procedures at WCI. "Why should I? We've never had any problem." At the end of the deposition, Gold's frustration was nearly palpable.

Defense counsel looked with schadenfreude at Gold's pitiful results, almost gleefully saying, "It's a shame your pathetic case is unwinnable." He could hear their mumbling about filing suit against him personally for the cost of defending their clients from his worthless case. Stakes against him were rising.

Gold returned to his office with Millie, who had attended the last round of depositions. They'd tried to glean from the medical staff valuable information, but they garnered nothing. Millie could see through Gold's veneer of positivity.

"We need help. Mr. Gold. We need somebody who will stand up for Honor, who will tell them she wasn't a drug addict and my family is good," she declared.

Alan assured her with a smiling face that it was still early, and good things could still happen. Just hang on. When she left, Alan closed the door, turned off the lights, and lay down on his couch, this time in a fetal position.

CHAPTER 39

WHEN ED AUBER TOLD the mayor that he and counsel for other defendants would soon file motions for summary judgment, Blandford summoned his loyal strategist. "Terry, I think it is time to update the Council on this matter. Ask the Safety Committee to call for a closed-door briefing by our public safety staff. I want you to personally prepare those from the safety department who will brief council members. They are to be brief, to answer as few questions as possible, and most importantly, to provide our councilmen with positive campaign talking points.

As Terry was about to shut the door, Blandford said, "Oh, and by the way, Terry, you might also want to mention to Chairman Baer that we and other defendants are about to file summary judgment." He quickly turned his head and returned to his desk where he feigned interest in a blank file folder.

* * *

In addition to serving on City Council, Lex Baer sold new and used cars. He sponsored and hosted weekly televised tag-team wrestling matches where he advertised cars for sale. In a ring below a colossal advertising sign for Baer's cars, two warriors battled each week. Between rounds, skimpily clothed beauties in high heels and fishnet stockings carried signs informing sotted patrons what round it was (there were only three). A black-trunked tattooed wrestler with long, black-dyed hair mercilessly thrashed his bleached blonde opponent in white trunks, who, after suffering what seemed to be horrific beatings, would miraculously muster enough energy to quickly pin the man in black just as the bell rang. After each match, Lex would take the microphone to interview the white-trunked hero. Sometimes a black-trunked villain would attack them during the interview, transforming Lex into a martyr to those whose loyalty was to men in white. The scenario repeated weekly. Lex sold lots of cars on high credit to those believing these fights were real.

Yet, despite the razzamatazz surrounding his theatre, there was another side to Mr. Baer. He had applied wrestling profits toward the purchase of a dignified residence in quiet northwest Columbus near Upper Arlington, fronted by a circular drive and adorned with white pillars, a slate roof, and copper gutters.

He was elected to City Council with Republican support. Although proud of his election, he felt his most noted personal achievement occurred a few years earlier when the Scioto Country Club, one of the oldest and most prestigious golf clubs in town, granted him membership. To convince its board to accept him (no small task), he agreed to pay the entire cost of rebuilding 18 greens in addition to its steep membership fee. He'd campaigned harder for his acceptance than for his election.

Among the upper crust, the club had an exclusive history: for over a half-century, it excluded blacks, Jews, and most foreigners. Lex believed membership immediately would transform him into a blue blood, a debonair man of elegance and charm. When accepted, he assumed a different style of speaking.

He later parlayed his membership to maneuver party leaders to schedule the county Republican Club annual dinner, the biggest political event of the year, at Scioto's main dining room. For the occasion, he bought a black mohair suit and a black and green silk rep tie atop a starched white shirt, just like the attire he once saw worn by a gentleman leaving the club. On the advice of a club trustee and a Republican committeeman, he grudgingly left his cigars at home. When Terry told him that the City was about to file its summary judgment motion, Lex knew the good

Lord was allowing him to reduce the matter of Honor to a divot on the course.

Upon arriving at the gala on a surprisingly warm night, Lex parked his wife with her friends and started working the room, glad-handing contributors, bigwigs, and wannabes who could influence his reelection. He kept up cocktail banter with as many as he could while keeping an eye out for the judge. Lex needed to chat with Stuart Rumsfeld...alone.

Finding the tall jurist proved easy. Even in the dim confines of the 19th hole, he stood high like an aging sunflower bending over for liquid nourishment. Since his wife had died, Stuart's friendship with Johnnie Walker Black Label had become ever closer.

"Good evening, Judge. So glad you could come tonight. I know I speak for all the members when I say that our club feels honored to open our doors to fine members of the bench like you," Lex oozed.

"Well, thank you, Lex," said the jurist in his gravelly voice. "It's a pleasure to be here and chat with many dear friends. You know, I'm on the bench so much, I just don't have enough hours in the day to keep up acquaintances that I truly miss. Seems like I'm working all the time. The club looks great, by the way."

"Why, thank you so much, Judge. We are rather proud of it. Let me show you around. We have done a few things to fix up the place. I paid to rework the greens a while back—just a little gift. But I'm not the only one helping. Other members bought new porch furniture that we took out for this evening. Come, let me show you."

With that, Lex put his arm over Judge Rumsfeld's shoulder and directed him outside onto an empty veranda and closed the door. "We just remodeled this patio, Judge. Looks good, huh?" He paused in the night as both looked out onto the silent course and let the still night surround them in darkness. Not even a bird chirped. He wished he had his cigars. Each waited for the other to speak and break the silence.

Finally, Lex said, "Glad to hear you're busy on the bench, Judge. Must not leave you time for much else. I've got to tell you, Stuart, your work is being noticed by some pretty important people. Yes, indeedy. Good judges are hard to find, and many of us on the party selection team have been looking your way for that Court of Appeals slot opening next year. I believe you'd do well there."

"Well, thank you. I'm honored to be considered, although next year is a lifetime in politics, as you well know." Rumsfeld had always relied on the party for his elections; he would not exert the effort to mount his own campaign. In past elections, the party would buy him television ads, and he attended political events like this, where drinks flowed freely.

"Don't I know that? I run this November along with the mayor and others. We're looking good to win, and then we will be there for you when that Court of Appeals slot opens. One hand feeds the other, you know?"

"But right now, Judge, we have a little problem that maybe you can help us with. Now I don't know much about law, and I don't try to pretend I do. And I certainly wouldn't try to tell you how to do your job. Why, the respect I have for you would not permit me even to take a tiny step in your shoes. No siree. Your work, Judge, is far above my pay grade. I can't tell you how much I admire your brains and dedication. I'm still proud that some friends and I helped put you on the common pleas bench in the first place. You know, sometimes we all need a little help. You know what I'm saying?"

Without waiting for an answer, Lex went on.

"It's not easy sitting on Council. Pressures from all sides. This one wants one thing, while that one wants something else.

And problems come out of the woodwork. I mean, let's just take as an example, Judge. You know, a hypothetical, I think they call it.

"Suppose the city might have to defend a lawsuit about some Negro girl who died at our workhouse, and let's also suppose her death causes a rumble in the jungle—if you know what I mean. Why, that sort of thing could cause riots in the streets, death and destruction in the city, even when nobody could've done anything to save her anyway. The druggie was going to die no matter what, God bless her soul.

"But for the good of the community, if that sort of thing ever happened, we would need judges who preserve law and order and have the guts to stop a bloodbath before it begins. A problem like that has got to go away—and go away fast—you know, for the good of a city. Voters would want that too. They admire judges with courage. I declare we will not forget strong judges preserving law and order. I can guarantee you that.

Judge Rumsfeld remained silent, lifted Johnny to his lips for a long swallow, and stared into the night. Lex pressed on.

"You might recall I recommended you to the central committee when you first ran. Law-and-order judges are special. They move up to bigger and better things. Those judges might even get a pass from Democrats and run unopposed. We hope you are still one of that kind of law-and-order judges."

"Who, may I ask, is the included 'we'?" asked Rumsfeld, as he looked out into the night, exhaling a puff of smoke from his ever-present cigarette, and swallowing more Johnny Walker Black. Lex smiled slightly, like a fisherman feeling a tug on his line. He paused a moment, hoping his catch would not let go of the bait. Turning toward the judge, he asked, looking straight into the man's bloodshot eyes,

"Who would you want to be included?"

"I would like to think you are including Mayor Blandford and Mr. Foxx as part of the 'we', aren't you?"

Lex took a step closer and whispered into Stuart's ear, "If they are, then do we have a deal?"

"Lex, I have always tried to be a law-and-order judge and do not plan to change." With that declaration, Lex Baer nodded his head and shook hands with Stuart Rumsfeld.

"Great. Now, let's get some dinner. I have a couple of folks I'd like you to meet, and others I need to talk to."

Together, they returned to the party dinner. After dessert, Lex brought to Judge Rumsfeld two gentlemen of prominence. The judge first shook hands with Mayor Blandford and then Chesterton Foxx. Each looked him in the eye, as they said, "I support law-and-order judges."

History was made that night. In the clubhouse of the Scioto Country Club, Baer and Rumsfeld each scored a hole in one in the darkness of night.

CHAPTER 40

GOLD WAS SURPRISED TO receive the defendants' motions for summary judgment, which asked the judge to dismiss Honor's case before trial. As he read their motions, Gold could not understand why counsel had filed them before discovery was complete. He still had time to depose others, although he had not scheduled any. Judge Rumsfeld was only permitted to dismiss before all discovery was completed where he found that Gold could not win, regardless of remaining factual differences. Failure to name an expert, as instructed, came to mind as a potential game-loser.

Auber's motion mainly attacked Gold's civil rights claims, while Livingston and Chase denounced his malpractice claims. The city argued plaintiffs could not prove that it violated Honor's constitutional right to medical care. It even refused to accept that Honor was included among those entitled to benefits under the Supreme Court's decision. It also contended that WCI's policies, as administered by its staff, did not demonstrate "deliberate indifference" to her condition or treatment. Further, because the nurses were under the control of Dr. V, a private contractor and not a city employee, the city should not be held responsible for acts done under his direction. Finally, it asserted the mayor and safety director did not know what had taken place at WCI and weren't required to, so they could not have deprived Honor of anything. In sum, blame the doctor or the nurses.

Dr. V's motion argued that he should be dismissed because Millie's family could not prove he acted below medical standards, particularly without expert doctor testimony. And by its silence, the city approved all his actions. So, blame the city.

In their joint motion, both nurses argued they should be dismissed because they were under the control of the doctor, and Gold could not prove that either nurse had acted against the doctor's orders. So, blame the doctor or blame the city; just don't blame them.

Despite finger-pointing at each other, all three motions united in asserting that regardless of anything else, the family could not prove any act of any defendant had caused Honor's death, which they declared was an act of God. Even if someone had done something wrong, all agreed that she was doomed to die anyway. In other words, Gold's case fails because he cannot prove causation.

Alan's heartbeat raced as he read. He only had a month to respond and doubted he could find a doctor to testify by then. Even if he uncovered wrongdoing worse than mere negligence, he had no case unless he could prove the wrongdoing was the cause of her death.

Gold sent Frank to the OSU medical library to explore any medical arguments they might use. After stumbling through thick books written in jargonic medicalese, a librarian took pity on Frank and directed him toward a section where he might find answers. A D&C procedure ordered as part of her six-week checkup could have removed cancerous tissue from the womb and prevented death. Honor's autopsy showed that the unremoved and fast-growing type of cancer tissue had spread to the brain. So, Frank reported to Gold that a timely D&C while she had been incarcerated might have prevented metastasis.

He and Frank spent hours writing his response to Judge Rumsfeld, justifying their complaint and their need for a jury trial where her peers would make the final decision. Gold loaded his brief with affidavits, deposition transcripts, rules, and regulations, arguing that the defendants blatantly and deliberately violated Honor's civil rights and good medical practice. Night after night, they labored to find the relevant cases, the appropriate analogies and precedents, and precise wording to persuade the court to let Honor's case go to trial.

Alan became energized just by describing what Honor had endured at WCI and the plight of others incarcerated there. Advocating for Honor's cause was a medal he would always wear proudly; despite his foolhardy dream that he could beat the big boys. *Let's be honest*, his head reasoned with his heart. *No one beats the big boys.*

But what Gold could not do was add a doctor's affidavit to his brief that her cancer was treatable and curable.

* * *

A few weeks after the Republican gala, Judge Rumsfeld arrived late to his chambers behind his courtroom. His trusted bailiff, big Ben Walton, informed him that a case set for trial that day had settled, clearing his docket for the afternoon. Rumsfeld instructed Ben to hold calls and visitors; he wanted to spend the day alone working on pleadings, motions, and other paperwork. He entered his quiet chambers, closing the door behind him, and retrieved from his right-hand desk drawer a large roly-poly glass. Then, he called upon Johnnie Walker Black to come forward and do him an overworked favor—help get him through what would be an emotional day.

Although he and Johnnie were becoming closer, he felt he could cut off their relationship at any time. He told himself Johnnie was just a friend who provided comfort in times of need, nothing more. To him, Johnnie in his high hat and cane was like a political acquaintance; a very close, convenient friend when needed, but should their friendship ever cause him a problem, a near-stranger.

Which made him think of Lex Baer. If Lex could get him that seat on the Court of Appeals, privately he would treat Lex as a very dear friend. But if anyone found out about their law-and-order understanding, well then, his response would be that he scarcely knew the boor.

His comparison of Johnnie Walker to Lex Baer was quite simple. *Johnnie asks little from me,* he reasoned. *A small contribution at the liquor store buys his entrance into my home. Once there, he only wants to sit quietly in a cool dark place where he can be happy.*

I have a similar understanding with Lex, he continued. *He simply wants a short decision written by my clerk that might pass muster on appeal and remove a complicated case off my docket plus save the city from whatever it was that Lex said it needed saving from. That might be all I will have to do to move up to the appellate court where nobody will bother me.*

Lex's deal might not feel good inside when I look in the mirror, but then sometimes, I don't feel so good on some mornings after a night with Johnnie either. It's just part of a day's work, part of the life I live.

It had not always been so. When Rumsfeld left law school and joined the prosecutor's office, he was full of bright, visionary dreams of achieving true justice for all. But time and circumstance slowly faded his clear notions of morality into colorless vagaries. The death of his wife after her long illness did little to help him frame a notion of universal fairness, leaving him adrift in the sea of justice.

Also, living alone was hard for him. He found himself drinking instead of eating, instead of living. He disliked interacting with antagonistic lawyers. If only he could be on the Court of Appeals, he would only have to listen to their banter a few hours a week before returning to the quiet of a plush office.

Lex was offering him a getaway he could not turn down. After carefully putting away his glass and flask, he sent for his new law clerk. Sounding like he had seriously deliberated the merits of the case, he instructed the young man to write his first opinion for him, granting summary judgment to all defendants because there was no reason to keep the case on his docket.

"Her death was unavoidable," he admonished the young man. "The family can't prove damages. They just repackaged their medical and nursing malpractice claims into one of these newly proclaimed civil rights violations. They haven't found a medical expert, and ... well, you take care of the rest. And have the first draft on my desk by Monday," he said, trying to sound businesslike, almost impressing himself with his legal acumen. The clerk rushed back to his cubicle, excited by his first major assignment.

Stuart Rumsfeld leaned into his high-backed leather chair and called on Johnnie Walker for an encore. By end of the following week, the judge had filed his decision, the Clerk of Courts had mailed it to the attorneys, and, unless a successful appeal, the case was closed. Just like that.

CHAPTER 41

IT TURNED COLD THAT CLOUDY Saturday morning in late spring when Gold came to his office to clean up a few things. The mailman had dropped off an official envelope from the Common Pleas Court. His fingers trembled as he ripped the sealed flap. Rumsfeld's decision was only three pages long. Gold jumped immediately to the last page, "In conclusion, the Court finds that there are no material facts in dispute, and defendants' motions for summary judgment are granted. The case is dismissed." He sank into his chair and wept.

He had not cried since he was a child, but the hole in his soul was so great that tomorrow no longer mattered. He was too green in trial practice to have experienced a complete defeat from a summary judgment motion. Why had he gotten so involved? He learned long ago to stay detached, provide a cool head, and never, never lose sight of the reality that every case belongs to the client. He was merely their advocate and counselor.

But somehow during the many hours working on it, he had practically absorbed the Rivers' lives and suffered the inmates' conditions. He found himself no longer just their attorney but their champion. He had unwittingly transformed himself into someone else, someone he did not know.

Foolishness had found him. Rearranging his entire practice for the big show and giving up representation of Cynthia Carlton, his primary source of income, were proving costly. Now, after all of that and just as he was going to don his trial day armor, Judge Rumsfeld had locked the doors and turned off the lights. He cried for losing what could have been. He swore to himself would never stray from Lake Mediocrity again.

He could not avoid informing Millie that the judge had dismissed their lawsuit and shattered their dreams. Sharing bad news with clients was nothing new. He'd gotten used to his less-than-stellar strikeouts in other cases, but this decision, more than any other, proved to him that he was not, and probably never would be, ready for the big leagues. He no longer felt worthy even to hold a bat.

Before she went to work Monday morning, Millie came to Gold's office. Her smile and warm brown cheeks showed dimples on either side of her white, shiny teeth. She sat in front of his desk wearing tan scrubs and started talking about her weekend, the kids, and her job—little things that came to mind. She chattered lyrically about Winston taking steps and Miles joining the school band. In the middle of a sentence, her twinkling black eyes happened to turn toward his, and she withdrew her smile. She knew.

"We got the decision?"

Gold slumped down in his chair, nodding, staring at the side wall, motionless.

"He threw the case out?"

Gold nodded again, tossing the court papers toward her side of the desk without changing his stare. Millie didn't move. There was no need to read it. Just words on paper. The end. Conclusion. They sat in silence, hearing only the tick-tock of a wall clock in the other room. It began almost unnoticed, but their continued silence seemed to increase its volume until the tick-tock clamored.

He knew he must get past his letdown and face the future. She, in turn, knew that she would have to explain to her children why they lost and listen to Duke remind her she never should have picked Gold. Neither knew where to start, but tick-tock would not let them adjourn.

"Mr. Gold, what do we do next?"

"We appeal."

"And then what?"

"If we beat the odds and win on appeal, we go to trial," he said without changing his gaze.

"What are the odds?"

"Less than 20 percent," he mumbled. Another long silence. ... *tick-tock, tick-tock.* Finally, she rose, leaned over his desk with arms firmly planted on it, her dark eyes flashing in his face as if they were backlit.

"Then, let's do it! It's the only way we'll get justice for Honor. Look at me, Alan Gold," she said in a firm voice. "You're down. I'm down. My family is down. My people are down. But we're not out. We'll have to get those appeals judges to face what's wrong. Make them change what that judge did and then make the jury face what the city did to Honor and my family. When we do, we'll then make people in this town face their jailers and tell them to stop what happened here before it happens again.

"And you...you are the man who must do that. You hear me? You've got the soul to change things. I feel in my prayers that the Lord will provide for us. Please don't ask me why, but I still believe in you. But what I feel doesn't matter. The real question is, do you believe in yourself?"

Alan stood up suddenly and raised an arm, as if revived, reborn, redeemed, shouting, " Millie, I know we can win. Let's get to it!" She left his office quickly.

Both were excited; neither was convinced.

CHAPTER 42

MILLIE WAITED UNTIL HER family finished dinner before she broached the decision. She wanted them to clear their dishes and their minds. Best to talk over dessert. She started slicing her fresh-baked sweet potato pie.

"Went to Mr. Gold's office this morning. He said we'll appeal."

"Appeal?" asked Duke. "Appeal what?"

"Well, as he explained, there is this motion thing. I don't understand it completely, but the city and others filed papers asking the judge to throw out our case. Mr. Gold said the judge agreed with them and threw it out. So, we must appeal to bring it back in. He says we'll have our trial after the appeal judges turn it around."

"He lost again, Mama?"

"Well, he's doing the best he can, and he's going to start working on the appeal right away."

"Ain't it time we get ourselves a real lawyer? I mean, they got so many hotshots fightin' us. We need one of our own. How can a honky tell our story anyhow? I mean, look what's going on around us. Honky lawyers, honky judges, honky mayors, honky television, honky teachers. Mama, how we ever gonna win?"

"Well, child, as bad as things look, they used to be worse. It may be slow, but some things are getting better. Not much, and not great, but I still hope. Unlike Reverend King, I don't have a dream, and I'm not sure about a promised land, but I see a light in the darkness. All I want people to know is Honor was no drug addict, and we are good people. If that happens, then we win."

"You'd call that a win?" asked Duke. "That don't put food on our table. It don't pay for diapers on Winston's ass. It don't get honkies off our backs. It don't get me and others no jobs. Mama, to win, we got to take to the streets and take what we need. If we can't break into the system, then we gotta break the system."

"Now, Duke, don't be talking that way. I lost one child in jail, and I will not lose another. You sound like some of them crazies out there. No, we're going to find a way. We've got to."

She went upstairs to pray. Billie finished slicing Millie's pie, but there was nothing she could do to sweeten it.

CHAPTER 43

GOLD EXPLAINED TO FRANK the procedure of the Court of Appeals. As appellants, they would have 30 days to file a brief showing what was wrong with Rumsfeld's decision. After the defendants responded, they would file a rebuttal brief limited to telling the court why the defendants' briefs were mistaken. There would be only argument at hearing before three judges: no jury, witnesses, or new evidence. Frank's job was to provide relevant cases, suggest arguments, and edit Gold's work when he finished writing.

Each went to work separately. Frank continued his study of federal cases. He hoped to find overlooked among constitutional cases he had already discovered, hidden gems to mine, then to explore malpractice cases and review standards of medical treatment of inmates awaiting trial, which in combination would prove the judge wrong.

Gold began writing the brief. First, just a simple outline of vague statements of law inconsistent with Judge Rumsfeld's ruling. Then he applied the facts in Honor's case, later adding Frank's carefully researched cases for appropriate quotes, and finally, a powerful conclusion. Gold kept adjusting, refining, and reworking his arguments to fit the facts and the law.

For days, they toiled ceaselessly. After discarding much and rewriting nearly every sentence at least twice, Gold found some of his arguments convincing. Words were his paints; sentences, his brush strokes; paragraphs, his shapes. He wrote and rewrote, anticipating how the judges would respond to his main arguments and his response to anticipated defense challenges. He titled his completed brief "a Rembrandt of legal argument." After three weeks of composition and touchup, he gave it to Frank for a final edit before going home to sleep.

Thursday morning, he rose and took a refreshing shower. He was renewed and more enthusiastic about the future. Although he had no court hearings that day, he wore his best suit and shoes. Frannie presented him with his typed brief as soon as he entered his office. He poured himself a cup of coffee before sitting down to review and admire it one last time before Frank filed it. He began reading his Rembrandt, holding each page with reverence.

His pride began to fade as he read his masterpiece. Today, he could no longer find its genius; it was nowhere near as compelling as he recalled. Instead of confidence, he now had serious doubts that it would convince the court to reverse.

Disproving Honor would have died anyway was highly problematic. Because the disease was rare, compelling statistics to suggest she was capable of treatment and cure were not available. The law concerning prisoners' constitutional rights to medical care was so new, none of Frank's cases hit the jackpot. His entire brief now seemed fragile, including a lame procedural argument he'd added at the last minute, that the court had not allowed him his full discovery time to find experts. He told Frank to file it anyway, although Alan's fears now overwhelmed his prior bravado. It was the best he could muster when his time ran out.

A few weeks later, Gold received defendants' reply briefs. He quickly recognized their efforts had been coordinated. Like lions attacking a water buffalo, they assumed different roles. One pushed one of his arguments into the waiting trap of another, each contributing to the kill. Not one of his arguments did the pack leave intact. He imagined them after his impending fall gorging themselves on his spoils. But he also remembered Millie's words and vowed to keep fighting. Gold awaited a hearing when he could argue for reversal, his last chance.

During the long weeks before the hearing, Gold could think of nothing else. He related everything in life to his upcoming thirty minutes of argument. Articles in newspapers, comments, and even attorneys' discussions about unrelated matters directed him back to this case. He should have written this; there must have been a better way to say that. He wrenched his gut, beating himself up about how he might have done better.

To his surprise, Gold received notice that a hearing was scheduled in a few weeks. The clerk's office had mistakenly put this case ahead of many others. He was sure that although the mayor and his campaign would want to delay the case, Auber would not be able to convince the court he would need time to prepare because the briefs were already submitted, and only oral arguments were left.

All counsel in Gold's case were required to be in the courtroom at 9 a.m., as were attorneys for the two other cases scheduled that morning, even though one-third of them would not argue their case until 11 a.m. The Court allotted each side 30 minutes, and the chief judge's bailiff watched the clock to enforce the schedule.

CHAPTER 44

WHEN GOLD ARRIVED EARLY, the bailiff told him his case was first. He sat at the appellant's table and looked up at the walnut bench where three judges would listen to him talk from a podium standing between the two counsel tables and wondered, *Why isn't this a waste of time? If the judges read the trial judge's decision and the briefs, wouldn't they already have made up their minds before I could say a word?*

Making their grand entrance, the defendants' legal warriors, including young associates tagging along, strutted toward their table. Their sheer number intimidated Alan. The ratio was eight to one against him. During his argument, if judges would look around the room, they might decide whatever Gold said was wrong, simply from the number of defense lawyers in the room shaking their heads. When Millie entered, he gestured for her to sit with him and Frank at the counsel table, but she opted to sit in the back.

At 9:00 a.m., upon the call of the bailiff, three black-robed judges entered from the side and mounted the bench. All rose and remained standing until the chief judge instructed them to be seated.

"Are the parties ready to proceed?" the chief judge asked.

"Yes, Your Honor."

"Very well, counsel for the appellant, you have selected to use 20 minutes of your half hour now and leave 10 minutes in rebuttal. Please proceed."

"May it please the court, I would like first to present Millie Rivers, administrator of the estate of Honor Wilson and the appellant in this case. She is seated in the back.

"Ms. Rivers' daughter, Honor Wilson, died awaiting trial in the Women's Correctional Institution, owned and operated by the defendant, the City of Columbus. She was an innocent victim of the deliberate indifference and negligence of the defendants. They are represented today by these many attorneys, all pursuing the same objective: to deny her and her family their fundamental right to a trial in which we would hold them accountable."

As he was about to expound upon his opening salvo, a judge interrupted Gold quietly but firmly,

"Counsel, aren't you simply saying the judge ruled in favor of defendants' motion for summary judgment, a legal procedure used for decades to weed out unworthy cases? Isn't the issue here whether the judge erred in granting that motion, rather than your claim of denying plaintiffs their fundamental right to trial? If so, please confine your argument to the issues at hand."

"Yes, Your Honor," Alan said, wincing from the sting of having been scolded for invoking emotions into a discussion of logic. Did he hear snickering? For the rest of his allotted time, he kept to his prepared outline. Near the end, the elephant-in-the-room question came from the chief judge.

"Counselor, plaintiff has the burden of proving that the appellees' actions caused the decedent's death. This proof necessitates expert testimony by doctors and perhaps prison experts, showing both that appellees breached their duty of care and that their breach caused her death. Reviewing the record, we found no testimony or affidavits from an expert doctor. Without this proof of causation, how can your case go forward?"

Gold had anticipated this question for months. "Your Honors, the trial judge did not allow us our full time to identify expert testimony. By the trial court's own schedule, we had another week or two of discovery to produce the needed expert testimony. Defendants jumped the gun and filed their summary judgment motions before the discovery period ended, thereby depriving us of the time allotted to provide experts and affidavits. The rules of procedure are quite clear on this. The trial judge, unfortunately, ignored our plea to grant us our full discovery time."

"Counsel, are you saying that within three weeks, you would have named a doctor who would testify that defendants could have prevented the decedent's death?"

Gold, not anticipating that question, blurted out reflexively, "Your Honor, that is exactly what we are saying."

"So, Counsel, you are representing to this court both that such expert testimony exists, and you would have introduced it at trial."

"Yes, Your Honor. That is my representation." He lied to the court with the straightest face he could muster. He continued his practiced posture and facial expression, looking directly into the eyes of each judge during the interminable silence that followed. Finally, the judge said,

"Thank you, Counsel. Anything more?"

"No, Your Honors."

In their 30-minute response, defense counsel was straightforward, relying on simple contentions that this was a useless appeal. WCI followed the approved policies. The medical staff had done all they could have for Honor. Most importantly, Honor Wilson's condition was incurable, and nothing the prison medical staff could do would have changed that or saved her from death. To suggest otherwise was meritless. Gold's bodacious claim, they seemed to say, was too weak to spend much time arguing. Honor had only been in WCI about a month before she died. Their clients were helpless in so short a time to save her from cancer.

"How did you prove her condition was incurable? Did you provide medical testimony?" one judge asked.

Gordan Chase hesitated. "Uh...not yet, your honors. Plaintiff had not provided required expert testimony."

"Anything else for you, Counselor?"

"No, Your Honors."

When the judges left the bench after Gold's rebuttal, defense counsel discussed among themselves who would bring disciplinary action against Gold before the Supreme Court. Frank Pearl turned his back on Alan and walked out alone. Gold's frenzied lie had taken the case to a whole new level.

For the first time since Alan Gold became an attorney, he was scared. He realized he faced a no-win situation. If the Court of Appeals ruled against him, the case would be lost and, with it, his reputation. If, instead, the Court of Appeals reversed and sent it to trial, he would also lose when he failed to produce the promised doctor testimony that the defendants caused her death, and then he would be further subject to sanctions for lying to a court. Unless he pulled a rabbit out of a hat, his career was over, and Millie's case would be history.

He tossed and turned between 2 and 5 a.m. most nights after that, awakening exhausted to face another day. During the night, he sometimes dreamt of riding in a gondola floating down a silent river in a dark cavern, looking toward his mute gondolier, wearing a black robe with a hood. They floated ever deeper into a cavern until the gondola fell forward, like over a waterfall. Suddenly, Alan would sit up in a pool of sweat and open his eyes widely. He'd adjust the covers, roll over, and begin his endless self-questioning. *Why did I lie to the judges? Where will I find a doctor-expert? What will I do after they take away my law license? Why am I such a failure?* His self-berating questions went on and on as he drifted into a light sleep until the alarm went off.

His bathroom mirror showed his hair graying, his skin ashen, and new lines forming on his face like a map of highways and secondary roads. He became sullen and shattered, paralyzed in self-doubt. Should he continue the folly of looking for a doctor to testify in a dismissed case and waste his efforts, or should he wait and pray for a favorable decision but then have little time to find his rabbit?

By sulking, he opted to wait, proving paralysis can also be an option. Every hour became a day, every day a week. Life was in slow motion. He walked past people conversing and heard nothing. He shivered in sunlight. Meals tasted like pablum. He excused himself from his Monday night card games. After checking his mail, he would sit at his desk and stare at the walls. At home, he walked across Broad Street into Franklin Park, looking for vitality in gorgeous spring flowers. But Alan could no longer see beauty. His treks through the park began increasing in tempo and effort. Instead of taking casual moments to experience the splendor, they became brutal exercises of self-flagellation. Every week, he lost another pound or two.

CHAPTER 45

THE POSTMAN DROPPED OFF the decision five weeks later when no one else was in the office. Alan placed the manila envelope from the Court of Appeals on his desk and sat down to stare at it, pretending he was divining its contents through concentration alone. He left the envelope—and his fate—sealed for the moment.

After a tasteless cup of coffee, he finally opened the envelope. Sometimes one can sense a life-changing event is about to occur, and Gold knew this was one of them. Slowly he pushed his thumb under the flap containing too much mucilage. It would not separate. Frustrated with his inability to simply open an envelope, he ripped it, tearing both the envelope and its contents. On his hands and knees, Alan put the ripped sheets together to make sense of what he had torn in anger. After rearranging the papers in proper order, he rushed to the last sheet to read the result. It said, "The trial court's decision is reversed, and the case remanded for proceedings consistent with this decision." Still on his knees, Alan reached toward the heavens, not thanking his god for this decision but praying for a miracle.

* * *

The sun's rays danced on Millie Rivers' wooden porch when Gold bounded up her steps and knocked on her door. He could have telephoned the news, but he wanted to deliver it personally. As an attorney, he had never made a house call. All might come crashing down later, but this was their celebration moment. Besides, he was curious about her home. Homes can say a lot about a person. He recalled today was Millie's day off and hoped he could surprise her. Several sets of eyes at different windows peered at the white intruder before Millie opened the door.

"Mr. Gold, what brings you here this morning?"

"I have good news. May I come in?"

"Sure. Want some tea?"

"Thank you."

Alan stepped into the small living room, his nostrils embracing sweet lavender. He sat on a clean, well-worn, overstuffed chair across from an old brown couch and relaxed while Millie went into the kitchen. Across the room, pictures of Martin Luther King and John F. Kennedy stared back at him. Duke and Billie wandered into the room, looking cautiously.

"Good morning. I've come by because I want to share some news, but I don't want to start until your mother returns. How are you guys doing?"

"Fine."

"No school today?"

"Nope. Teacher conference day."

"What's that?"

"Don't know, but no school."

"Well, I guess it doesn't matter why, so long as you're off," Alan said with a smile, trying to relax but feeling awkward.

Millie returned with a plastic tray and a paper napkin. She put them beside Alan on an imitation wood and brass TV table.

"I forgot to ask you whether you take sugar, so I brought a cube for you. You said you had good news?"

"Yes, I received the decision from the Court of Appeals today. They unanimously reversed the trial judge."

"What does 'unanimously' mean?" asked Billie.

"It means all three judges agreed. Judge Rumsfeld goofed when he dismissed our case."

"Does that mean we'll go to trial?" asked Duke.

"It does, but only if we can find a doctor who will say Honor's disease was curable and treatable and that the City's treatment of her was improper."

"Improper? She died without nobody helping her except to lie and say she was a druggie. What's proper 'bout that?" asked Duke.

"Hey, I'm on your side. But the law says we must bring to court an expert to say it."

After a long pause, Millie said quietly, "You already have an expert, don't you? I thought I heard you tell those judges you did."

"Well, I hope to have one," said Alan, clearing his throat while averting Millie's intense stare. Her black eyes and furrowed brow had a mother's way of burrowing through mendacity with the precision of a neurosurgeon. Alan took a sip of tea and looked into his cup, trying his best to avoid Millie's glower.

"Well, I hope you will too," she said, not as a form of encouragement but more like an accusation.

"Yes, uh, we'll need to do a lot of trial preparation before our court date. Please let me know if you hear anything that can help us. Thank you for the tea. I must be going, but I wanted to share the good news with you today. Have a great day."

"Yes," said Millie, "Thank you for coming over. Most of it sounded very good."

Gold grabbed his briefcase, and Billie walked him to the door.

"Mama, was you saying Mr. Gold lied to the judges to get them to give us a trial?" asked Duke after Gold left.

"I'm afraid so, Duke."

"Damn, that dude is all right! I never thought no honky would put hisself out for us. He could get in trouble, couldn't he?"

"I s'pose so. Duke, it's not right to lie, even if he did it for us."

CHAPTER 46

THE TRIAL WAS SCHEDULED TO BEGIN in two months. Alan spent hours gathering information about internal systems at WCI, particularly how guards and medical staff were to treat inmates. He called Sweet Willie occasionally to get updates. He followed up tales from inmates who claimed to have been sick, but they seldom yielded usable evidence. He called all the trial attorneys he knew, asking if any of them had in their stable of testifying doctors one with choriocarcinoma experience. Frank wrote memo after memo anticipating defense motions and objections.

Defense counsels were preparing as well. Both sides were playing out the chess game of litigation. Unfortunately, one side was still missing the queen, an expert doctor.

Gold left the office late and picked up some take-out before heading home. After changing out of his suit and into casual clothes, he ate, then got on board the good ship *Cutty Sark*. He poured one over ice with water, turned on his stereo, and drifted out to sea. In his lounger, his favorite place, he listened to America's album "Hideaway." The chorus from "Today's the Day" suddenly struck him as prophetic. He rewound and played it twice, hoping that trial would be the "today's the day" that would come true.

Alan was neither religious nor superstitious—if there is a difference. He had long believed things don't happen for a reason;

they happen. People foolishly add meaning to happenstance. They aren't placed on earth for a purpose, he believed. They seek understanding from random placement. Occasionally, he asked himself what his purpose was in a haphazard world. He tried to do good for its own sake, not for any later reward. He believed that goodness had its own intrinsic value, even when unappreciated.

Honor's death had changed all that for him. He never wanted this case, but he heard a clarion call to action, despite his inadequacies. He doubted his ability to convince a jury that Puddin's accusations or those of others at WCI were true. Who would believe her or them? Why should a jury believe me? If life were random, why did Millie pick me to take her case? All he had wanted at first was recognition from fellow attorneys of his competency, but without victory, this case might define him as the incompetent fool he feared he was.

To stop his falling again into self-debasement, Alan rose from his lounger, stretched his thin torso, and looked around for something to keep his spirits up. He noticed his answering machine was blinking. He hadn't checked in a few days, so he pushed the button. He listened to the pleas of bill collectors, clients waiting for his return calls, and advertisers and was about to turn it off, get onboard the Cutty, and return to the land of self-pity when he heard a voice he didn't recognize.

"Mr. Gold, Dr. Harrison here. You called Dr. Faraday at OSU Hospital a while ago, asking for someone with expertise in choriocarcinoma, and he put your message on the board. So it may not be worth much, but I recently attended a lecture by Dr. Karl Steiner from the University of Cincinnati. He reported successfully treating several late-stage choriocarcinoma patients. Don't know much more about him, but maybe he could answer your questions. He is part of the clinical faculty of U of C. Hope this helps..."

Stunned, Alan rewound the tape and listened to the message again. He could hardly wait for the sun to rise.

In his office early the following day, he dialed the University of Cincinnati Medical School

"This is Dr. Steiner's office."

"Yes, good morning. Is Dr. Steiner available?"

"Whom should I say is calling?"

"Alan Gold, calling at the suggestion of Dr. Harrison of the Ohio State University Medical School. I'm an attorney in Columbus."

"Please hold."

"Hello, this is Dr. Steiner."

"Good morning. My name is Alan Gold. I'm an attorney in Columbus with a tragic case of a woman who died of choriocarcinoma. Dr. Harrison from OSU heard your recent presentation and suggested I give you a call. He said you have treated women who survived the disease."

"Yes, that is correct. Some of my patients have survived. What happened in your case?"

"Well, as I read the autopsy report, the cancer the coroner found in her brain began in her womb. Does that make sense to you, Doctor?"

"Yes, it is not unusual for this disease to metastasize to the brain from the uterus."

"Is it treatable when it gets to that stage?"

"Yes, I have treated such patients."

"And they lived?"

"Some did."

"Well, this one didn't. She was an inmate of the Women's Correctional Institution here in Columbus. We believe she died due to lack of care."

"I see."

"The doctor who saw her while she was confined neither examined her nor diagnosed her symptoms."

"I would need to see her medical records to understand more."

"Yes, of course. Can you meet with me soon and look them over?"

"Let me look at my schedule." There was the sound of papers rustling. "Well, I might see you for a few minutes tomorrow afternoon after I complete rounds, say around 3 p.m."

"Thanks, Doctor. I'll bring the records with me. I hope you can make more sense of them than I have been able to. I really appreciate your taking the time to talk to me."

Gold bounded out of his office in an unusual burst of enthusiasm and began pacing back and forth by Frannie's desk, thinking aloud.

"Frannie, I need you to make me a copy of Honor's medical records, WCI rules and regulations; its medical procedures; the depositions of Villanueva, Hill, and Kratz; and any medical articles that we have collected about choriocarcinoma. I need them by the end of today. Then, call Frank and tell him I will update him tomorrow evening. We will need to retain an expert from a nursing school to testify on improper nursing record-keeping and nursing procedures and maybe an ex-warden to criticize WCI prison standards. We will also need another expert to testify about her lost income. Cancel my haircut tomorrow. Let's see. I must take with me a state highway map showing UC's campus..."

"Would you mind telling me what's going on?" Frannie asked, crossing her arms.

"Oh, I'm sorry. Didn't I mention it? I just made a 3 p.m. appointment tomorrow to talk to an OB-GYN cancer doctor in Cincinnati. He's treated multiple patients with choriocarcinoma, and they survived. Wish me luck."

Just then, she saw on his face something she had not seen for a very long time: a smile.

CHAPTER 47

GOLD WANDERED THROUGH a labyrinth of university halls before finding Dr. Steiner's office.

"Are you sure you brought me everything? Where are the doctor's notes?" asked Dr. Steiner, looking over the few documents Gold brought.

"There are none. He took no notes on any patients he saw."

"The nursing notes you were to bring—all I see are several 3x5 cards with Wilson's name on it and a few words. Where are her recorded vitals?"

"No vitals were recorded because they took none, according to the nurses' depositions I've included. No pulse, blood pressure, temperature, weight, height—nothing."

"The card says she claims she had a stillborn. Well, did she?"

"The nurse who wrote that card called a friend who worked in the OB/GYN ward and told her that Honor had not been there, but we recovered the attached Grant Hospital records showing she delivered in the ER, not up in the ward. The hospital records also show that it scheduled a six-week checkup for her, and she informed the nurses at WCI that she was missing it. The nurse admitted in deposition that when she uses the word 'claims,' it's her shorthand way to tell the doctor a patient was lying."

The doctor sat back in his chair, shaking his head. "That checkup could have saved her life. I am so sorry for her. You probably don't know much about me. I came to this country from Austria to learn the finest medical practices in the world. But when I see this, the practice of medicine in American prisons where people don't care about inmates, I wonder whether I'm not observing the worst medical practices in the world."

Turning Steiner's attention back to the reason for his visit, Gold said, "Doc, defense counsel claim there was nothing that could be done, that she was too far gone, based upon something about the multiplication of cancer cells. Unless I can prove otherwise, my case is lost."

"Mr. Gold, you can tell them that several years ago, I had a patient who presented at this hospital already comatose for several hours due to enlargement of her brain from choriocarcinoma. After treatment, she survived, her mind intact, and even had another child. Medicines and treatment for this disease have been known for years."

"With your permission Doc, I will set up a deposition here in your office in the next few weeks and give you the privilege of telling them yourself. Thank you so much."

At his deposition, Karl Steiner, M.D. did just that. Gold finally had the expert he needed.

CHAPTER 48

ED AUBER ASKED TO MEET with the mayor. He specifically requested that Haskel Gross not be invited nor City Council members, and he wanted only Director Puchik and Terry Prince to be with the mayor. Ed's trial preparations cast doubt on his ability to defend WCI procedures.

Politically, mayoral optimism had taken a pass. Since the Court of Appeals overturned Rumsfeld's decision, Blandford had taken big hits in the black community. Editorials from *The Call and Post* and frequent pickets at City Hall were hurting him in the polls. In his briefings to the mayor, Terry reminded him obliquely of his prior warnings that the death of Honor would not go away, but he knew better than to say to his boss, "I told you so." A sinking ship drowns more than the captain.

The mood at City Hall became somber. From Terry's polling briefings, the mayor recognized that re-election prospects were slipping. Led by Sweet Willie Moss, WVKO was awash with listeners reporting personal tales of abuse. On slow news days, other radio and TV stations (excluding Foxx's WBNS) would run one of Sweet Willie's interviews, for which WVKO charged nothing. Campaign staff reported to Terry that Pastor Jenkins was encouraging his colleagues to step up accusations that the mayor was incompetent. The accusation that he "can't even run a workhouse" also began to resonate in the white community.

Experience told Ed Auber it was time to talk settlement, even though he had participated in many negotiations that turned sour. Sometimes merely suggesting settlement would lead some plaintiffs to believe the defense was folding, causing them to inflate the value of their cases. If an offered amount was too low or the littlest flaw in the presentation upset plaintiffs, negotiations would fail, sometimes ending all further settlement efforts. On the other hand, City Council rejected offers it considered too high, which cratered any future negotiations. But Ed concluded that despite all obstacles, settlement of this case would still be better than a public trial.

Before the meeting, he ran his plan by Terry Prince to discuss settlement. Prince thought it worth a try but refused to be the front man, should the effort turn sour. Ed agreed to lead the effort.

"What the hell changed?" the mayor railed when the meeting began. "You told me this was an open-and-shut case. Our defense, as you described it, was that an inmate died from an incurable disease that could not be altered by any actions of WCI staff."

"Gold somehow found a doctor who, in deposition, opined that her cancer was treatable and curable. He now has other experts who testified that our medical staff should have done more. In short, his case is getting stronger," Auber softly replied. "I think it's time to discuss settlement with him."

"Mayor, we don't need more public exposure on this," Terry Prince offered. "Remember the Columbus school desegregation case? It cost millions in legal fees when the board lost at trial and then appealed it all the way to the United States Supreme Court. The school board lost each time, and the board members lost. We cannot afford either the expense or negative polling. Your numbers are no longer that high."

"Ed, what are you thinking we should offer?" asked Director Puchik.

"Well, of course, our offer should be as low as possible yet still high enough to tempt them to respond. Our office doesn't have much experience settling this type of case because, before recent

Supreme Court decisions, we were immune. After contacting colleagues in other cities, I haven't found any place that has faced our problem. So, unfortunately, we have no settlement comparisons. That's the first problem.

"Second, I haven't discussed with other defense counsel whether we would make a single offer from all defendants, make three offers, or go it alone. If we all kick in for a single offer, the amount would sound higher and perhaps tempt them more. If accepted, all defendants would be dismissed. If I had my choice, I'd favor approaching plaintiffs with a single offer from all, but that remains to be seen. Now, Mr. Puchik, as to the amount, here's how I calculate it.

"On the low side, we have factors we might use to our advantage. Wilson did not graduate high school and was on welfare without a job, charged with crimes involving drugs. On the other hand, she got her GED, which a jury might see as an upbeat show of ambition. She was probably arrested in error, but we are not sure if we can keep out a possible false arrest. She appeared to be in the wrong place at the wrong time, and we have no proof yet that she was using drugs except marijuana.

"What a jury would do with all of this is anyone's guess," Auber said with a shrug. "What we can be sure of is neither side can realistically predict a jury's reaction to this case. The case is a first, and as the old saying goes, uncertainty invites settlement."

"So, how much we should offer?" the mayor said impatiently.

"Well," Auber continued. "We calculated her income, assuming she worked until 65 at minimum wages and worked maybe 30 years. Then we took away taxes she won't pay on the settlement and reduced it to its present value. Add money for pain and suffering, which could be substantial, and we should be around $100,000 as a possible jury verdict.

"But the family is struggling. The mother works as an aide supervisor in a nursing home and now has another infant to raise. I think our starting offer should be somewhere south of half. The family might accept $40,000 and drop the case. Hell, it's a lot of money for these people."

The mayor ran his fingers through his hair. "The public might see it as a lot of money for the death of a potential criminal. It's probably more than she would have made," he mumbled.

Ed continued. "You're right. The jury might find she would have stayed a welfare mother and never worked at all, but then again, Mr. Mayor, there is always the other side. If we split it with the insurance companies for the doctor and nurses, the city might end up paying only twenty or twenty-five thousand, plus saving the cost of doctors or other experts. For that, we could be done with it."

Another long pause before Puchik asked, "Of course, you're the commander, Mayor, but do you really want to give that much money to some darky who has never earned $5,000 in a single year of her life? Don't you think we should run it by Council before we start down this path? I am not sure how Lex would react."

"That depends on how we present it to Council," Terry interjected. "Money paid to the family must go through probate court and be divided partly for the child's good. Isn't that right, Ed?" Before Ed answered, Terry added, "We should stress the money would support and educate the child of the deceased. Our position would be the city has acted charitably toward an unfortunate one," Terry suggested. "That should help ease Council fears."

There was another long pause before the mayor announced, "Proceed, Ed, but do not say you have our authority. Before that, please work with the other defendants to present a single offer, keeping our share as low as possible. Then tease this out with the family's lawyer. Tell him any agreement we come to must be presented to City Council for approval before it's a deal. Get him to go out on a limb. I don't want the city to look like it's the one making the first move."

CHAPTER 49

"GOOD MORNING, MILLIE. Thanks for coming to my office on such short notice."

"I can't stay long."

"Okay. I'll get right to it. Assistant City Attorney Ed Auber called me, asking if we would be open to a financial settlement. You might remember him. He took your deposition."

"I don't understand. How do we clear Honor's reputation without a trial? And what about the people who treated her so badly?"

"One way to look at it is that if they offer a settlement, they think our case is strong enough to win. Another way is that they are willing to pay instead of exposing the problems that contributed to Honor's death."

"What do you say?"

"Well, this case is going to be very hard to win. I have always told you that. Judges and juries favor police officers, prosecutors, and government people over those who sue them. So, at trial, we would be swimming upstream, and our risk of completely losing is possible, even probable.

"On the other hand, if we get a jury on our side, the sky's the limit. But that is very unlikely. Columbus is not a town where past juries have gone wild.

"Let me be frank. Millie. Demographics do not favor black families, if you see what I mean. We chose to file in state court partly because jurors from Franklin County mostly live in Columbus. If we had filed in Federal court, jurors would be residents of 23 counties in the district, most of which are rural, and blacks fare even worse there. I know it's unfair, but we've got to face reality.

"Also, appeals would be very likely, no matter who wins. With the number of changes to the law relating to this case, either side might end up appealing. Given the circumstances, a financial settlement might be the best thing to do, and it would certainly help you raise little Winston and your other kids."

"If I agreed to talk, how would it work?" asked Millie.

"The usual way is they would make the first offer. Then we raise it, and both sides would keep negotiating until we arrived at a settlement."

"What should we ask for?"

"Well, to keep them negotiating, we can't make our counteroffer too high, or negotiations will stop. Our expert will testify that if Honor worked for ten years at minimum-wage jobs, rose to higher pay jobs, and retired at 65, she would have made over $300,000. Now there are a lot of 'ifs' there. We don't know whether cancer would have impaired her lifespan or employment possibilities, nor can we be sure of convincing a jury that she would have worked all those years because she has no reliable employment record. We also don't know how much a jury would award for pain and suffering. We have little experience with how much juries have awarded to family members claiming wrongful death of a loved one while incarcerated. We'd also have to calculate…"

"Stop!" shouted Millie, slapping his desk and rising to her full height. "All you talk about is money, Mr. Gold. You still don't get it, do you? Our family not only lost Honor, we lost our dignity. *The Dispatch* said to thousands of people that my daughter was a druggie, a worthless, no-account welfare mom. Some kids at school told my son we are money-grabbers, trying to take advantage of the death of his no-good sister. The press runs stories against my community saying I—which means we—am using my daughter's death for political advantage. And all you're doing is calculating wages she didn't make. I know you're trying, but you're missing it. You want to get us the most money, and I thank you for your efforts. But don't you see? What we want most is our dignity."

"Look," Gold responded, "Courts can only do so much. Settlement can't bring back your Honor nor restore your dignity. But neither can a trial. All a jury can do is award money. That's all it's got to give. It's a means of exchange, a way—meager as it is—of converting the dignity and Honor you lost into something else of worth—money. It's a poor excuse, I agree, but it's the best we've got to restore something to those claiming lost.

"Millie, a trial is about different things to different people. To some, it is a day off work sitting in a jury box. For others, it is another workday, recording words spoken in a courtroom. Some find it one of the most memorable times of their lives, while others find the whole experience bland and forgettable. What I'm trying to say is a trial is not one picture for all. It is a panorama of many images, big and small, for many people.

"I want to make you and your family proud and to enable you to hold your heads high with your dignity restored and your loss compensated. But I would not be doing my job if I told you a trial is the only way to do it. It doesn't always work like it does in the movies."

Slowly, she returned to her seat, and Gold leaned forward.

"Suppose we lose. Suppose the jury finds her death unavoidable or the actions of the prison people were excusable. Suppose the jury finds your daughter's life financially was of minimal value. Wouldn't you be more brokenhearted with that result than a fair settlement? Suppose we win at trial, but they reverse our victory on appeal, just as we reversed their dismissing our suit. Or suppose years go by without a final decision or payments to you and Winston. You may not be able to keep it together financially for that long. Would years of delay be a victory for you, no matter the outcome?

"Whatever happens, Millie, I want you and your family to have no regrets. Let's try this. Let's add to our settlement a demand for an apology from the city. Would that satisfy you?"

Alan looked at Millie, hoping to find a way toward a resolution, including a written agreement but with something more. Millie turned away. She needed a moment to think. Deep down, she knew that no matter the outcome, her daughter would never return. Winston needed money, and her family needed closure.

But to her, settlement meant retreat. Alan seemed sincere, but she still had doubts. More discussion with her family would only incite their differences with her in picking him, and she knew what they would say. No, she must decide and hope her family would accept her decision, and she had to sort things out.

She asked to use the bathroom. When she returned, she said, "OK. Put in the largest amount you think a jury might award but add that the mayor himself, and maybe with the safety director, but absolutely the mayor, must go on TV and tell folks Honor Wilson was not a druggie and did not die of an overdose. He must say it; no one else. Then make him tell people what specific steps the city will take—and take soon—to stop this from ever happening again. If he does that, we will accept that settlement. Mr. Gold, they can Jew you down on the amount, but we will not move on the rest."

He tried not to wince at her unintended slur but to remain focused on convincing her that her family and her community would remember her efforts to settle, while it was defendants who refused to compromise.

"I doubt this will make a deal, but it's a start. I'll do my best."

Millie rushed to work, while Gold tried to figure out how he could settle this ordeal.

CHAPTER 49

AT SETTLEMENT CONFERENCES, COUNSEL often dance with two partners. Before the ball, counsel for plaintiff bemoans to clients the overwhelming difficulties of winning and the virtues of a certain and final settlement, as Gold did to Millie. At the ball, during negotiations with defense counsel, that same attorney will launch into a fit of bravado, predicting an outrageous victory over worthless defenses.

Likewise, defense counsel at pre-settlement conferences with clients will, in mirror image, extol the strength of plaintiff's case, as did Auber. But when he meets opposing counsel at the party, the same attorney will dismiss the plaintiff's claims as laughably worthless. After a first dance without a prize, clients often complain, 'But I thought you said...'

Then, they reengage and schedule another prom, practicing the same steps for a new dance. By the time they reach the final song, both counsel often will have waltzed, bowed-and-curtsied, do-si-do'd, boogaloo'd, and sometimes even performed an electric slide before they settle.

Negotiations in the City Attorney's "government plush" conference room started pleasantly. Frederick Livingston and Gordon Chase came to settle the claim against the doctors and nurses while Ed represented all other defendants. Neither side brought their clients. They sat casually between light blue-gray walls with little adornment, save for portraits of the City Attorney, Mayor Blandford, and an old print of Abraham Lincoln. The heavy, well-worn, wooden conference table was surrounded by

The Matter of Honor

halfback jury chairs with unpadded seats and arms curled in front. Defense counsel sat across from Alan Gold, three facing one. Auber began in a relaxed tone.

"Thanks for coming, Al. Good to see you again. We haven't talked much since those recent depositions of those experts you found. I hope today that we might spend a little time trying to find a settlement we can all live with and avoid war. Of course, our people don't think we are at fault, and we think Judge Rumsfeld will again dismiss your case when your trial presentation is over. We believe our hard-working employees and our devoted doctor and nurses will win over a jury who will agree with us that no wrongdoing occurred," he continued, leaning back in his chair.

"Your case on behalf of a black, unemployed inmate charged with purchasing drugs seems weak. And we don't think you will get very far with your local so-called experts, compared to our world-renowned cancer professor you already deposed.

"And if you got past liability, which is nearly impossible, we don't think a jury would give you much without proving actual damages. A welfare mom facing a possible prison sentence is not quite a poster child for a big award, Alan. Unfortunately, there is too much for you to overcome before you can look at the prospect of a big pot.

"If we win on liability, which we think we will, neither you nor your clients with empty pockets will be pleased. Gordon has tried hundreds of these cases over his many years, far more than you or I, and he says he has never seen a case as weak as yours."

"That's right," Chase intoned with the certitude of a practiced trial lawyer. He began like he had just been given a tag to enter the ring for a wrestling match at Lex Baer's Saturday fracas. But instead of satin shorts, wrestlers in this event wear worsted wool. "Speaking very frankly, Mr. Gold, your malpractice claim that a prison doctor failed to cure a prisoner's rare cancer who died just a little more than a month later sounds extraordinarily lame. How you think you can pull it off is beyond me."

Livingston said, "I reviewed more than 67 cases without finding a single case where the plaintiff won. I advise you, Mr. Gold, to listen carefully to our offer."

"Anyhow," Ed continued, nodding to his colleagues that the tag-team match was about to end with his landing a crushing blow on Gold, "The bottom line is we don't think you can avoid Judge Rumsfeld dismissing your case, but if you did, you still would not win a large damage award.

"Listen, Alan, we understand your predicament. We've all been in your spot, needing a way out. So, I talked to the guys, and we spoke with our clients asking them to come up with something meaningful for your trouble and find a reasonable solution we know you can sell to your clients. We want to help you out.

"We propose to give your clients, in exchange for a release of all claims, the sum of $33,000 cash paid within 30 days, subject to City Council approval. Now, I need to explain that Council has not voted on it, and the mayor has not yet committed himself. This offer is preliminary, but I am confident that with your clients' acceptance, we can make this happen. Taxpayer money is hard to come by these days.

"So, basically, Alan, you have two choices: you can take the cash now and end this, or you can continue your quest, only to lose in court later. The choice is yours. But remember, we are trying to help you out. What do you say?"

The three leaned forward, padded suit shoulders together, awaiting Gold's response. The bell had not yet rung on the match.

Gazing across the table at the three of them, each nearly panting in expectation for his response, Alan suddenly sensed a remarkable change in position. They wanted settlement now more than he. Experience in other negotiations taught him the one in control is the one who wants a deal least. He relaxed and savored the moment for the first time in a long while. His lips curled, half in whimsy. He rose from his chair and paced slowly about the room as he responded.

"I appreciate your offer and will relay it to my client, as I must. As for your advice, Freddie, I suppose we can all use it, even when gratuitously offered.

"Let me be clear. Our view of this case differs drastically from yours. We see lost wages at nearly half a million, plus pain and suffering, though my clients are not bent necessarily on maximizing financial return. We will prove to the jury that WCI is a cistern of medical neglect run by incompetents with no idea of how to deliver proper medical care. The people of our city will become aware of what is going on in their government institutions. You know, as do I, that an extensive public trial—and it will be extensive—will disclose what a lousy job the mayor has done. Honor's death reflects the mayor and the city ignoring the serious medical needs of prisoners. It started with a terrible doctor and incompetent nurses, and we'll show how the stink rose to the top.

"My client wants Columbus citizens to see this trial as a day of reckoning. So, before we meet again when you present us with a more realistic offer—and I think you will want to meet again—my clients require, besides a much, much more significant settlement amount, two things not related to money. We demand an apology on TV delivered personally by the mayor, and his disclosing specific prison reforms he will enact immediately, including those that will improve medical care at WCI.

"Gentlemen, I think we have gone as far as we can today. I will inform you of my clients' decision regarding your initial offer, but I'm certain they will reject it. Please tell me the mayor accepts the two non-monetary terms. If he will, we can meet again to resolve money issues. I hope we do. Thank you, Ed, for bringing us together. Gentlemen, until our next meeting, let me wish you all a good day."

With that, Alan Gold put his yellow pad in his black leather briefcase, stood very straight, and walked out without looking back.

They were stunned. Auber was the first to speak. "I cannot believe that man. He must be on a suicide mission. I expected him to up the ante a little, but surely, he must know that his demand for a personal apology, coupled with specific and immediate reforms, is a deal-breaker. Doesn't he know the mayor is running for reelection? Does he think Blandford would give up his reelection bid just to improve life for a few prisoners? I swear, Gold has gone mad."

"Let us know what happens with City Hall, Ed. We gotta go now," said Livingston. As the two attorneys left Ed's office, Gordon whispered to Livingston, "Let's talk."

CHAPTER 50

ED AUBER SET UP ANOTHER meeting the following morning with the same clients he'd met before to discuss Gold's counteroffer. Puchik was beside himself in anticipation.

"Well, did she accept?" he blurted out.

"Not yet, I'm sorry to report. Negotiations proved to be very interesting. While Gold demanded more money, he said his clients have other requirements."

"My concern is timing, Ed," said Terry. "Just tell me. Will a few more bucks make this go away before our next poll?"

"More money is not all Mr. Gold said his clients want. They made two other demands."

"I don't get it," said Bruno. "What else but money do they want? Isn't that all those goddamn people ever ask for? First, it's welfare, and then when cops arrest them, they sue us. What else do they want, a trip to the Bahamas?"

"No, Mr. Puchik. Al says their other demands are not just for them."

"Let me guess. They want us to donate to the Nation of Islam, right?" asked Bruno, a smirk across his face.

"My turn," said Terry with a wide grin. "She wants us to make Martin Luther King's birthday a holiday. Do I win a cigar?"

"Not even a consolation prize. Their two demands are: number one, that the mayor make a public apology on TV, and number two, he must announce specific prison reforms to take effect immediately, ensuring that this will never happen again."

The shock came so fast that it wiped the smiles off the men's faces. They sat silently for a few moments.

"Do you think this is some kind of stunt, a fake to divert attention from their money grab?" asked Bruno.

"I don't think so. Mr. Gold sensed our offer still had some gas in the tank. He seemed sincere in saying his clients considered those other demands a key part of the settlement and will stop further negotiations if we don't accept them." Ed returned his gaze to his three puzzled listeners.

Bruno began, "Mr. Mayor, if it would get rid of this case, my office could pretty up some rules without wasting too much time. Set a few goals in lofty terms. Fluff like that."

"We'll say these rules were long in the making and they do not reflect a policy change, only a clarification," added Terry.

Ed interrupted. "I think Mr. Gold will want to review those rules before they are issued, and my guess is that he will want to see real reform, not administrative gingerbread. What about the apology?" asked Ed, turning toward the mayor.

"That is out of the question," Terry interjected. "An apology would admit the claim. I can't imagine what would lose our campaign faster than an apology. People would start talking about race and discrimination instead of jobs. Jobs win us elections. Race doesn't. You know, Jenkins gave that eulogy at Honor's funeral. I bet he put her mother up to this. Or maybe it was that Sweet Willie Moss who's been stirring up trouble on his radio show. This is nothing short of blackmail, Mr. Mayor."

All eyes were focused on the mayor, who remained silent, no doubt anticipating the consequences of either a trial or an apology. This was not the first time merciless Fate had thrust him between a rock and a hard place. He knew Terry was correct; an apology could be a fatal blow to the campaign. But he also knew if the family would not relent and insisted on going to trial, he might instead die by a thousand cuts. Each night at 6 o'clock, some news shows would report on some municipal error or misdeed related to prisons or law enforcement and then follow up on the 11 o'clock news with his reaction to his own administrative error.

Days before the trial, reporters would begin man-on-the-street interviews with those who had called into WVKO. It would be incessant and disastrous. His strong ties with the Foxx family would not be enough to stop them. Foxx Media would have to join the rush to condemn because their television stations could not go dark, while their competitors grabbed the spotlight. Business is business. He foresaw it all. His choices were grim.

"Mayor, what shall I tell Gold?"

Blandford said calmly, "Tell him I will appoint a blue-ribbon panel to review all procedures at WCI. Tell them the chairman will be black. Raise our part of the offer by $5,000 and tell those insurance lawyers to do the same. Give the family three days to accept this as our total package, or negotiations will cease. Is there anything else we need to discuss? If not, thank you, Ed, for your help." He left quickly.

Ed communicated the city's position to the two insurance lawyers whose clients authorized them to raise their offers. Armed with extra cash, he called Gold and gave him the combined response. Gold then met with the family. While the kids discussed what settlement would mean to them, Millie was in her own zone, recalling the funeral, Pastor Jenkins' eulogy, and the song about Paul and Silas. Later, she told Gold no deal without a public apology and prison reforms.

Ed reported the stumbling blocks to the insurance attorneys and the mayor's office. The city could not accept the song and left the dance.

The insurance companies were not so constrained. Their agents agreed that local politics were getting in the way of settling, and they wanted out. The cost of hiring experts and additional attorney fees alone would more than justify increasing their offers. They authorized their attorneys to call Gold and make a deal. After all, his clients wanted an apology from the mayor, not their clients.

Gold treated their counteroffers as a new opportunity. A partial settlement from them—without giving up claims against the city—would allow him to use part of the settlement to help pay for depositions, experts, and other expenses. It would allow him to use "house money" to finance a trial against the city only.

Millie agreed to settle against the medical staff only, as did the probate court, which authorized this partial settlement. Malpractice and negligence cases against Dr. V and the nurses were settled. The plaintiffs' claims remained against the medical staff in the context of their suit against the City of Columbus, but the plaintiffs could not collect any more from them. The only defendant who would have to pay, if plaintiffs won, would be the City of Columbus.

Without insurance defense attorneys at counsel table to share the work and impress the jury, the City Attorney hastily pulled Ed and his team off the case and instead hired special counsel from Philadelphia to represent it, the famed George Russell Stone. The City Attorney, who also was up for reelection, wanted no criticism should things turn sour. Counsel, in emergency session, agreed to Stone's enormous retainer contract.

Negotiations ceased. The family would go to trial against the city only, and Alan Gold would face George Stone, *mano a mano*.

CHAPTER 51

A DAY OR TWO LATER, JOHNI, in her new routine, sat alone in the dining area with her back to the wall. Word among inmates had gotten out that she was collecting information for Gold, and she set this time and place for anyone who could help to talk to her. Guards did not notice what she was doing, or if they did, they ignored her. Some may have even wished her success.

A few inmates tried negotiating with Johni as if she were a prosecutor, offering to tell her who killed Honor in exchange for release. She told them to get out of her face. Occasionally, someone would bring her a pitiful tale unrelated to Honor's case. Those stories wouldn't help win Honor's case, but they encouraged Johni to keep pushing.

Today, nobody came. She was about to leave when a white inmate came by with a pot of coffee and one cup. After pouring the brew and handing it to her, she stood over Johni, facing the wall with her back to the camera, making sure her face could not be viewed.

"You still helping the lawyer for the dead girl?"

"That's right. Why?"

"I know some stuff—a lot. Have him come see me. I won't talk to nobody else."

"What do you know? I'll tell him."

"Not you. I'll only talk to him. Just remember. I pour coffee for a lot of people, not just inmates. Name is Molene Jones; in case you don't know."

With that, she walked away.

CHAPTER 52

GOLD SAID GOOD NIGHT TO Frannie, who left a little early after a tumultuous day to take a night out for herself. She was wearing a smart beige blouse over slacks.

At his desk, he took a few minutes to ponder recent events. He'd been afraid he might cave during settlement negotiations. Their offer had been tempting. Take the cash and run, avoid the stress, return to restful sleep, and, most importantly, skip the chance of losing. Now, he reveled in having stood his ground.

But his exhilaration popped after he received from the court a Notice of Change of Counsel; George Stone would be replacing Ed Auber. Gold had once attended a seminar on trial techniques at the University of Michigan law school. The sponsors proclaimed George Russell Stone as one of the finest defense attorneys in America. In mock trials there, Gold watched as Stone flawlessly demonstrated how he could turn a hostile jury to his side after a single slip-up by plaintiff counsel. He still recalled the look on one counsel's face after Stone humbled him, undoing everything he had proudly established on direct examination of a witness. *Will I now be the one to slip up?* Gold wondered. *But I'm in too deep to look back*, he tried to convince himself.

It was getting dark when he started to leave the office. For a second, he thought of skipping a call coming in, but after several rings, he picked up the phone and, with his practiced professional voice, said, "This is Alan Gold."

"Mr. Gold, I'm Sgt. Mitchell, you know, from over at the Women's Correctional Institution? You may not remember me, you being so busy. We met at that witness meeting a few weeks ago when you asked me a bunch of questions with that court reporter, and you gave me your card."

"Yes, yes, I remember. You were the officer who called the squad for Honor?"

"Yeah, you got that right."

"What can I do for you?"

"Well, Mr. Gold, I don't know what to say. It's sort of like this. I'm having some problems, but I don't want to lose my job. Been there for many years and worked my way from guard to sergeant—a chance at lieutenant, well not much of chance—but maybe. Anyway, I got to stay on the good side of my boss."

Alan muttered, "Uh,huh" and listened for more, putting his coat and briefcase down and taking a seat.

"But you see, I've got other problems. I keep thinking about her. Hearing her screams from the cell, seeing blood running from her. I recall what I said to you, and I'm having problems with it all. So, I'm torn, and I'm not sure what to do."

"Sounds very hard for you. Must be tearing you up. If I recall, you said you thought she OD'd. Am I recalling it right?"

"Yes, sir, that's what I said. And that's where I'm having problems."

"Go on. Tell me about them."

"Well, you see, the thing is, I ain't no doctor. Maybe she didn't take drugs. I found out the other day she had cancer."

"Yes, that's what the coroner says. I know you're not a doctor, but why did you say she OD'd?"

"Well, I guess it's sort of 'you gotta do what you gotta do,' you understand?"

"No, not really. What did you have to do?"

"Well, I got to keep my job. I made sergeant. Did it on my own. You know what I'm saying?"

"I think I'm starting to get it. You're having problems because you thought by saying she OD'd, you were saving your job. Am I getting closer?"

"Yeah, closer."

"Uh, did someone else think she had a drug reaction and mentioned it to you? Or maybe someone told you to tell the squad she OD'd? And so, you did it to keep your job? Am I getting warmer?"

"Yeah, warmer."

"And you're torn because you don't think what you said to me was true, particularly after you learned from the coroner's report that she didn't OD and didn't have other drugs in her. And now you feel bad and think you're stuck in the middle of someone else's dirty work. How am I doing?"

"Gettin' hot, sir."

"And what you swore to me as true is now haunting you. If you stick to that story, you're scared about what might happen to you, but you're also scared you might lose your job if you testify to what you think really happened. How close am I?"

"Mr. Gold, I think you're readin' my mind."

"Well, first, let me thank you for calling, Sergeant Mitchell. I can see you're in a tight spot. I'll tell you what I will do to help you get out of it. I'll issue a subpoena for you to testify at trial. Don't worry. I am going to issue lots of subpoenas. You won't be the only one. When it's your turn to testify, the judge will put you under oath and order you to tell the truth. If you do, the Civil Service Commission will protect your job. Then, you will feel good that you did the right thing."

"If I testify, will the city fire Mr. Gross?"

"Probably. Civil Service does not protect him."

"I feel torn. I'm still not sure."

"Not sure you will be protected?"

"No."

"Not sure Gross will be gone?"

"No."

"Not sure you'll no longer feel torn?"

"No. Not sure I can do it. I ain't that strong."

"I see. Sergeant, trust me; you can do it. You will do it because it's the right thing to do and because it's the only way to rid yourself of this problem. You've got a monkey on your back, running through your gut and into your mind. So really, what's your choice? You're not a person who can live a lie. It'll eat you up. You can rot your whole life living a lie. It will haunt you when you go to sleep, when you go to work, and when you pray at church. You go to church, don't you? What I'm saying to you, Sgt. Mitchell, is peace will come only after you tell the truth."

"Well, thank you, Mr. Gold. I'm not sure but thank you. I'm so confused; I got to pray. Good night."

CHAPTER 53

WHEN BAILIFF BEN WALTON first read the complaint, he scheduled an additional pre-trial conference near trial time to allow an additional opportunity to resolve what might become a complicated trial. Since then, settlements with the doctor and nurses had simplified this case. No more malpractice claims, insurance considerations, or possible confusion from having so many lawyers involved. Judge Rumsfeld still wanted to use this conference as the final opportunity to settle. If the City and plaintiffs could resolve the remaining claims, he might land back in the good graces of Lex Baer and the judicial nominating committee. But he was hampered by not knowing either counsel or what would entice either them or their clients to compromise.

Ben gladly rescheduled the date and hour of that conference to accommodate George Stone's business plans without allowing Gold to object.

Alan arrived first on the rescheduled date, took his usual seat, and avoided Bailiff Walton. He dreaded trying the case before Judge Rumsfeld, particularly after the Court of Appeals reversed his dismissal. Rumsfeld, angry for being told publicly his decision was wrong, might vent his ire on Gold.

When Stone arrived, Walton escorted him into the conference room, talking to him as if they were old friends. Gold looked up from his papers to see his tall opponent clad in a tailor-made blue sharkskin suit that accented his coiffed silver hair. Gold rose to shake his hand. Stone turned slightly from Walton and extended his left hand, exposing a gold Rolex below a pearl cufflink.

The Matter of Honor

"Good afternoon, I'm George Stone," he said before turning his back and resuming conversation with Ben. Gold sat down awkwardly.

The two continued talking, excluding Alan, until the judge arrived 15 minutes late. Putting his hand on Stone's back, Walton said, "Judge, I would like you to meet George Stone, who just flew in from Philadelphia to attend our final pre-trial conference. He told me how helpful a bailiff in Chicago had been during his recent victory. I told him I would do my best to be just as helpful in this case. I told him if he had any concerns whatsoever to give us a call, and that it would be my pleasure to be of help in whatever way I could. Please sit here, Mr. Stone," the bailiff said as he pulled out the chair for Stone. "You already met Alan Gold, the plaintiffs' lawyer. Can I offer you some coffee? If not, I'll leave you now."

"How was your flight?" asked the judge.

"Fairly routine. When he saw turbulence south of Lake Erie, my pilot changed our itinerary to come into Columbus from the southeast. Thanks for asking, Judge."

"Well, glad you got here safely. Now, today is our final pretrial conference. Counsel, are there any outstanding issues?"

Gold was dumbfounded. "Yes, Your Honor. Three motions are pending."

"Well, tell Ben about them after the conference, and I'll get to them. Any witness problems? Are all experts testifying through video depositions? Any other concerns? "

"You don't allow jurors to take notes, do you?" asked Stone.

"Not usually. Why, would you want them to?" asked Rumsfeld.

"No, thanks. I had a case recently in Milwaukee where the judge allowed notetaking. One juror spent so much writing, she stopped listening to me. But we won anyhow," he said with a smile.

"Oh, Mr. Stone, I'll bet you have lots of stories from your cases across the country," said Rumsfeld, sitting back in his chair.

"Funny that you mention it. My staff and I are compiling notes of my years in court, and I'm planning to publish my memoirs next year. My agent is negotiating with several national publishers, and I expect his report when I return."

"Really? I can't wait to read it," said the judge.

"It's not complete yet. Who knows? Maybe I will add you as well."

"Me? Then, for sure, I will read it," said the judge, giggling.

Gold cleared his throat.

The judge resumed a serious posture. "Have you boys had a chance to talk settlement? Your clients might want to wrap this up. It could end up a mess. Listen, I'll be happy to do whatever I can to help you boys settle this case. It might be in your client's best interest not to try this case but find some mutually agreeable resolution."

Stone replied, "My understanding, Judge, is those discussions resulting in settlements with the doctor and nurses ceased before I was retained. We've tried our best to continue negotiations, but I was told that plaintiffs were unwilling."

"Well, Mr. Gold, are your clients refusing to negotiate further, forcing this case to trial? Of course, a court can't require settlement or force unwanted negotiations, but neither do I look favorably on obstinacy nor appreciate long trials when a fair settlement is possible. You have made that clear to your clients, have you not?" asked Rumsfeld in an unusually firm voice.

"Without disclosing the nature of settlement issues, Your Honor, I must clarify the record. The city is refusing to negotiate," responded Gold.

"In my long experience with the city, Ed Auber and the others in the City Attorney's office have always been most willing

THE MATTER OF HONOR

to negotiate. Continue trying. Please let me know if there is anything my office can do to assist."

"Yes, Your Honor."

"If nothing else, then we stand adjourned. I want you boys to keep trying to settle. I look forward to hearing from you one week from today regarding your progress. Mr. Stone, will you please let Ben know the status of your efforts?"

"I would be happy to, Your Honor."

CHAPTER 54

GOLD CONTINUED VISITING helpful inmates whenever he went to WCI, creating an effective network of inside informants and messengers. Anything said to a person in authority was relayed to Gold. Likewise, during a visit with one inmate, he could communicate with many others through messengers carrying the word.

He avoided direct meetings with Johni to protect their relationship. Her mother would call him with Johni's news. But her memory was slipping, and sometimes she forgot all that her daughter had told her, and when she visited her daughter, she could not write it down for fear of being caught. When Johni relayed Molene's request, her mother couldn't remember her name. She told him Johni told her an inmate wanted to talk to him but forgot the details. She could not remember her name, maybe Marlene or Marna, or something like that.

Gold met in WCI with a client, advising her to take a plea to one count of prostitution. She had no choice, with two kids who depended on her. Since Honor's case, he had become even more uncomfortable being part of the system imprisoning these women for prostitution both because of the danger when they were confined and because of the fundamental unfairness of the crime itself. A few judges who pitied helpless defendants also had qualms about putting them in jail but feared being labeled "soft on crime" at reelection time. Before ending his client conference, he tried to find out from her the name of that potential witness.

"By the way," he asked the woman. "Do you know somebody in here named Marna or Marlene?"

"Say what?"

"Moni, or something like that. Momi? Molly?"

"I don't know no Moni. Who she?"

"She wants to talk to me about some other case. Well, anyway, I spoke to the judge and the prosecutor. They say you must get out of the business."

"How do I do that? I got no job. Can't afford school. I got me two kids. What they say I'm s'posed to do?"

"They didn't. Never do. But they did say they would let you out of jail if you'll pay a fine of 50 bucks. Can you handle it?"

"Got no choice, do I? I'll find it somewhere. When do I get out?"

"I'll try to talk to them tomorrow if you can find the money. I gotta go. Getting tired. Sure wish I had a cup of coffee."

"Thanks, Mr. Gold. Say, is you looking for Molene? She gives coffee and stuff to guards and folks like that."

"Molene. Yeah, maybe that's the one. Thanks. If the judge will see me tomorrow, I'll get you out real soon."

CHAPTER 55

SINCE COBBLING TOGETHER A NETWORK of inmates and guards, Gold had made real progress. Starting with a jigsaw puzzle of at least 196 unknown witnesses, seemingly worthless medical records, bland rules and procedures, and lots of rumors (mostly useless), he had assembled a credible narrative. When he began, he did not know which inmate or guard had any helpful information. Slowly, he had put one piece loosely together with another to give it some form. A seemingly trivial fact later proved critical; a seemingly obvious lead proved worthless. But he would always harbor the haunting question of every litigator after trial: *Did I miss a piece?*

Gold now looked forward to trial with the same bravado as Barry displayed in poker games when pulling for an inside straight. Just like Barry, Alan suddenly had received divine wisdom. He now disputed what he had long known: that luck is fleeting, fickle, and phony.

Today he believed, as only a true gambler-believer can, that genius, not providence, brought Dr. Steiner and his other witnesses to him. Genius alone would propel him to victory. Somehow, the evidence and laws, which had seemed so daunting, now juiced him up. He could already hear the heart-rending words he'd say to the jury about injustices inflicted upon Honor by uncaring defendants who caused her senseless death.

His great aids had been inmates and guards who, at tremendous risk to themselves, helped him insert puzzle pieces and shape facts, while Frank provided him a current guide to the ever-changing law.

Focusing on her cause of death, he laid out a chart of what happened to Honor day by day and how defendants mistreated her. He learned of other inmates and their troubles and arrived at a startling conclusion. He now agreed with Dr. V, the nurses, and Haskel Gross that Honor had been treated like other inmates. But the more devasting fact, he concluded, was they mistreated all inmates. At WCI, mistreatment was systemic. He began to understand what Justice Marshall meant by his phrase "deliberate indifference."

As he crafted the trial narrative, he constantly reminded himself that facts must dominate his presentation of Honor's treatment. He needed both to convince the jury and lure them into wanting more, as a good book informs readers yet entices them to read the next chapter. He hoped jurors would respond not only with a justifiable decision but also with gut emotion. Carefully fitting each piece of evidence into what the law required him to prove, he worked on carving an unforgettable emotional narrative for the jury.

He and Frank met for hours, creating an amalgam of fact and law they hoped would prevent Judge Rumsfeld from dismissing the case again.

CHAPTER 56

LIKE A MOVIE DIRECTOR ON SET, Gold began extracting emotional impact from the testimony of each witness. He meticulously entwined every scrap of evidence with appropriate elements of law and then tied the entire package with an emotional cord so strong he expected to see tears flowing from jurors' eyes.

He dealt with drama questions he had never thought about before: *How does the arc of Honor's story change by rearranging the order of witnesses? Would the jury be more moved if this witness introduced a document instead of that one? Are there more emotive ways to evidence a fact than through this witness? How about using photos to enhance jury response?* Nuance gained importance as he reworded questions to encourage juror reaction.

But unlike a movie director, Gold could not pick his actors, props, or scenery. He had to use dislikeable witnesses when he could not prove a fact without them and could only call likable witnesses when he could find something relevant for them to say.

His greatest fear was Judge Rumsfeld. Gold prepared for him to tilt the trial in every possible way. He had two adversaries in the courtroom: George Stone and the judge. Anticipating retribution, he and Frank developed many Plan Bs.

To protect witnesses from intimidation, the list of trial witnesses he was required to provide opposing counsel included every inmate and guard. Stone's staff could not prepare nor warn prison authorities who, if any, would be spilling the beans. Gold prepped his witnesses with anticipated questions from Stone but avoided putting words into their mouths. He knew rehearsed testimony lost authenticity.

Next to his bed, Gold kept a pad to record late-night thoughts. He postponed other cases, read medical research articles on choriocarcinoma, studied government reports on prison standards, and watched TV dramas about prisons. He constantly second-guessed what Stone might do with his evidence to destroy his case. He planned for legal war with the same tenacity and detail as General Giáp had prepared North Vietnamese fighters for battle against French and American troops.

On the other hand, Stone had a distinct advantage in trial preparation. As defense counsel, he did not have to prove anything. Gold had the burden of proof. Stone could win simply by disproving Gold. Because Gold went first, Stone could react on his feet during the trial. His reputation was so impressive it was said that he could prove 2+2=5 if given enough time with a jury.

Stone reviewed condensed versions of earlier pleadings and depositions digested by his research staff, spoke briefly with WCI and City Hall officials, and interviewed experts his trial team selected. The rest he delegated, while off he went to another trial in Buffalo where other staff awaited him. There, he would try a different case, address lawyers as a lead presenter at two seminars, and then meet in New York City with insurance executives about defending their companies against claims of asbestos poisoning.

Before leaving Columbus for Buffalo, Stone made three calls. Ed Auber told him that Gold must drop his demands for an apology and prison reform if he wanted a deal. On his second call, Gold told him the mayor must apologize publicly and institute real reform before his client would agree to a settlement. In his last call, Ben Walton improperly let him speak directly to the judge to whom he reported that a trial was unavoidable because the plaintiffs were unwilling to negotiate.

CHAPTER 57

THE CASE OF "*MILLIE RIVERS, Administrator of the Estate of Honor Wilson v Jon Blandford et al.*" was to start on Monday. Judge Rumsfeld began the jury selection process on the Thursday morning before.

Gold and Stone vigorously questioned potential jurors about their backgrounds, connections to political parties, attitudes toward prisoners and those accused of crimes, the death penalty, prison reform, and many other issues.

They probed into every lobe of jurors' brains and every valve of their hearts, trying to determine their attitudes and feelings about large awards, religion, political preferences, crime, city finances, even their attitudes about lawyers. They examined possible connections to the city and its employees and agents. Despite telling them they were seeking fair and impartial peers, each wanted biased jurors bent in their direction. Fairness is for fools.

While Gold asked potential jurors every question imaginable about their lives, thoughts, feelings, biases, experiences, and attitudes, Millie looked through their eyes and into their souls, mining lodes of compassion and empathy to assess their suitability as jurors. Together, Alan and Millie decided who to keep or strike.

As the litigators were picking jurors, Mayor Blandford, with Bruno Puchik and Haskel Gross standing behind him, held a huge news conference on Thursday afternoon outside WCI. Terry invited all the media he could and amassed over 75 spectators (mainly city employees who had been given paid leave) to emphasize its importance.

Blandford announced the result of his demand for a state investigation. WCI, he proudly declared, had met all requirements of the Ohio Bureau of Adult Detention for 1978-1979. He did not explain why he had waited until the eve of Honor's trial to announce the report that he had received three weeks earlier, what the requirements were, nor which cities failed (there were none). It was a headline, not a story, but Foxx Media ran the mayor's announcement as its lead story all weekend.

By 4:15 Friday afternoon, counsel had selected a jury of eight: two white women, a black woman, a Latina, three white men, and a black man. Two were retirees, two were college students (one had dropped out), one was a high school biology teacher, two were homemakers, and one was a college administrator. They also chose two alternate jurors—one black and one white. Judge Rumsfeld ordered all to return Monday at 9 a.m. to begin the trial.

CHAPTER 58

BY 8:45 A.M. MONDAY MORNING, every visitor seat in Rumsfeld's courtroom was taken. Because photographers were not allowed to take pictures inside the courtroom, they stood outside and took what shots they could get through the door window. *The Columbus Dispatch*, with instructions from Mr. Foxx, sent both a reporter and a sketch artist to cover the trial.

Gold arrived early to calm his nerves and adjust to the courtroom environment. Millie sat beside Alan and Frank at the counsel table. To his surprise, his otherwise meek client now seemed steeled, like a mother bear defending her cubs. She was set on proving that her daughter was not a druggie and defendants had hurt her family. Her family, all dressed in their Sunday best, sat in the front row of the visitor's section behind the wooden rail separating them from the judge and attorneys.

Stone and some staff who had flown with him on his plane sat at the defense table. Haskel and Bruno sat immediately behind them. The mayor was not present. Downstairs, jurors sat in their room, waiting to be called. All were set to go except for Judge Rumsfeld, tardy as usual. Bailiff Ben Walton finally called the jury to come upstairs and take their seats in the jury box at 9:45 a.m.

"All rise! The court is now in session. The Honorable Judge Stuart Rumsfeld presiding."

Rumsfeld took the bench, gaveled once, and asked, "Good morning, ladies and gentlemen of the jury. Is everyone comfortable? Good. Are counsel ready to proceed?"

Gold and Stone stood. "Yes, Your Honor."

"Counsel for Plaintiff, please proceed with your opening statement."

Gold went to the small podium placed temporarily in front of the jury box before the trial by Bailiff Walton. After spending nearly 16 hours together, introductions were unneeded. jurors knew who the attorneys were and what they wanted. Instead, Gold offered pleasantries, thank you's for their service, and a show of humility, asking jurors not to punish his clients if, during the trial, he offended anyone.

"The evidence will show that the city of Columbus and its employees and agents, from guards to the mayor himself, were deliberately indifferent to the serious medical needs of Honor Wilson. They deprived her of her constitutional right to decent medical care while at WCI. Her family mourns her loss. She was so young."

He introduced Millie and each member of her family, spending a moment or two describing something good about each one: an A in English, a member of the band, a job at Wendy's, etc. He then laid out his case, a time map of what he planned to present, promising a twist or two to keep the jury engaged.

"Honor's baby boy, Winston, is not with us today. Tragically, he can no longer look into his mother's eyes, feel her touch, and receive her love and attention. He is less than two years old, a baby without a mother. We will bring little Winston to court later; he is now a part of Millie's family."

He paused to look into the eyes of the jurors. "We are here to see justice done for Honor and her family. Fate has given you the power to dispense justice through your verdict. You will find the proof you need to render that verdict from this witness stand and documents that the judge will admit as evidence. While Judge Rumsfeld will rule on law and procedures, you will make the final decisions on liability and how much the award will be.

"Later, we will discuss ways you might wish to use in calculating the award amount. For some of you, these may be some of the most profound decisions you will ever make. I have confidence in you. You are up to the challenge of creating history; you will make the right decisions. Thank you on behalf of Honor's family, including baby Winston."

George Russell Stone rose to his full six-foot frame and slowly walked to the podium, displaying his perfect teeth set in a warm smile and his light blue-gray eyes that matched his perfectly tailored suit. He smiled at each juror, winked at a lady, and nodded to a gentleman as if his short walk were a grand parade. He brought no notes to the podium.

Stone began mildly and naturally, moving the narrative in an entirely different direction from Gold's. He heralded the duty of members of law enforcement to protect citizens like them from criminals like those incarcerated at the WCI.

"From fearless police to dedicated guards at WCI, they all take their jobs seriously and do them very well. They rise to the challenge daily, acting responsibly and according to the law. And they do it for you and you and you," he said, walking from the podium to point to each juror. "Why, to accuse these professionals of indifference of any kind is to insult and disrespect not just them but each of you whom they protect. It's an insult to this city and all its law-abiding Americans—indeed a travesty—that these defendants, your dedicated public servants protecting law and order for your safety, should be on trial at all!"

He then introduced each defendant present who stood when called. He described their positions in exalted tones and thanked them sincerely on behalf of all the citizens of the entire city for their work. The mayor, Stone said, was at City Hall working on important government business, the people's business. He admonished them to distinguish the mayor's political beliefs, with which they might disagree, from his dedication to serving the people of Columbus.

Causation was a central theme of his opening statement. "That fact is—and I say this only with the utmost grief—and the evidence will show (expressing feigned condolences to the family of Honor for their loss) that her death, unfortunately, was inevitable. The deceased, bless her soul, had received the death sentence of (whisper and wince) "cancer." Using practiced and polished gestures, Stone leaned forward toward the jurors and whispered and winced every time he used the C-word as if the very word were contagious.

"We will show you later a video deposition of one of the world's greatest cancer experts, who will explain to you an undeniable fact, a fact that undercuts everything plaintiffs will try to present, a fact so important that it calls into question why plaintiffs want to take up your valuable time even to hear their highly questionable claims. That fact is plaintiff cannot prove anything any defendant could have done to prevent the inevitable death of the deceased."

"Unless Mr. Gold can prove the defendants caused her death, he has no case at all. He has nothing but claims and accusations. But he cannot prove causation. Nor can he prove indifference, his weak attempt to snatch a large award drawn from your taxpayer coffers."

Gold stood. "Objection, Your Honor."

"Overruled."

Stone looked away momentarily, shaking his head at Gold's objection to Stone's reference to taxpayer coffers paying for the trial. "Well, I just want to say thank you for your service as jurors, protecting those whom Mr. Gold has falsely accused. I know you will use critically good judgment when you listen to whatever stories Mr. Gold might compose."

The two opening statements had bewildered jurors. Contrary facts overly flavored with fortified adjectives had overwhelmed them, and they wondered whether Gold and Stone were talking about the same case. As Orwell put it, "If thought corrupts language, language can also corrupt thought." Jurors settled in for a long trial, expecting each lawyer to corrupt communication.

After opening statements, Judge Rumsfeld ordered a 15-minute break and excused the jury. Alan asked Millie her thoughts on opening statements.

"Well, I haven't been to a trial before, but the jurors' faces seemed sad after you finished. I saw one woman dab her eye with a tissue. Is that a good thing or bad?"

Gold nodded. "I hope it means I got through to them."

"After Mr. Stone was done, however, I wasn't sure what they were thinking. I suppose after they hear all our witnesses telling them what happened, they will know the real score."

Gold froze. He had forgotten to interview one inmate, the one who served coffee. Rising from the counsel table with a feigned smile, he left the courtroom and rushed to the restroom on the floor above the courtroom, avoiding public contact. To prevent hyperventilation, he breathed into his hands, telling himself to remain calm. There would still be time to see her if he went after trial today. But he was overwhelmed by the prospect of her having been released.

He washed his face in cold water, leaning over the basin and talking to himself. Finally, he stared directly into the mirror, trying to persuade himself to get a grip. He forced a faux smile. After wiping his face, he marched back into the courtroom, wearing the aura of a winner.

CHAPTER 59

GOLD CALLED THE CORONER as his first witness and introduced as Exhibit A Honor's death certificate. The coroner testified that her cause of death was choriocarcinoma, not a drug overdose. Except for a finding of marijuana, Honor Wilson's toxicology lab results revealed she was clean of drugs. Because marijuana can remain in the body unmetabolized for as long as a month, he could not testify when she had consumed it. He acknowledged medical articles that Gold showed him, revealing studies of a few patients suffering this type of cancer who reportedly had been cured.

When Gold finished his direct examination, he was sure jurors would conclude her death was from cancer, not from drugs, and the disease was treatable and curable. Coming from a publicly elected government doctor of the same party as the mayor, Alan was sure jurors would find the coroner's testimony convincing.

Millie was also pleased. In her mind, Gold had used the coroner's testimony to prove that Honor was not a druggie, which to her was the heart of their case. Of course, she wanted money for Winston, but her family's reputation was paramount. The coroner had just told the jury Honor was not a druggie.

To her, his testimony proved that the newspapers were lying, particularly the largest one. She sat back, expecting tomorrow's front-page headline of *The Columbus Dispatch* to read, "Franklin County Coroner Says Honor Wilson Not a Druggie," and somewhere in the article, she would find an apology to her family. Correcting false accusations and an apology from all accusers would make the trial worth the effort, even without a large jury award. The coroner's testimony accomplished her mission. She relaxed.

Cross-examination followed. Stone went after the coroner like a spider ensnaring a wasp. With charm and self-confidence oozing from his pinstriped worsted suit, he asked the coroner roundabout questions regarding his education and experience to size him up before commencing his attack. He employed only yes or no questions, starting with the toxicology report.

"Isn't it true, Doctor, that your tests do not detect some drugs? Isn't it also true that some drugs metabolize so fast that had she taken them before her death, your tests would not detect them after she died? Isn't it true the evil drug, marijuana, detected by your office, provides some proof she might have ingested it while she was incarcerated at WCI? So, she could have been taking illegal drugs even while confined, couldn't she? Didn't a sergeant at WCI report she might have taken drugs? If Honor were taking drugs that went undetected and unreported in your toxicology report, then your report would not prove the sergeant wrong, would it?

"Doctor, the decedent claimed to have lost a child at birth. If true, that loss can cause depression, can't it? Sometimes, depressed people turn to drugs, don't they? If her claim of having a stillborn were true, that loss could have motivated her to take drugs, couldn't it? In short, she could have been motivated to take drugs undetected by your tests even while in prison, couldn't she?"

The coroner had offered one-word responses, agreeing to everything Stone asked. The silver-haired attorney moved on to the subject of causation.

"Cancer (whisper and wince) is a deadly disease, is it not? And as is true of many cancers, the tragic truth is there are no cures for many of them, are there? The disease can be literally a curse of death, can't it? You are not aware of any studies measuring the effect of psychotropic drugs on cancer cell growth, are you?"

On and on it went. Stone making statements in the form of questions to which the coroner agreed. Finally, Stone summed up succinctly.

"So that the jury is clear about your testimony, Doctor. As Franklin County coroner, you cannot deny Ms. Wilson's unavoidable death could have been caused, in whole or in part, by her taking undetectable illegal or illicit drugs, correct? Her stillbirth could have motivated her to take drugs, correct? Your opinion on her cause of death is based upon minimal information and, unfortunately for us, inadequate research of illegal drugs by medical experts. Isn't that correct, Doctor? You would agree, as would we all, that it is a pity we don't know more about drugs, causation, and cancer (whisper and wince)?"

After he concluded his assault, Stone gestured his profound regret to the jury that Alan's crystal-clear evidence was, in truth, blurry, distorted, and filled with many unknowns. He sat down, his back to the jurors, and smiled to his staff, unobtrusively reveling in his performance.

Millie's eyes were afire, while her heart was broken. How can he live with himself, making nothing into something? So cruel. She overheard Frank say to Alan, "Wow, that was impressive!"

Judge Rumsfeld continued the trial until the next morning while he attended to other matters.

CHAPTER 60

AFTER TRIAL THAT EVENING, Alan rushed from the courtroom to WCI, praying Molene had not been released. He quickly interviewed an appointed client charged with stealing a welfare check before returning to the front desk.

"Er, officer, there's another inmate I need to see, but I can't remember her last name. I think her first name is Molene. You know who I'm talking about?"

"You're working late, Counselor. We are getting near lights out. The only Molene I can recall is named Jones. Can it wait?"

"Molene Jones. Yeah, that's the one. I need to talk to her briefly. Can you send her out? I'll be quick."

"Just be a few minutes."

"Thank you," he said, taking a seat in the waiting room before letting out a quiet sigh of relief.

Soon, a short white woman with her hair in a bun stood nearby with her right arm across her chest and her left hand covering her mouth. She stood there looking in all directions. He nonchalantly walked toward her, asking, "Are you Molene Jones?"

"Who are you?"

"Alan Gold. I understand you need to talk to me about some matters. Let's go to the attorney conference room. It's empty."

Molene was uncertain about what to do and who he was. She walked hesitantly toward the only private conference room in WCI, stopping at the door—now with both arms crossed.

Alan said quietly, "I'm the attorney for Honor Wilson's family. Johni told me you wanted to see me. Please come in and shut the door, so we can talk privately."

Molene sat. "I'm not sure now if I should be talking to you. I may get into trouble."

"No, you did the right thing. I may already be aware of what you can tell me about Honor's case, so it may not be new information. But her family is very grateful you called, as am I."

Molene relaxed a little while Gold got out his yellow pad.

"Tell me a little about yourself, Molene. Where are you from?"

"Neffs, Ohio."

"Never heard of it. Where is that?"

"Belmont County, over by the river, near Wheeling."

"What brought you to Columbus?"

"My daddy got a job here at Jeffrey Manufacturing. He brought us here. Things were okay till he got hurt on the job, and he filed a worker's comp claim, so they fired him. Never worked again."

"How long have you been in here?"

"About three months. I'm doing six months on a federal charge of cashing welfare checks."

"What do you do at WCI?"

"I work in the kitchen and other odd jobs. Most often, I make coffee and serve it to staff. Sometimes I deliver food to inmates in the Hole. It ain't much, but it keeps me busy."

"Did you know Honor Wilson?"

"No, sir. I never talked to her, but I seen her in there, in the Hole."

"OK, so why did you tell Johni you wanted to see me?"

"I heard that people from WCI said they did all they could to save her. That's a damned lie, and I wanted you to know it."

"How is it a lie?"

"Well, you learned she was in the Hole, didn't you?"

"I learned that guards moved her there before they took her to OSU."

"Well, did you know she had been there before then? That was her second time in cell block. The first time I brought her dinner, I almost dropped her tray when I saw her lying there in her pee, shit, and blood. She smelled worse than a honey-dipper's load.

"When the guards came, she woke up, and they brought her stuff, like clean clothes and a Kotex, but then they made her clean up her cell first and then the whole cell block. She looked like death warmed over. She could hardly stand. It wasn't right, making her work like that. And I don't think the guards called the nurses until after they gave her a mop and bucket. I just knew they still thought she was a'fakin, but I can tell you, that nigger girl was really sick."

"Faking?"

"Yeah, faking. That's right. Nurse Kratz told a guard over coffee she didn't think she was sick at all, and she said something about checking out her baby story. But I can tell you, anybody with me in cell block that night would know that poor thing was mighty sick."

"Was anyone else aware of Nurse Kratz's actions or Honor's illness?"

"Yeah, I heard staff in the breakroom talking about the case. Dr. V and Mr. Gross knew for sure.

"Were you there the second time Honor was in the Hole?"

"No, but Sgt. Mitchell said it was the worst thing she'd ever seen. She said the girl was screaming and in so much pain she pulled some hair out of her head. I just had to tell you what happened. Nobody should be treated that way. And anyone who had a hand in it should be locked up. Hey, I'm doing time for what I did wrong. Why ain't they?"

"Molene, you're right. Why aren't they? You may be just the person who can make that happen. I will ask you in the next few days to tell the jury just what you told me. You are right. You're damned right!"

Gold returned her to the guards just before lights-out. As he walked to his car, trial thoughts swirled in his brain like lights from a glittering from a disco ball. Now he had someone to upset the city's version of what happened to Honor and maybe to others.

CHAPTER 61

THE NEXT DAY, GOLD CALLED several defendants to testify "as on cross-examination" to answer his questions yes or no, using the same technique as Stone had used to cross-examine the coroner. But Stone's team had schooled these defendants to demand a chance to explain their answers and to try to foil Gold's efforts to convey his side of the narrative. Throughout the trial, Gold and Stone had each vigorously fought to gain the power of narrative, the melody each attorney wanted jurors to hear among the cacophony of witness chatter.

During trial, Gold gently but persistently described to each defendant what happened in short sentences ending each of them with "Isn't that correct?" or starting with "Isn't it true that...?" Before the trial, Frank had practiced for hours with Alan, training him to keep a cadence of short Q&As that would force witnesses to answer only yes or no and provide no further explanation. When Frank, posing as a witness, wiggled with a question that might allow a judge to permit witness explanation, the two would rewrite the question to eliminate that possibility. Their goal was to use a witness to tell the story their way without allowing the witness to contradict it. Each point they wanted to make was reduced to many simple yes-or-no questions, requiring the witness to simply confirm their narrative through one-word answers.

Throughout the day, Gold went through his narration at his practiced pace, gliding along so smoothly that jurors stopped listening to witness one-word answers. Instead, they heard only

The Matter of Honor

Gold's questions. While each defendant fought to avoid answering yes or no, none could control the conversation.

When Acting Superintendent Gross took the stand, his testimony seemed particularly stiff and coached. He feigned ignorance of the term 'the Hole,' which quickly tarnished his credibility. He said he only knew of the location's name as "cell block." His justification on budgetary grounds for using cell block for both medical and punitive purposes was weak, despite presenting City Auditor projections of the cost to build a separate infirmary. Anticipating his response, Gold quickly threw in questions showing the city could afford to provide Gross with the unrestricted use of an automobile when he only drove to and from work. He added other questions showing the city had money to buy what it wanted when it chose to.

Despite his best efforts, Gross could not justify the abuse caused by not having separate facilities, nor could his answer be anything but 'no' when asked if he did anything to protect ill prisoners abused in the Hole. Instead, he testified that he was not aware of any such abuse. While that answer caught Gold by surprise, he recovered instantly and turned it around by asking, wasn't the superintendent supposed to know if such abuse happened?

Dr. V and the nurses were, of course, aware that the settlement by their insurance companies freed them from further financial liability to Honor's family. However, they still had to protect their professional licenses and their jobs. They testified that the most common complaints at WCI were headaches and gynecological issues. In a well-rehearsed effort to break Gold's cadence, Dr. V paused after one of Gold's yes or no questions about his not examining Honor and assumed a cogitative pose before stating firmly that in his medical judgment and under the circumstances, there was no need for him to examine Honor.

Further, he opined, six-week checkups rarely produced meaningful results.

As its principal author, Nurse Kratz defended the manual of medical procedures. It was adequate for a city prison, she declared. In response to Gold's persistent questioning whether specific procedures in the manual were up to medical standards, she responded that it was written for a jail, not the Mayo Clinic.

Nurse Kratz found Honor's explanation that she had given birth to a stillborn untrue. She acknowledged she could have obtained Honor's medical records from Grant Hospital, but only at significant expense to the taxpayers of Columbus. Her way was cheaper and quicker—reasonable under the circumstances. Still, when confronted with Honor's medical records from Grant Hospital, she was forced to admit that obtaining medical information by calls to nursing friends had produced a false result.

Nurse Hill was the only one who broke a little, saying if she had been Kratz, she would have scheduled Honor to see Dr. V a little earlier and probably would have ordered medical records instead of making a call to a friend.

Gold's nursing expert, a local nursing school professor, testified that many of the nurses' actions constituted textbook negligence. Further, Kratz's overall actions regarding Honor's illness constituted making a diagnosis, which is illegal for Ohio nurses.

Neither she nor any other health expert on either side could testify as to what constitutes "deliberate indifference to a serious medical need." They all agreed it was a legal term not used in healthcare, leaving Gold's federal claim in doubt.

In the days following, Gold called to testify inmates and guards who bolstered his position or disproved the defendants' denials. Some seemed convincing, others not so. Judge Rumsfeld ordered jurors to disregard inmates' accounts of gut-wrenching stories of their experiences in WCI that did not pertain to Honor.

Puddin, who laid off drugs for the entire day before she testified, told jurors in her gritty way how guards had forced Honor to clean cells in the Hole when she could hardly stand. She recalled Honor's dying day, lying in agony, first her cries, then her gurgling. Yet no one helped. She told them that the last thing she remembered was a guard bending over in Honor's cell to pick up a tuft of her hair Honor had pulled from her scalp before she died.

Johni wore her shiniest red dress to court. She described, through thickly painted lips, Honor's declining condition over the weeks and relentless complaints for medical help, which went unheeded. Sweet Willie's Stack of Shellac had provided Gold with a few other inmates who had been incarcerated before and after Honor, and who swore they had been treated the same way as Honor, showing a pattern of mistreatment.

Alan spent hours with Tonya Gates before she testified, trying to stop her from talking about her own maladies and to concentrate only on what she knew about Honor. He held his breath as she testified. To his surprise, she answered his questions without turning it on herself and perhaps helped to explain how Honor had been ignored at pill-call by Nurse Kratz.

During his cross-examinations of each of Gold's witnesses, Stone again tried to change the narrative. He practically ignored their earlier responses to Gold's questions and spent most of his inmate cross-examinations impeaching them for who they were, not for what they said. He spent hours making sure jurors knew each of Gold's witnesses was a prostitute, a welfare defrauder, a check bouncer, or worse—dishonest and unworthy of belief. Inmates who had been convicted of more serious offenses faced an onslaught of questions about their crimes, emphasizing how those crimes involved lying, deceit, or lack of trustworthiness.

Gold also brought several guards who testified against their employer. Sgt. Mitchell bravely admitted that Haskel Gross told her to say Honor may have OD'd and admitted she lied to protect her job. She explained she had been intimidated before by Gross but was halted when Stone objected to her describing Gross unzipping his pants during her promotion interview.

Judge Rumsfeld agreed with Stone and instructed the jury to disregard it. Without his thinking it through, Stone later slipped up in his cross-examination and brought up that episode when he previously objected to it.

Using quick yes-or-no questions put to Mitchell to which she could only answer 'yes,' Stone switched tactics from what Mitchell said to why she said it. "You applied for a promotion? You were denied the promotion? You were not happy that you were denied the promotion? You felt you deserved the promotion. You felt you were sexually harassed? It is possible, is it not, that jurors could consider your testimony today as your attempt to get even with Mr. Gross for what you consider to be his harassing you? Nothing further."

Gold objected to Stone's asking questions on a matter that the judge had instructed the jury to disregard, and Rumsfeld overruled his objection without comment.

Plaintiffs' case continued for several more days as Gold introduced members of the Columbus Fire Department Emergency Squad, as well as the OSU ER doc who testified that Mitchell's false OD information had impaired his ability to save Honor.

Even though expert doctors, except the coroner, testified via video, their testimony on the question of causation was the most dramatic. After trying to prove defendants were "deliberately indifferent to Honor's serious medical needs," (without a single medical provider willing to use the term), Gold moved on to proving that defendant indifference caused her death, that critical point on which his case rested.

Gold played the deposition of Dr. Steiner from Cincinnati, who described how he saved a patient suffering from the same disease as Honor, already comatose from choriocarcinoma metastatic brain cancer, when she presented at the Cincinnati hospital. With government-approved drugs, she lived and later gave birth to a healthy child. Dr. Steiner explained that various cancers were neither alike nor were they all fatal. Choriocarcinoma could be cured; for years, some doctors had successfully treated this rare disease. He opined that failing to examine a patient complaining of pain in her uterus, particularly within six weeks after a stillbirth, was malpractice and that Honor's death had been preventable and curable.

In the video, Stone countered by again changing the narrative from Steiner's opinion on causation toward his lack of research experience, pointing out that as a treating doctor, he conducted no cancer research, had not graduated from an elite medical school in America, and had not written a single medical article on treating and curing any type of cancer in any peer-reviewed medical journal. To Stone's question, "You have never braved a moment of your time, as does Dr. Villanueva weekly, to protect citizens by treating patients at a correctional facility, have you?" Steiner admitted he had not.

During the trial, Gold objected when he caught Stone flirting with a juror and was overruled. He objected when he learned that Stone and Ben Walton had gone for coffee together and was overruled. Judge Rumsfeld sided with Stone on nearly every technical point throughout the trial, giving Stone a considerable advantage. Gold faced a constant challenge, knowing that arguing with a judge when the jury listened would be as foolish as a bicyclist fighting for right-of-way with a semi-driver. He suffered in silence.

When it was his turn to present his case, Stone introduced the State Inspection Report announced by the mayor; Gold objected. It had not been on Stone's exhibit list of trial documents, and from what he saw, the report did not concern any matters relevant to this case. For example, it did not cover medical procedures, only the number and educational background of personnel. WCI barely complied; it had a part-time doctor and two nurses on staff, the minimum requirement.

Outside the hearing of the jury (to prevent jurors from being swayed, should the judge keep the evidence out), Gold asked the judge to recess the jury and conduct a hearing on the admissibility of the state report. He knew the document could persuade some jurors that WCI "passed inspection." Judge Rumsfeld listened to the counsel's arguments for less than two minutes before denying a hearing and overruling Gold's objection. Stone introduced the report.

Stone, with great fanfare, showed the video deposition of the noted cancer research expert, Jonas Farber, M.S., M.D., Ph.D. Farber told the jury his credentials: his teaching awards at Duke University School of Medicine where he was currently a professor of cancer research, his M.S. degree from MIT in statistical analysis, his Harvard medical degree, his graduate research work in cancer cell replication at Stanford and his many, many peer-reviewed articles on cancer. From his years in the classroom, he conveyed the image of a learned man.

After patiently explaining cell reproduction in terms no one understood, Farber gave his opinion that based on multiplication rates of cancer cells, Honor could no longer be helped, at least from when she started complaining of headaches. He swore to a reasonable medical certainty he was aware of nothing that the defendants did or could have done that would affect Honor's life expectancy. He described in detail his many peer-reviewed articles verifying his cell growth calculations. In short, the Fates had cursed Honor. Her tragedy was reality, her death unstoppable. Sad, but inevitable.

Gold dared not touch Farber's educational background but noted it was only in research. Farber did not treat choriocarcinoma patients; he analyzed numbers. Gold judiciously questioned the use of cancer cell multiplication rates to predict cancer death, using a medical article he found that challenged its accuracy. It wasn't much, but the best he could do with his limited resources.

Stone called defendants to retell their stories in a way favorable to them and cleverly insinuated in his questions that they were helping to protect citizens, like jurors, and law and order. He called as witnesses guards who impugned inmates' credibility with incidents that showed inmates lied to get favors like extra food or phone calls. Then Stone rested.

It was Gold's turn again. Gold saved the best for last. This time, he was limited in the scope of his questions to rebutting defense testimony; he could raise no new topics. He called a few witnesses to dispute one fact or another before calling his star witness. Molene Jones took the stand.

He carefully set the stage for each episode by placing her near the defendants as they drank coffee or in the cell block when she found Honor. He made sure the jury understood she could see and hear clearly before she testified. She also swore she had not heard or read any trial testimony, so she was not aware of what anyone said in the courtroom.

Then Gold asked questions regarding each defendant's testimony. Jurors could see he was trying to quote the exact words each defendant used when they testified because he kept looking at his trial notes. When he finished asking Molene what she heard witnesses say about quotes from witness testimony, her responses contradicted the testimony of nearly every defense witness who worked or visited WCI and drank coffee. More than once, a juror raised an eyebrow when Molene told them what prison guards, medical staff, and prison officials said over coffee, often the exact opposite of their words on the witness stand.

Gold's apparent dilemma: He could introduce inmates' testimony contradicting defense testimony, but he could neither undo their convictions nor stop Stone's unceasing impugning of their credibility. While their testimony was powerful, he doubted the jury would believe his motley crew of criminals.

CHAPTER 62

BOTH SIDES RESTED. BEFORE closing arguments, Judge Rumsfeld conferred with counsel. He would instruct jurors on how to treat evidence after the attorneys made their closing statements and before jurors began deliberating. Days earlier, Gold and Stone had submitted draft instructions for Rumsfeld to consider.

In the judge's chambers, as they went through the instructions individually, each attorney argued for Rumsfeld to choose his. The judge listened and almost immediately accepted nearly all instructions suggested by Stone. He only accepted one of Gold's that declared Honor had a constitutional right to medical care while incarcerated, and then, only after Gold submitted a seven-page memorandum citing a recent U.S. Supreme Court case and one trial court decision only five weeks old that Frank had uncovered.

Rumsfeld expected to read to the jury his chosen instructions the following day after lunch, assuming Gold and Stone finished their closing statements before the lunch break. They had one night to incorporate into their closing statements those instructions selected and cut any references to those rejected.

The next morning, jurors, lawyers, courtroom staff, and a packed audience assembled for closing statements and again had to wait for Judge Rumsfeld. When he took the bench, he tried to look away from those in the courtroom, but everyone could see his bloodshot eyes. By the time he was to read instructions to the jury, Rumsfeld hoped that all the coffee he drank would wash away the cotton he tasted from the night before.

"Plaintiff may proceed."

Gold rose from his chair and walked slowly to the podium, his hand to his chin. He looked into the eyes of each juror, creating a deafening silence in the courtroom but instilling in them, he hoped, a feeling of courage toward their consequential decisions that might change the course of local history. He quietly thanked them for their time and attention and apologized again if he had offended anyone.

Using simple words, he began recounting specific, undeniable facts, starting with Honor's arrest. He reminded them Honor had been convicted of absolutely nothing, that the only reason the state kept her in WCI, instead of allowing her to be home with her baby, was because she was too poor to post bond. Responding to anticipated jurors who might regard his comments as those from an idealistic do-gooder who ignored criminals roaming the streets, he quoted President Johnson:

> *The defendant with means can afford to pay bail. He can afford to buy his freedom. But the poor defendant cannot pay the price. He languishes in jail weeks, months, and perhaps even years before trial. He does not stay in jail because he is guilty. He does not stay in jail because any sentence has been passed. He does not stay in jail because he is any more likely to flee before trial.*
>
> *He stays in jail for one reason only-he stays in jail because he is poor.*

Alan asked them rhetorically if they agreed Honor must be considered innocent before her trial. Did it make a difference to them if innocent people were treated the way Honor had been? Their faces told him nothing.

He described Honor's family in detail, first her brothers, then her sisters. All were there except for Baby Winston and Ella, who had a test at school. Mentioning Winston only briefly, he promised to talk more about him later. Locking eyes with mothers and fathers on the jury, he extolled Millie's strength to continue after losing her first child and overcoming her depression.

"Her daughter came back to her and her family. Then, in a flash, she was gone before she started her new life here."

His implied question for each juror to ponder was their verdict if Honor had been their daughter or sister.

Turning his attention toward the defendants seated behind the defense counsel table, Gold looked at them and back to the jurors. He stood straighter; his voice became more robust. "And what of the defendants?" he asked.

He began laying out his case against each defendant and the City of Columbus, starting with Kratz's Medical Procedures Manual, which Doctor V approved without reading. By contrasting it with model regulations written by commissions studying prison medicine, he demonstrated precisely how WCI's rules were woefully inadequate. He recalled for the jury the testimony of his nurse expert, who opined that medical staff obviously had designed the WCI's manual for their convenience, not for the needs of sick inmates.

Gold emphasized that those regulations were official policies of the city. They denied Honor her constitutional right to medical care while incarcerated, found in the eighth amendment prohibiting cruel and unusual punishment. Explaining the jury instruction that Judge Rumsfeld was about to give them on that issue, he discussed the reasoning of the Supreme Court when it used the phrase "deliberately indifferent to the serious medical needs" of those incarcerated.

Quoting directly from the high court decision, he explained that providing medical care to prisoners is but one of the "broad and idealistic concepts of dignity, civilized standards, humanity, and decency" embodied in the Eighth Amendment. He continued to use "deliberately indifferent" for the remainder of his closing statement, hoping that his repetition would give it acceptance, despite having no witness who could define it or use it in testimony.

He declared that the sheets showing Honor standing in pill-call 23 times and Steiner's video testimony about her medical condition since confinement proved Honor had presented a "serious medical need to medical staff." After contrasting Kratz's pathetic efforts to obtain from a phone call Honor's stillborn history instead of ordering hospital records, he declared Kratz's actions "deliberately indifferent." He added that Kratz's decision not to refer Honor to the doctor when she requested it might even constitute the illegal practice of medicine. Honor's medical condition and her status as one awaiting trial could not, under any condition, justify guards forcing her to clean out the Hole. Guards were "deliberately indifferent," by ignoring her bleeding and releasing her bladder and her bowels. Gold packaged each witness and every piece of evidence into boxes individually marked "deliberately indifferent."

He told the jury Dr. V and the nurses knew or should have known how important a six-week checkup was for a woman who had just had a stillbirth. He argued that Dr. Villanueva's contention that complications at six-week checkups occur rarely was unjustifiable and downright dangerous. It was precisely then that choriocarcinoma could have been detected and, when found, eliminated with a D&C.

A patient, Gold declared, had a right to expect a doctor NOT to play the averages when dealing with her health. He gave them examples of colonoscopies, cardiographs, and other tests doctors routinely administered to asymptomatic patients, despite a low probability of finding anything. Yet they are part of proper medical protocol, and the consequences of not performing them are too significant to let slide. "Isn't that indifference?" he asked.

Even if she had not received a needed D&C, Gold listed lifesaving drugs described by Steiner available to save Honor. He asked them to consider their life experiences when they went to their doctors, whether they expected them to examine and test them only when a disease was likely, rather than when it was possible, even rarely.

He portrayed Dr. V as an indifferent quack, looking to get a buck without earning it, who took no pride in his work and did not try to provide adequate medical care to his patients. Gold proved that point with the testimony of many of his "patients" at WCI, who testified that he never examined them. His inattention when approving the regulations, failure to supervise the nurses, and ignoring Honor's complaints were proof of deliberate indifference, creating a medical swamp filled with sloth, laziness, and unsupervised violations of medical and nursing ethics. And what was the predictable result from such shoddiness? The death of Honor.

Gold went up the ladder. Gross's attempt to hide under his contention that "Dr. V ran his shop, and I ran mine" showed deliberate indifference to the medical concerns of patients for which he was also responsible. Further, Gross made no inquiry whether medical staff treated inmates at all. And Gross's directing Mitchell to lie about Honor suffering an OD was inexcusable.

Although Judge Rumsfeld instructed the jury to disregard evidence of Gross's sexual harassment—despite allowing Stone to use it to find motive when cross-examining Mitchell—Gold decided that less would be more. His only comment about Haskel's womanizing was, "And you recall female guards' testimony about fearing to be alone with Mr. Gross, don't you?" He just left it at that.

He dismissed Gross as a rank amateur who was not qualified and did not merit his appointment by Director Puchik to such an important position, even in an "acting" role. The people of Columbus deserved more than an unqualified hack.

He used this theme as he moved up the ladder. Puchik's initial appointment of Gross and then not replacing him quickly with someone competent was evidence of indifference by both Puchik and the mayor. They didn't care about the rights of inmates. They were ignorant of what occurred at WCI because they didn't want to know. This, Gold declared, was nearly the definition of "deliberate indifference."

He tied Puchik to abuse of the Hole. He told the jury, "By providing only one set of cells for treatment and punishment, Puchik and the mayor set in motion an official policy permitting staff to punish inmates like Honor just for being sick. You don't have to consider whether medical reports from WCI staff to Gross or Puchik were adequate, because there were none." Gold reminded jurors that Puchik had never met Dr. V before Honor's death, nor had the safety director even entered the doors of WCI more than once or twice since his appointment four years earlier.

Prisoner care didn't matter to the mayor either, Gold declared. Blandford was only interested in reelection. The jury could find both his and the city's indifference in their failure in six years to increase funding for WCI, even after the inmate population had more than doubled.

Gold did not run from witness credibility. He lauded inmates and guards who bravely testified about prison conditions, medical care, and the events leading to the death of Honor. He suggested that jurors might use the idea of gain or loss as one criterion for judging credibility. Highlighting Sgt. Mitchell's words, which he guessed jurors found most credible, he asked them, "We know she could lose a promotion for testifying, but what does she have to gain?" As to inmates, he declared jurors should treat inmate testimony as even more credible than that of any of the defendants. Gold reminded jurors that in testifying, each defendant had something to gain—job retention—while each inmate had nothing to gain and could suffer consequences later.

Molene was even more credible, he asserted, than any defendant who testified. She could not have made up her stinging, rebuttal testimony that directly contradicted almost every defense witness because she didn't know what any of them had said in court. He recalled Molene's testimony on why she risked her safety to testify. She simply wanted justice applied to those who broke the law, as it had been applied to her when she committed a crime. Defendants might have considered her a mere coffee server, but "servers have ears," Gold reminded jurors. He described her testimony as "devastating." He then posed a pivotal question to them, "If you believe Molene, then why would you doubt other inmates?" he asked.

He contrasted Dr. Steiner's hands-on experience to Farber's devising fancy theories and writing dull, little articles. "He spends his days counting cells instead of saving lives. So much for defendants' expert," he scoffed.

Finally, Gold dove into the question of damages. "Honor had her whole life ahead of her. She tried to find work to support her baby and help her family, and her untimely death took away that option." He urged them to heed his expert's calculations of her lost wages after graduating from a two-year community college. He declared Honor would have gone to college just as she dedicated herself to getting her GED.

As to Honor's pain and suffering, Gold asked jurors, "How can you find a formula to calculate in dollars what she went through?" He then suggested that they compensate her estate on a daily basis. She had suffered miserably in WCI for 29 days. He inched closer to the jury box as he asked them, "Would you suffer her horrendous pain, cruel humiliation, or anguish for $100 per day, $1,000? $100,000? When you get to the number where you would swap places with Honor Wilson in that hell-hole they call WCI for one day, then just multiply that number by 29. You may find that number a fair award for her pain and suffering."

Gold ended his summation by discussing Honor's family and their wrongful death claims. He recalled the words of family members describing how Honor's death had hurt them. Her siblings described her as their big sister, their second mom. How proud they were when she studied for and received her GED. How happy they were when she gave birth to Winston. After her divorce, they were delighted when she moved in with them. They truly loved her.

He left Millie and Baby Winston for last to emphasize her loss and combine it with the costs of caring for him for at least the next sixteen years. Little Winston was now part of Millie's family, he declared. Gold ended his closing remarks by having Millie bring Winston into the courtroom in her arms, his little fingers wrapped around a bottle.

Gold returned to his seat exhausted and satisfied but anxious to hear the response of George Russell Stone.

CHAPTER 63

AFTER A BREAK, STONE, TALL and stately, strode to the podium and looked back and forth at jurors like a lighthouse seeking ships at sea. Wordlessly, he drew them in, fixing their attention on his countenance. When he finally uttered in a firm, solid voice, "Ladies and gentlemen of the jury," nearly everyone in the courtroom leaned forward in rapt attention to what he was about to say.

"You should feel insulted. You have just witnessed an assault on the very foundations of law and order, on your mayor, your director of public safety, and the law enforcement officers who protect you. Plaintiff's counsel has, in essence, asked you to join him in attacking part of your safety net, thereby attacking your wall of well-being. On behalf of the mayor, the City of Columbus, and its officials, I say, 'Stand up to Mr. Gold. Protect your fellow citizens from plaintiffs' siege upon the public treasury.'

"This is not about Mr. Gold or me, but the people of Columbus. They are watching you. They want to know whether you are taking this assault personally, treating it as if your homes were being invaded. For you and the hundreds of thousands of people with whom you are fortunate to share this great city, I ask you to find for the city of Columbus and against Mr. Gold. Permit me to tell you why."

Stone then called into question every aspect of Gold's case. He praised the professionalism of the city's medical staff, who, he claimed, properly followed approved policies. He noted Gold had not proven that anyone, except his "Monday-morning-quarterback nurse" expert, ever criticized WCI medical policies before Honor, which had been in effect for years. Again and again, he urged them to review the annual inspection report of the State of Ohio that showed WCI had passed inspection with flying colors. Gold did not refute the report. He could not. The state of Ohio found that the city of Columbus was in compliance with the state's vigorous requirements.

"Instead of accepting the fact that even after its intense governmental inspection, the state found that the city had complied," Stone insisted, "Gold went out and found and paid people to say something else. They do not work to protect you and your loved ones, as do defendants. What were they trying to get you to believe? That what defendants have been doing successfully for years and had been approved by the state violated Ms. Wilson's constitutional rights. Can you believe it? Gold refused to grasp what we all know," he declared. "This is WCI, not the Mayo Clinic. A prison, not a hospital." Stone proclaimed. "The decedent suffered from a fatal condition, but Mr. Gold refuses to accept this sad truth. He did not and could prove that her death should have been foreseen or prevented by the WCI staff."

Stone ignored Sergeant Mitchell's and other guards' testimony. Instead, he focused on inmates. He cautioned jurors to disregard whatever inmates said because it was said by criminals. He hammered jurors with Judge Rumsfeld's instruction that when weighing witness credibility, jurors may consider convictions of felonies involving fraud or misdemeanors of "moral turpitude."

His golden voice rose as he declared that Gold's case was based on the testimony of criminals. "They're drug dealers, prostitutes, thieves, cheats, liars, murderers, crooks, perps, witches, vixens, Jezebels, and more—not even one of the lot is worthy of belief. Let me ask you," he said while leaning forward like he was about to tell a secret, "Would you trust any one of them in your home? With your children? Would you give her the keys to your car? If your response is no, then please don't give her the keys to the treasury."

He asked jurors to compare "those kind of people" to the good nurses and doctor—top-notch healthcare providers—who instead of seeking wealth and fortune, devoted themselves to caring for low-life criminals like Gold's witnesses. "Dr. Villanueva is a model of the American dream, coming to this country with little and working hard to become a Father Teresa in Columbus. It's an insult," he declared, "to impugn his fine reputation."

But most of all, Stone attacked causation, proudly recalling for jurors the learned opinion of the world-famous Dr. Jonas Farber. Stone urged jurors in the strongest words he could muster to consider Dr. Farber's monumental work in cancer cell reproduction as their guiding light. Stone implored jurors to believe him when he opined, "without reservation or hesitation" (not exactly Farber's words), the sad but undeniable truth: Honor could not be cured. Farber's written opinions had been peer-reviewed, he reminded them, meaning that other learned doctors and other noted experts who, before publishing, read his works and found that they met the standards of the medical society or school that published them. In other words, Stone suggested, other professionals agree with his views. "Medical experts trust his opinion," said Stone. "Shouldn't you trust it as well?"

Stone's disdain for Gold's expert doctor was obvious. "Dr. Steiner's half-baked ideas lack peer review and could not be said to represent our medical community's opinion. Steiner may have gotten lucky once and now professes he can save all patients suffering from cancer. Any real scientist would tell you his case is a statistical oddity, and his one exception only proves the rule.

He dismissed Steiner as merely some unpublished, foreign doctor from down the road in Cincinnati who got paid to suggest a hare-brained notion that cancer (whisper and wince) is curable. He certainly was not in the class of experts comparable to Professor Dr. Jonas Farber, who has dedicated his entire professional career to cancer research. "You must not believe Steiner's fish story," he told them. "Who has verified the opinions of Dr. Steiner? Absolutely no one," he asked and answered.

Again and again, he worked on narrative. Who will you believe? He kept turning each question into a choice between a law enforcer or lawbreaker, a doctor who may have gotten lucky or a cancer expert. He put each choice as between "them" or "us."

In a performance worthy of an Oscar, George Stone nearly wept as he leaned forward toward the jury box one final time in a grand eulogy. "The inmate had cancer (whisper and wince), bless her heart, and the Good Lord sent her to a better place."

Gold's response was striking. In claiming the plaintiffs were trying to destroy the city, Gold noted, Stone was referring partly to little baby Winston sleeping in Millie's arms. "How could Stone be so cold?" he asked.

He again praised inmates for their courage, like Puddin and Johni, who were no longer in prison, risking everything to tell the truth, regardless of what law enforcement might do to them later. Knowing that Stone could not speak again, Gold reminded jurors that Mr. Stone had ignored the testimony of officers like Sergeant Mitchell. Gold demanded, "Let Mr. Stone utter a sound now suggesting that the words of Sergeant Mitchell and other guards were not credible."

He rebranded Stone's description of Dr. Steiner's "fish tales" as real life, not ivory-tower theories. Unlike Farber, who tied himself up in theories like a first-time fisherman tied up his lines and unable to continue, Steiner actually caught the fish. He asked them whether Honor didn't deserve the chance to receive a D&C, plus the drugs and other therapies Dr. Steiner suggested that Dr. V. could have saved her had he simply performed a six-week check-up if he knew how, or, if he didn't know not, he could have sent her to a doctor who did.

Finally, Gold paused before going off-script, disturbed by Stone's narrative that the case was an assault on the government by certain disreputable elements, said, "Don't let opposing counsel do this to you or our city. This case is not about 'Us versus Them.' If we were to demean inmate witnesses, belittle their testimony, and ignore their calls for reform not because of what they said but who we think they are, we'd demean ourselves and our justice system. Honor deserves better than that. The people of Columbus deserve better than that. Instead, give them your best." The courtroom fell silent when Gold finished.

After a short break, Judge Rumsfeld read his instructions to the jury, and by late afternoon, the case was in their hands.

The judge told them to convene immediately and select a foreperson before starting deliberations at 9:00 a.m. the following day. He admonished them not to discuss the case with anyone, read or listen to any news accounts or anything else related to the case, and not to come to any conclusions until after they had discussed the case with the other jurors. All rose. After Walton led jurors from the courtroom, litigants, lawyers, and laypeople poured out.

In the public square around the courthouse, news photographers captured the likes of Pastor Jenkins and Sweet Willie Moss, who were drumming up crowds of protesters carrying signs reading "Justice for Honor," "Bail Reform Now," and "Close WCI." To avoid doing or saying anything that could cause a mistrial, Millie and her family, accompanied by Gold, found their way to their cars through a side door of the courthouse.

A. S. White

CHAPTER 64

MILLIE PREPARED A QUICK dinner for the family: hot dogs, baked beans, and hot cornbread. The trial hovered over the dinner table like a low cloud.

"I wish I could have been there today. What happened?" asked Ella.

Duke replied, "Lots of talk. They tried to show Honor was a druggie. Gold did good, but the other honky lawyer in the fancy threads and the judge picked at him. I couldn't tell what the jury was thinkin' when the lawyers was talkin'. That white judge ain't no friend of ours, you best believe. He looked sick. His eyes were red, and he kept drinking water. Every time that slick lawyer asked him for something, the judge said yes, but every time Mr. Gold asked, he said no. I didn't get what he told the jury to do, but it didn't sound good for us.

"I ain't as sure as I was before the trial we'll win. It didn't go down like on TV. Not as simple. They brought in some big-shot doctor who said Honor was going to die anyway, and that slick lawyer kept telling the jury to believe him, but Mr. Gold told them to believe his doctor, the one who saved other folks. Somehow, we're gonna get cheated."

"Mr. Gold did good," said Billie. "I think folks in the jury box liked us. Mama, what do you think?"

"We'll see, kids. The Lord will provide," Millie added. "At least we showed them Honor was not lying about her illness. I believe they killed her. And I hope the jury will provide for Winston. Now, you guys got homework to do. Come on, let's clean up and get started. "

A. S. WHITE

After they did the dishes, Millie changed little Winston's diaper and put him to bed. The trial had lasted nearly two weeks. She attended only part of the trial when she could get off work, but it was enough to see what Stone was trying to do. He wanted to give jurors as many ways as possible to find against her and her family. She asked herself, *Would lawyers make the difference, or would race decide it? Yes, race always decides it.*

CHAPTER 65

EITHER CITY ATTORNEY AUBER or his assistant attended the trial daily, and Ed updated the mayor regularly, lawyer to lawyer. Ed was not optimistic but remained hopeful that Stone and his staff would carry the day. Because Blandford knew that lawyers speak cautiously to clients, he discounted Ed's negativity, refusing to fall prey either to hope or despair. As a former judge, Blandford felt anticipation wasted emotional resources when results would soon be disclosed. Blandford concentrated on staying calm and evaluating alternative outcomes. From his days on the bench, he knew victory and defeat sit side by side in a courtroom.

After Auber reported to the mayor that the jury was out, Blandford had Terry share the news with the City Council. Lex Baer made a private call.

"Hi, Stuart. Lex Baer. Wanted to share with you an update on the nominating committee. We are still reviewing next year's appointments to the Court of Appeals; I want you to know that you're still in contention. I swear, some members are sitting on it like they're at a prayer meeting, looking for a sign to direct their choice. Well, maybe they will soon see the sign they are looking for. By the way, how's the trial going?"

Now sober and judge-like, Rumsfeld said, "The case is in the hands of the jury, Lex. George Stone did a nice job for the city. Gold, the inexperienced lawyer for the family, was surprisingly well-prepared. Believe me, Lex, I did everything possible within ethical boundaries to advance my law-and-order position."

"Well, that's fine, Judge. As the old saying goes, the proof of the pudding is in the eating. And I'm looking forward to a very tasty dish." The call ended amicably, neither hearing what he wanted. Receiving no reason for optimism, Lex warned his fellow council members of a pending disaster, suggesting they should keep their political distance from the mayor until they knew the verdict. "Be prepared to turn on a dime," he advised.

Sweet Willie had no hesitation and saw no downside to continuing his attacks. If the jury found for the defendants, he would rile the black community to unite against oppression. If the jury found in favor of Honor's family, he would continue his efforts to show Blandford as incompetent to run the city. His main goal, as it had always been, was to activate concerns for justice in law enforcement.

Pastor Jenkins likewise continued to urge pastors to pray with their flocks using bible quotes. He declared that Blandford and the city had offended God, citing the Good Book, Hebrews 13:3 "Remember them that are in bonds, as bound with them; and them which suffer adversity, as being yourselves also in the body."

The 6 o'clock news reported that jury deliberations would begin in the morning. The media recalled events leading to Honor's death, reactions on the street (including those described as "rioters"), and opinions of those at the courthouse today. While interviews with officials about the trial were extensive, no one in the media focused on prison conditions.

CHAPTER 66

THE EIGHT JURORS MADE themselves comfortable in their room, enveloped in the faint tobacco odor of past juries. They sat around an old wooden conference table large enough to seat twelve and covered with coffee rings. One long wall was interrupted only by a single bathroom door. No pictures hung on the hueless walls rising from industrial-grade taupe carpeting. Cold fluorescent lighting made their windowless surroundings only more austere.

No one was concerned about their stark environment because none expected to be there long. Obviously, fellow jurors had come to the same "obvious" conclusions, and soon they would render a unanimous decision. Oh, they may quibble about a few details along the way, but each thought it would take no time to render a verdict. By lunchtime tomorrow, they would be home, having completed their civic duty.

They took seats randomly as Bailiff Walton, who had led them into the room, placed a folder in the center of the table.

"Here are the judge's written instructions and verdict sheets for each of you to sign when you've reached a decision. In a minute, I will bring you all the admitted exhibits. Then, I'll leave you alone. After that, please flip this switch if you need anything. It will light up outside, and I'll come in. Good luck."

After a few used the bathroom, they settled in their seats. Chatter dimmed as they faced their awesome task. Soon, they sat silently. No one wanted to start; no one wanted to be the foreperson. Each waited for someone else to take charge. Jasper Peabody finally stated, "Well, I suppose we should pick somebody to be foreperson, so we can take a vote and get out of here."

Everyone nodded, but the tone of his comments did not suggest he should be elected foreperson.

"I agree," said Tammy Talbert. "We need the right foreperson. As our beloved president John F. Kennedy once said, *The times are too grave, the challenge too urgent, and the stakes too high to permit the customary passions of political debate. We are not here to curse the darkness but to light the candle.*" She sat back, proud that she remembered her recitation. Everyone nodded but wondered why she said it.

To Matilda Jameson, a member of the Upper Arlington Republican Club, who was wearing a pink and green flowered blouse from Talbots, Tammy's very mention of JFK sent her into a tailspin and almost bent the gold circle pin on her collar. Scratch Tammy.

Barney Wills sat his plump, soft body on a chair in the center of the table. He unknowingly had made the fateful move of leaning forward to glance at some of the exhibits that Ben brought in.

Everyone paused for a moment to consider his friendly countenance. Judson Kingman said what others were thinking, "This guy in the middle seems like he'd make as good a foreperson as anyone else." Barney shook his head with a smile, adjusting his wire-rimmed glasses, but before he could say anything, Elmira Snodgrass said, "I agree" and seconded the motion. "Let's vote." Her little Chihuahua, hidden in her purse, barked in agreement. All said aye, and that was how Barney was elected foreperson precisely because he displayed no strong opinions and therefore seemed the least objectionable.

Jasper Peabody renewed his motion to take a vote on the verdict. Barney paused, recognizing this to be his first test as foreperson. With a friendly smile that shone through his glasses, he mused, "I suppose all of us would like to be done with this, but didn't the judge say we should select a foreperson and begin deliberations tomorrow? Is that what you guys heard?" he asked. Others nodded.

"Now, to me, deliberation means talking things out, listening to each other, and keeping an open mind instead of accepting first impressions. Is that what you think it means?" Again, nods of approval.

"OK, so if we all agree, let's go home, think about what we saw and heard during the trial, and start deliberations in the morning. We'll get to know each other a little and talk this out. We need to be comfortable with whatever we decide."

While another day was unnecessary to him, Peabody could see in the faces of others their desire to return, particularly after Willie Bolden said, "I'm retired. I'm in no hurry." Jasper backed off. Barney switched on the light to inform Ben he had been chosen foreperson and they were going home.

CHAPTER 67

THE FOLLOWING MORNING, they arrived on time, except for Zoe, who came a few minutes late wearing bell-bottom jeans and toting a canvas handbag with a Walkman and tapes. She again sat at the table's end looking away. Barney remained seated in the middle rather than at its head. His well-worn sweater added to his cushy exterior.

"Let's go around the room and say something about ourselves. I'm Barney Willis. I retired as a librarian at Ohio State, working mainly in the fiction department, and I do a little writing sometimes for *The Columbus Free Press*."

"I'm Elmira Snodgrass," the Latina in a brightly colored dress and carefully coiffed hair said. "My husband Sam and I came from Toledo and began a beauty salon business here. Now I stay home and keep our house, and we like to cook and garden. We have no children, but I have Consuela," she said, petting the little tan dog in her soft, white leather purse.

"I'm Bill Bolden. Moved here from Mobile, Alabama, over 25 years ago to play football for Coach Hayes but later got cut after a head injury," said the dark-skinned man with the barrel chest, still muscled but with a paunch. "I retired from Dephi over on the West Side after I tore out my back. I like to watch my soaps, and I'm missing them today."

"Me, too," stated a woman wearing a small pink and green flower-print dress. "Which ones do you watch?"

"Me? I like *General Hospital*, *Days of Our Lives*, and *The Young and the Restless*."

"That's funny. So do I. Hi, I'm Matilda Jameson, but please call me Tilley," she said, happy that she'd found another soaper.

Suddenly, everyone relaxed and began making small talk with their neighbors until Barney corralled them back to introductions. The next juror, wearing a short-sleeved white shirt and red tie, leaned forward in his seat.

"I'm Jasper Peabody, but folks call me Jazz, which is kind of funny because I don't like jazz. I work in student relations at Otterbein University in Westerville, near our house. Excuse me, can we finish this as quickly as possible? I need to return to work."

The room was quiet. Tilley broke the silence. "I'm Tilley Jamison. I've lived in Upper Arlington all my life. "I'm divorced, and my dog is a pedigreed Pembroke Welsh Corgi."

"I'm Judd Kingman, a graduate of South High School here in town. I teach biology at the Columbus Academy for Boys. My primary research area is biological taxonomy," he said, adjusting his thick bifocals. He pivoted on his left elbow to allow the next juror to speak and unbuttoned his dull, corduroy jacket.

Zoe was listening to her Walkman, apparently paying no attention. Fourteen eyes were staring at her. "Huh?" She removed her earplugs. "Oh, I'm Zoe, Zoe Whitman. I used to go to Columbus Technical Institute. I like listening to Barry White. My favorite of his is 'It's Ecstasy When You Lay Down Next to Me.'"

"Hi, everybody. My name is Tammy Talbert," said the next young woman, waving as if she were saying goodbye. She looked perky in her red Ohio State t-shirt and frayed jeans. "I graduated from Bishop Hartley High School. I am a junior at Ohio State, majoring in political science and black studies. When I graduate, I plan to join the Peace Corps. "

"Thanks. Now, who wants to share their thoughts about the case?" asked Barney. "And let me suggest, if nobody objects, we allow each person to speak without interruption, and we listen politely even when we disagree. So, who wants to go first?"

After a brief pause, Tilley said, "I think it was unfortunate what happened to her. I mean, she was so young. She may have lost her way a bit, but it was very sad she died the way she did. I've heard drugs are a big problem in that community. It's just a shame."

"Drugs are all over campus, too," said Tammy. " By the way, musicians of all colors have used drugs at least as far back as the turn of this century. Drugs and the arts generally have gone hand in hand since way before modern jazz. For example, composers like Berlioz took opium, as did poets like Edgar Allen Poe, while Mussorgsky and Beethoven were alcoholics. I learned that in my course on "Art, Drugs, and the Creative Process."

"Why are we talking so much about drugs?" asked Elmira.

"I agree," Bill Bolden said. "This ain't about drugs, but mistreatment."

"Well," exclaimed Tilley, "I thought I heard them say that girl Honor (isn't that an odd name?) was on drugs, and I was just saying how drugs are so bad for them. It's ruining their community."

"What community are you talking about?" asked Bill. "Are you talking about a black community? Didn't you say you live in Upper Arlington? That's nearly all white. I don't know your community. How do you know mine?"

Judd Kingman interrupted, "I have the coroner's toxicology report here, Exhibit D. It shows Honor had no drugs in her system, except for trace amounts of marijuana."

"Look," said Jazz, "let's not pussyfoot around about how much she took this day or that. We all know what she was about and why she was in jail. We'll be here for a week if we waste our time looking at details. I say, if you commit a crime, you do the time, and that's all there is to this case."

"She wasn't convicted, was she?" asked Barney. "Wasn't she awaiting trial? Do you think we must decide if she committed a crime before deciding liability? Should we assume she was innocent until proven guilty? Does it matter? I am not trying to sway anyone. I'm only asking, so we can be sure of what we are doing."

"What I'm doing is getting a headache," said Elmira, petting Consuela.

"I think I need to use the bathroom," said Judd, rising.

Jazz mumbled something to himself as he looked toward Zoe, awash in the whispers of Barry White on her Walkman.

When they reassembled, Barney suggested another topic. "What about the doctors and nurses? What are your thoughts about them?"

"Well, I never heard of a doctor's office that didn't keep clear medical records," Elmira said. "I mean, how can you monitor a patient if you don't keep track?"

"But this isn't a doctor's office, it's a prison. Didn't you hear that prison nurse say it's a jail and the rules on the outside don't apply?" responded an exasperated Jazz.

Judd said, "Yes, but the judge instructed us that prisoners have a constitutional right to medical care. Wouldn't that mean medical care like on the outside? Are there two types of care, one for those on the inside and another for the rest of us? Is that what you are saying?"

"Seems right to me to have only one standard. Medical care is medical care," said Bolden in his deep gravelly voice.

Jazz was becoming more frustrated. "Are you saying you think a prisoner should get the same kind of care as a citizen?" he asked. "For example, should the city pay for her surgery while she's locked up?"

"Why not, if she needs it?" answered Elmira. "Who said prison means taking away her health care, particularly when she was only awaiting trial? It's not like she was convicted or anything. I don't understand what you think prison is for, Mr. Peabody."

Jurors declined Barney's suggestion that they read the judge's instructions. "I heard what he told us; I don't need to reread them," said Jazz, looking away from the others, exasperated.

"What about that Nurse Kratz?" asked Judd. "No sympathy in her. That poor young girl told her about her stillborn and described her symptoms, but Kratz didn't seem to care."

Tilley asked, "But if their medical care is the same as ours, wouldn't some people go to jail just to get medical care? If they need care and can't afford it, why wouldn't they steal something to get into WCI and take advantage of the system?"

"What kind of a system is it that denies anyone medical care in the first place?" grumbled Bolden.

Barney struggled to get the conversation back on track. Then again, maybe it was on track. Perhaps they had to sort through these things to get to the heart of their deliberations. He had never been on a jury before, and trying to decide the real issues, in this case, was not as easy as he or others had realized. He tried again.

"What about her condition? Would treatment have saved her? You heard the experts. One said that Honor would have died by the time she stood in line, while the other said he'd saved a patient or two worse than her."

Tammy added. "Some said the doctors and nurses were up to standards, while others disagreed. What's the truth?"

"I don't care too much for so-called experts," said Judd. "Each side pays them to say what they want said. Why did the judge let them talk anyway? Expert testimony is like paid testimonials."

"I couldn't understand that doctor expert from Duke who counts cancer cells," said Elmira. "I mean, how can you compare whatever he was calculating to the Cincinnati doctor who saved a patient in a coma? If he saved her and others, maybe he or another doctor could have saved Honor."

"But I wonder if the patients he saved used drugs," said Tilley.

"Ms. Jameson," corrected Judd, "the toxicology report showed no drugs in her except marijuana. I don't think it would be fair for us to assume she used drugs because we have no proof of that.

"The guard who told the emergency squad she used drugs said she only told them that because Superintendent Haskel, whatever his last name, made her do it. And he said he told her only because he thought somebody else said it. It's all rumor.

"Personally, I thought Haskel was trying to save both his ass and the city's by trying to blame it on drugs. But, whatever, I don't see any proof she took drugs other than marijuana."

"After those awful things Haskel did, messing with guards; I wouldn't believe a word that nasty man said," said Elmira. "I've known only too well men who take advantage of women working for them. They are garbage. *Podrido*, as we say in my country."

"Oh, yeah," asked Bolden, "Where you from?"

"Mexico," she answered.

"What brought you to Toledo?"

"We were agricultural collectors, we used to joke. We traveled the country. In late fall, the last crop we picked was tomatoes, and the last farms we worked were south of Toledo. One year, after my father got hurt lifting a heavy basket of tomatoes, we quit picking and stayed near Toledo. I went to a regular school after that. It was bilingual. In a few years, I was speaking English like I was born here."

"Your family was migrant workers?" asked Tilley. "How interesting! I've never met a migrant worker before, but I did see the movie *Grapes of Wrath*. Was it like that?"

"Migrant workers are not a type of people," Tammy interjected. "And *Grapes of Wrath* was about people from Oklahoma, not Oaxaca. I took a course on 'Movies and America in Transition.'"

"We just did what we had to do, like everyone else," said Elmira, ignoring Tammy.

"Anyway, we must stop thinking of Honor as a druggie," Judd repeated. "It's confusing us."

"Well, I guess when I kept hearing it, I started to believe it," said Tilley.

"Can we agree," asked Barney, hoping to make some progress, "there is no proof she took drugs, except marijuana?" All eyes turned to Jazz.

"Well, I think she was a druggie, and the toxicology report only tested her one day. But I agree that as jurors, we have no proof she used drugs other than marijuana," said Jazz.

Barney smiled while others sighed in relief that they had overcome at least one hurdle.

"What can we say about the doctors and nurses? Are they responsible?" asked Barney.

"That's a tough one," noted Judd. "I mean, they need to sort out who is trying to get special treatment from those with real medical needs."

"Criminals are not trustworthy," said Jazz. "How can you stop prisoners from lying to medical staff for drugs, favors, or other stuff? They might say anything to keep up their habit. How is a nurse or doctor to know what to believe? Those people can be devious, and that's a fact."

Bolden sat up in his chair. "They still have a responsibility to treat everyone right. After all, the poor girl complained of bad headaches, and she nearly fainted and was found bleeding. You think people in jail are different from us? You don't believe patients on the outside lie to doctors to get what they want? To pass an insurance test? To dodge the draft? To qualify for a job?

"Jazz, do you think your doctor should ask you first why you came to him before he treats you? And if he thinks you are trying to put one over on him, should he send you away? Why do some folks apply different rules to 'those people'? Isn't it because we don't think 'those people' are as good as us? I say again, medical treatment is medical treatment, and it doesn't matter whether it's for these people, those people, or whose people."

"Didn't that nurse expert say the proper way to find if a hospital treated Honor is to ask for the hospital's records?" asked Elmira. "That Nurse Kratz said she just called a friend in the OB-GYN department. To me, that sounded sloppy. And I thought she was *brusca*,...ugh... how you say? Snippy?"

"She sure didn't care much about Honor, even after she was told of the stillbirth," Tilly added.

"But they did call the EMTs," Jazz said.

"Yeah, when she was almost dead. Too little, too late," said Judd.

"You got that right," Bolden added.

"So, what are we saying here?" Barney asked. "Was the city negligent?"

"If I recall what the judge said," noted Judd, "negligence isn't the test, but let me review the judge's instructions. Just to be sure. Here they are. Yes, we must find that the city was 'deliberately indifferent.'"

"What does that mean?" asked Tilley.

"You're right. I stand corrected," said Barney after scanning the instructions. "It sounds like a higher standard, doesn't it?"

"Whatever the standard, I think the city should have done more," Elmira added.

"Let's not forget," said Jazz, "if we award money against the city, the money it will have to pay will no longer be available for future medical services. So, what would an award accomplish?"

Judd nodded but with his eyebrows furrowed under his bifocals. "I see where you are coming from, but I've got problems with your analysis, Jazz. First, I believe we all promised when they selected us that we would not let a defendant's ability to pay cloud our thinking on the amount of judgment. Second, if jurors like us accept what you said—and I don't fault you for your concern—then how could anyone ever win a lawsuit involving a large amount of money?

"Juries would worry that the price of a new car would go up if they found against a carmaker or fear that doctors would stop practicing medicine or raise fees if they found against a doctor. That would be not fair to plaintiffs. And third, the city probably has insurance, so it might not make much financial difference anyway. And finally, didn't you say you lived in Westerville, Jazz? You don't pay Columbus taxes anyway. So, I don't think you can go there."

"I still say, medical treatment is medical treatment, and it doesn't matter if it is at a doctor's office, hospital, or jail," repeated Bolden.

The conversation continued to ebb and flow, sometimes about the case, other times about personal matters, like gardens, recipes, job stories, and soap opera plots. As a group, they continued to drift.

"I'm not sure," sighed Tilley, "I mean, this is so hard. I didn't think jury duty would be this difficult. So complicated, it's giving me a headache. I just don't feel right about judging them. What do I know about what they do? I'm just a widow. None of us are medical professionals."

"I know what you mean," said Elmira. "When I was studying for my citizenship, they told us jury duty was one of the most important jobs of a citizen. Juries protect our country from dictators and stuff like that. It sounded so noble. But here I am on a jury, trying to recall what went on for the last two weeks and what this one said and did, this opinion and that one, this document and that one. Noble duty is hard work."

"Nobody told you noble work was easy, did they?" asked Barney, smiling.

Bolden asked, with a twinkle in his eye, "If, like the judge said, he decides the law, and we decide the facts, then we got us a fifty-fifty deal, right? So how come he gets paid more than us?"

"Well, I've made my position clear, and I don't think it's that difficult to decide," Jazz said. "How about it, folks? How long are we going to debate this?"

"Are we ready to vote?" Barney asked.

No response.

"Okay, everyone who thinks we should vote, raise their hand."

Two hands went up.

"Then I guess we continue deliberating," said Barney.

Elmira looked at her watch. "It's noon. Let's call the bailiff. I'm getting hungry."

After they ate, the discussion continued. Barney asked the judge for a copy of the testimony of Nurse Kratz. They also reviewed the OSU-ER report, Exhibit S. Still no conclusions. They quit for the day.

CHAPTER 68

IT WAS COOL IN THE JURY room the next morning as jurors took the seats they'd occupied the day before. Jazz again called for a vote to end it all and return to work. Barney asked those in favor of voting on the verdict now to raise their hands. The vote was three to four, with one abstention.

Zoe was already listening to Barry White with her eyes closed. The judge had not instructed Barney what to do with a non-participating juror. Barney could not say she refused to deliberate; she responded adequately the last time he asked her a question. He let it ride, hoping she would be ready when they voted on a verdict.

"As I understand it, and correct me if I'm wrong, we first must decide whether each defendant is liable, like the acting superintendent, the safety director, and the mayor; and if so, then we need to assess damages and come up with a money figure. Is that your understanding too? I've thought about it overnight. Unless we find liability, we don't need to decide damages. Does that make sense to you?" After some hesitation, five heads nodded.

"Good, now, can we also agree if none of the people are liable, then the city would not be liable either because their actions are the actions of the City?" More nods. "OK, then, do you agree we decide the liability of the City last?"

Nods again.

"Great. Then if you also agree, let me suggest we decide first whether the nurses are responsible, then go to the doctor, then the acting superintendent, the safety director, the mayor, and then the City. If we find anybody liable, we can then turn our attention to damages. Are we still in agreement?" he asked, looking around the table.

"Yes," said Peabody. "Let's just get on with it."

Barney turned to him with a disarming smile. "Let's start with you, Jazz. What are your thoughts on the liability of the nurses? Would you hold them responsible?"

"No" Jazz snapped back. "I would not find them or anyone else liable."

"Okay," asked Barney, calmly. "Can you tell us your reasons?"

"I heard those inmates talk, but did you listen to why they were locked up? I don't think that kind of people can be trusted to tell the truth. They're whores, cheats, and I don't know what all. Did you catch that one inmate who was in for trying to murder her boyfriend? Working at WCI must be like living in a jungle," he said, his clip-on bow tie nearly popping off his collar. "It's a wonder the staff can provide any medical care to that kind of people. They're liars and schemers. Who could those nurses believe? I think they did all they could under the circumstances. So, if we all agree, then why are we wasting time? I would like to vote and get out of here."

"But, Jazz," asked Elmira, "please tell me how women at WCI could ever get a fair shake if jurors like us think they're all liars. Growing up, I heard the same kind of talk about us pickers. 'Those wetbacks are liars,' I used to hear all the time. I heard you, Jazz. Now please listen to me," she insisted before he could interrupt.

"Each woman in there has a story. Did you hear one inmate say she turned to prostitution after becoming addicted because a drug seller fed her stuff? And the one charged with welfare fraud said she used the money to feed her kids. And the one you said was charged with murdering her boyfriend—did you hear what she said he did to her first? Kicked her in the belly when she was pregnant? What would you have done? Huh? What would you do if you had no money, Jazz, and you had to feed your children? Are you sure you wouldn't turn to prostitution, welfare cheating, or even murder?"

Tammy added, "Crime is related to economic conditions, and study after study has shown more people with low incomes are convicted of crimes than rich people. We studied that in my criminology class last year."

"Those kinds of people?" repeated Bolden in baritone. "I swear! Let me tell you now, people arrested are no different from you and me. They are often the ones caught only because cops get to choose who they gonna arrest. Jazz, let me ask you a question. Do you think the Good Lord created different kinds of folks, them and us?

"A bunch of white Christian men rounded up my grandaddy for raping a white woman- no matter he wasn't even in the county at the time. A mob raided the jail and took him out to a tree. Would you say we can't trust all white Christian men?

"My brother got into trouble for stealing insulation from the back of a K-Mart to plug holes in his kid's bedroom room in their drafty apartment. The landlord wouldn't do a thing unless the government forced him to, but my brother's kids were freezing. Would you stop believing all landlords? Can any of us say we never committed a crime? As kids, didn't we all do something that could've got us in trouble if the police had arrested us?"

Others shifted in their seats, cleared their throats, and looked away.

"Well," Tammy said, "I smoked pot. Just like Honor, I guess. Except I was at a frat party, and no police came."

"When I was a teenager," laughed Judd, "me and my buddies snuck into a home in the neighborhood to party because we knew the owners were out of town. The police collared me and dragged me home to my parents at two in the morning. I was so ashamed. They grounded me for the rest of the semester and made me cut the grass of that out-of-town family. But I never was arrested." They all laughed at their little follies and murmured.

After a while, they heard a little voice.

"I did worse," whispered Tilley. The room went quiet. Sweet Tilley? How could she have done anything wrong? She's from Upper Arlington, a member of the UA Republican Party, perhaps a DAR. What crime could she have committed? Armed robbery was obviously out of the question, as was assault with a deadly weapon. They expected her confession to be a faux pas, like wearing white after Labor Day.

After what seemed like a decade of silence, her voice quivered as she said, "I had an abortion." She sobbed. "In my senior year of high school, during Christmas break, I told my friends I was going on vacation to Europe, but instead, I went to Washington, DC. My father knew a doctor there who let us into his office one night after hours. It was horrible. I returned to school and pretended like nothing had happened. I was so ashamed. I've never told anybody until now. It's been so many years." She blew her nose into her Swiss-cotton, laced handkerchief. The jurors were stunned. Elmira put Consuela down and went over to console Tilley.

After they took a break, deliberations resumed.

"Jazz would not find any of the defendants liable," said Barney as he tried to move the conversation forward. "If I understood what he said, he thinks the staff was doing their best, considering that inmates are liars. Is that your point, Jazz?"

"Well, sort of, I guess," stammered Jazz. "Say, I didn't mean to cause all this, and I was hoping we could wrap this up quickly. At Otterbein College where I work, we're having a show next week, and I oversee the stage crew, lights, and sound. I'm just trying to get back as quickly as possible. Perhaps I am pushing things a little too fast.

Jazz took a deep breath. "Now that you mention it, I stole Jimmy O'Reilly's bike when I was a kid. He was always showing off his fancy bike, and it made me mad. One night, I went over to his house, took his bike out of the backyard, and threw it in the lake. At the time, I thought it served him right for being such a show-off, but now that Mr. Bolden put it the way he did, I suppose I, too, could have been an insider."

"Let's review the evidence," suggested Barney. "Elmira talked about the procedures manual the nurse wrote, which Doctor V approved. The manual did not require medical record-keeping. Elmira said having no medical records was wrong. But from the sheets they did keep, we learned that Honor stood in the pill-call line nearly two dozen times before seeing a doctor. Then, after Nurse Kratz called her friend on the OB/GYN floor, she told the other nurse and Dr. V. that Honor was lying when she said she had a stillborn at Grant. Because of that, Dr. V did not even examine her. Is that your understanding? Do you think the nurses are responsible?"

"I sure do," said Bolden. Other nods.

"What about the doctor?" asked Barney, sensing movement in the group.

Judd responded quickly. "As doctor, he was captain of the ship. A nurse or somebody else may have prepared written procedures, but he still approved them. If those procedures prevented inmates from seeing him or getting their basic medical information before him to review, then he's responsible. And no matter what a nurse told him, I think he should be responsible when he didn't ask the patient about her stillborn, take a quick look at her, or do that six-week checkup thing. Don't forget the testimony of the other inmates and one of the guards who witnessed the sick-call line when the doctor met with patients. All of them said he rarely examined a patient. I'd say yes, he's liable. What the hell was he getting paid for anyway?"

Barney asked, "Are there any other comments?"

Tilley hesitated before saying, "I'm not a doctor; I'm just a housewife. But it seemed to me he wasn't living up to his medical standards, but maybe I'm wrong. I think he should have examined her, and with an exam, he would have known she had been pregnant."

"What about the Acting Superintendent, Haskel Gross?" asked Barney.

"Well, he's not a doctor," said Tilley, thinking over the trial. "But he is a creep. I was appalled at his advancements toward that female guard. Isn't what he was doing to her considered harassment now?"

"He's also caught up in this," said Bolden, "Don't forget. He was the one who told Sergeant Mitchell to say Honor OD'd. He told her to lie and say Honor was a druggie. That lie caused the docs at OSU to wait, which cost her life. I would sock it to him too."

"And he and the superintendent should be responsible for what they called 'the Hole.' Punishing her for being sick was barbaric," added Elmira.

Judd was looking at the wall, pondering. The jurors stopped talking, waiting for his thoughtful response.

Judd said, "Don't you think we should be careful about casting too broad a net? The superintendent oversees the guards, the office, all processing of inmates, the physical facility, preparation and serving of food, security, and a bunch of other things. How can we be sure he should be personally responsible for this?

"When Jazz complained about the city picking up the tab, we reminded him we were not to consider the ability to pay. But can we ignore it when it comes to individuals? Suppose Puchik must pay for this himself? Are you comfortable including him on the judgment he can't afford when he may not have been aware of what happened?"

Tilley sat back in her chair, fanning herself. "I'm getting a headache again. This is just too much thinking for my brain."

"We didn't ask for this job, Tilley," said Elmira, moving closer to her, "but we've got to make the right decisions. Hang in there, girl. You can do it."

"I took a course in business organization," said Tammy. "I thought the personal liability rule was that a business supervisor could be personally responsible only if he did something wrong outside of what he was supposed to be doing for the company. We didn't learn if it's the same for prison officials."

"School doesn't teach you about a lot of things, young lady," said Bolden. "It just shows you how to learn what you don't know."

The jurors had grown together, like crew members moving their hull together as one unit, but it was slipping away as they considered the liability of Safety Director Puchik and higher-ups. Discord could affect earlier understandings and tear all asunder.

Barney did not want to vote just yet, sensing they were heading toward a stalemate and fearing it might later cause his fellow jurors to resist changing positions and lead to a hung jury. He brought Zoe into the conversation for no reason other than a desperate attempt to escape their predicament, although he wasn't sure she had paid attention during the trial or these deliberations. But her vote was equal to that of any other juror. Besides, a new voice might unify thinking, or so he hoped.

"Ms. Whitman, you've been very quiet," he said. "We would like to hear your thoughts."

Zoe looked up, her big dark eyes headed first toward the ceiling and then made a circle like a school child called upon to report on a book she hadn't read. She paused, slowly removed her earphones, and wound up the cord while thinking about her response.

"I ain't into details. I'll just tell you what I feel, Okay? This trial was about what I already know. This tale ain't new to me. It's been happening since before my mama was a child. Honor may not have been in jail before, but she be from jail. Didn't Malcolm say, 'If you're born in America with black skin, you're born in prison'? They've been putting us in jails ever since we was freed from plantations. White folk just found new ways to store us. Barry White, my Barry White, did time when he was 16, yet he is now the greatest singer there ever was.

"Honor couldn't raise bail money to stay out of jail. So? Most poor folk can't. Most blacks are poor. The Man makes bails high to keep us in, and that helps convict us. Even those of us with jobs, families, and apartments can't make bail. When we sit in jail and wait, we lose all we got. What they done to her ain't no big thing. It's what we know.

"Most cases don't go to trial no how. They end up in some kind of deal after a cracker cop hits us with too many charges, so they can get us to plea to something less just to get out. But those deals could be made on the day they get arrested, and those who get probation could return to their families and jobs without losing nothing. No, it wasn't right she was in jail, or she died, if that is what you're asking me.

"Now, you folks have been looking at this rule or that and trying to figure out what one person or another did at WCI. But it don't take no Ph.D., MD, or even a GED to know the doctor and those nurses and superintendent were put there by folks who don't give a damn if prisoners got treated right or not. What's surprising 'bout that? We don't see the best doctors and nurses either 'cause they don't treat welfare patients. Our babies die, our old folks die, and we are sicker than white folk. I guess I'm saying yes, they killed Honor, but she's just one of many.

A. S. White

"I s'pose that is just the way of things. I can't change the way folks behave. That's why I let my sweet Barry sing to me, 'I'm his First, his Last, his Everything.' Every day, I think Honor or somebody like her could be me. Every day, I think about whether I'll go to jail, or my brother or my mama. But I don't pay it no mind. Instead, I listen to my Barry. I know he be jiving his soft, warm mouth at me, but his sweet talk makes me feel really good. And I like to feel good."

With that, Zoe put on her headphones and turned away.

Later that day, they took their final vote. When completed, Barney flipped the switch for the bailiff.

CHAPTER 69

JUDGE RUMSFELD ORDERED Stone and Gold to remain in the courthouse while jurors deliberated. Gold worked as best he could upstairs at a table in the county law library while Ben found Stone a large private room in the courthouse to set up shop for his entourage. Frank returned to law school to catch up on his studies before finals.

Gold accomplished little up there. He spent hours alternately beating himself up for taking the case, spending thousands of his own money, and devoting nearly a year of his life. And for what? *Did you think you would enhance your career with a defense verdict and the media ripping you apart for pursuing a worthless case? Can't you see the mayor announcing when it's over that the city had spent a "gazillion dollars" defending its "hard-working employees" from "scurrilous claims" made by "greedy attorneys" trying to "profit" from "unfortunate occurrences"? What were you thinking?*

Occasionally, other attorneys passed him in the library and said something like, "Good luck, Al. Hope you win." He knew behind his back they were sighing, "What a fool. What a fool." He would smile and say thanks, but a Bob Dylan song would play in his ear about people who've got a lot of nerve, wanting to be on the side that's winning.

Other times, he flipped into a luxuriated stupor from an award so large he would be forced to stop Judge Rumsfeld's efforts to reduce the amount. There was never a similar award against the city of as much as $100,000. This award would be so large he would be invited someday to sit at the gilded table within his imagined Attorneys Hall of Fame and over brandy and a good cigar, trade stories with the likes of Thurgood Marshall, Clarence Darrow, and William Jennings Bryan. Back and forth between two fickle extremes he went, consuming himself in meaningless monologues as he waited for eight ordinary people to decide his fate and that of his clients.

Millie did not have Alan's luxury—or curse—of idle time. When the jury began deliberating, she went back to work. She had her family to feed. Oh, she mused about the verdict as she changed linen or helped a new employee assist a patient out of bed. Of course, she wanted money for her grandson; his welfare meant everything to her. Now that he was part of her family, she had to rethink how that change would affect them in the long run. Maybe the jury would award enough money for Winston to go to college someday. That was her dream, unlike Alan's imaginary Hall of Fame.

Her notion of success was far more nuanced than his. If the jury awarded a lot of money to Winston only, how would she justify her children spending money on Winston but not on them? How could she prevent their resenting him? How could she stop from spoiling him?

But if the jury did not find for the family, she would be crushed because it would mean the jury, and so the world, deemed her daughter a drug addict, a welfare mom, worthless. And destroying the reputation of her family or any member might also destroy her. She went about her daily duties stoically, but the outcome was eating her up too. Soon, she would learn the fate of her loved ones and perhaps find peace.

CHAPTER 70

AFTER BAILIFF BEN WALTON TOLD Gold that the jury would announce its verdict the next morning, Gold called Millie, and they agreed to park on a side street near the courthouse and walk together to hear the news.

The 11 o'clock news sizzled with the imminent verdict announcement, and by morning, a growing crowd of reporters and protesters had gathered on the courthouse steps. Reverend Jenkins and some of his congregants held homemade signs and sang. Sweet Willie's Moss Mobile was parked amidst the swelling crowd.

Gold met Millie and the kids by her parked car. He took her arm. "Our moment, whatever it might be, has come," he said as they walked to the courthouse. When they turned the corner of the courthouse, reporters shouted questions, photographers snapped pictures, and news crews filmed their every step.

"No comment," came the words from Gold's staged smile as they made their way up the courthouse steps and into the elevator. Having learned from her mistakes, Millie raised her head high as television camera eyes stared at her, hoping to catch her again in an unflattering pose. Like it or not, she and her children had become part of this year's mayoral campaign and perhaps the history of Columbus.

Gold led Millie to the plaintiff's table. The courtroom quieted as jurors took their seats.

"Ready?" Gold asked Millie.

"As ready as I'll ever be," she said.

"All rise!" Bailiff Walton shouted. Judge Rumsfeld entered and took his place on the bench. The jurors and others sat down after him.

Judge Rumsfeld was also anxious. He figured the mayor was behind the call from Lex. If the jury hit the city hard, then Mayor Blandford might lose reelection and take down with him all Republicans running in the city and, next year, all Republican officials in the county. His appointment to the Court of Appeals would be lost. While concerned, he could only imagine what Jon Blandford was going through. He was younger, more ambitious, and far more vulnerable than Rumsfeld.

"Has the jury reached a verdict?" the judge asked the foreperson, trying to appear calm.

"We have, Your Honor," Barney Willis said.

"Did you fill in the jury verdict forms, as I instructed?"

"We have, Your Honor."

"Have at least two-thirds of the jurors signed the forms, as instructed?"

"Yes, Your Honor."

"Very well. Please give the forms to the bailiff."

Ben Walton rose from his seat, took from Barney the envelope containing the verdict forms, and handed it to the judge, who opened the envelope, laid the forms flat on his desk, and read silently. Six jurors had signed the verdict.

When he finished, he looked out among the crowd and said, "Will the parties please rise."

Gold with Millie and her family stood, as did Gross, Puchik, and Stone with his cadre of counselors. Judge Rumsfeld read from the jury form,

"We, the jury, find for the plaintiffs and against the City of Columbus and all other defendants in the sum of $150,000."

The courtroom burst into applause. Pastor Jenkins shouted, "Hallelujah, it's a new day!" Reporters scribbled in their notebooks. Then, Barney spoke again but could hardly be heard above the din.

"Your Honor," Barney nearly shouted. "The jury has a request, but we had nowhere to write it on the forms."

The courtroom quickly hushed as the participants wondered what this was all about.

"What is your request?" asked the judge.

"We would like to know if you can convene a grand jury to prosecute this matter criminally."

Applause exploded into pandemonium. Newsmen ran to call their offices. Pastor Jenkins shouted, "Hallelujah. Great God almighty, change is acomin'! Join me outside, brothers and sisters, for a prayer of thanksgiving." His followers began to sing "We Shall Overcome."

Judge Rumsfeld pounded on his gavel for order to no avail.

CHAPTER 71

IN ONE OF HIS MOST DIFFICULT moments, Ed Auber met with the mayor and Terry Prince to give them the grim news.

"What the hell happened? I can't believe it. You hired the best attorney in the country, you said," screamed Terry at Ed.

"We did our homework, but Stone couldn't work his magic with the facts he had to work with. A young mother died, leaving a tender infant. Juries are unpredictable. We can always appeal. I'm sure we can find issues to raise."

"And be on the defensive? Hiding behind legal technicalities? It would make us look unrepentant and unsympathetic," Mayor Blandford said.

"Agreed," Prince said as he calmed down. "Probably best to eat it."

The mayor nodded pensively.

"What about City Council?" asked Terry.

"I'll deal with them directly."

Terry turned to Ed. "What about this business of a grand jury?"

"It was only a request. The jury has no authority. It'll go nowhere."

"Good. We can't afford another trial," said Terry.

A few minutes later, the city auditor called the mayor, suggesting his budget director revise the city budget. Soon after, Lex Baer stormed past Polly Gibson into the mayor's office, chewing his cigar like a hungry calf on its mother's teat.

"Goddammit! Now you got one hell of a job explaining to the people of Columbus why your doctor didn't examine his patient, your nurses didn't keep records, and your superintendent lied to the emergency squad. And you got to do all this in the middle of an election year. If I may say so, Mr. Mayor, your tit is in the wringer, and you better not pull us all in with you. How in the hell are you going to get us out of this mess?" Lex said, without bothering to sit down.

Fortunately for the mayor, Terry was at his side. As the mayor's fixer, Terry showed his worth, quickly taking charge of the situation.

"Thank you for coming in to bring us the news," Terry said to Lex. "We are working on a response now. Fortunately, we already missed the morning news, so there is time before 6 o'clock to prepare. I have some feelers out to sense public concern. We will likely ask Council for prompt action in appointing a blue-ribbon commission to study WCI activity. We may need your help with that. I am about to call Bruno to deliver a press statement. The mayor will be unavailable for comment for at least 24 hours.

"Now, Lex, let me ask you, do you have any suggestions? We want the benefit of your advice. Perhaps you might wish to talk to Judge Rumsfeld, your friend, to get all the trial details. We certainly welcome your ideas as chairman of the Council Safety Committee if that is why you came by.

"If not, I hope you will let us continue our work. I personally will keep you apprised. Thank you so much for dropping by," Terry said as he hurried Lex out the door. Once Lex was out, Terry instructed Polly to lock the door.

"Well, Mayor, we have several alternatives," said Terry, pacing back and forth. "We can attack the jury, which was composed of some non-city residents, attack Judge Rumsfeld for some of his procedural rulings, let Bruno accept responsibility while attacking Gross for providing us false information, or prostrate ourselves on the steps of City Hall and beg forgiveness, promising never to do it again. While there are other alternatives, we need your instruction in the general direction you want us to take."

The mayor mumbled, "Occasionally, words must serve to veil facts. But let this happen so that no one becomes aware of it; or, if it should be noticed, excuses must be at hand to be produced immediately."

"What's that, Mayor?"

"Oh, nothing, just a little quote from Machiavelli. Terry, let's look our best. Please prepare something for Bruno to say that will incorporate your suggestions along that line."

"Will do. We've got a lot of work to do before the election. Bruno will be here in a minute or two, and I've got to do some quick figuring. Are there any federal grants we received recently or other good news we can announce? We need other issues to divert attention."

On the 6 o'clock news that night, Safety Director Puchik described the mayor's disappointment with the jury's verdict and his taking action to prevent anything like this sad tragedy from happening again. "The mayor," he said, "was deeply disturbed by the decision, which two jurors opposed and several others who aren't even Columbus residents approved." Puchik then announced the mayor would appoint a blue-ribbon commission to review any problems at WCI and keep Columbus the greatest city in America. "The mayor intends to get to the bottom of this!" he declared, sounding like someone about to cook another Masserole.

If the City chose not to appeal, as Puchik urged, then he accepted full responsibility for what happened, despite receiving false reports from WCI officials regarding conditions there.

"Meanwhile, in other news," the announcer then droned, "The mayor today announced the start of a new garbage collection program designed to cut the local rat population by 23 percent over the next five years."

CHAPTER 72

DESPITE CARPING BY MANY city officials, including Lex Baer, who scurried to avoid political contamination, the city folded and agreed to pay. The award triggered a new set of concerns for Millie and her family. How would it be divided? The jury had only awarded a lump sum to "plaintiffs," not determined how much each would receive. Her estate would be entitled to what Honor would receive had she lived, including pain and suffering.

Family members had wrongful death claims: Honor's son's claim for the loss of his mother; Millie's and Lucky's for the loss of their oldest daughter and Millie's burden of rearing Winston; the siblings for their loss of a sister.

Deciding who gets what percentage of the wrongful death claims was left to Franklin County's probate judge, not Judge Rumsfeld. Gold filed probate papers to set a hearing where those decisions would be made, along with approving his fee.

Gold arrived for that probate hearing hoping they could resolve all issues that day, avoid a family fight, and approve his fee award. Unless all parties agreed, his fees could be held captive until a final resolution of the other issues. Appeals can take years, and after all his work, delayed payment would cut him deeply.

When the family emerged from the elevator onto the probate floor lobby, Gold sensed a certain excitement among them, which might not bode well. He noticed that Lucky was absent.

"I want to get me a car," he heard Duke say. "Now that I'm 16, I want a Camaro with dual pipes."

"I want some pretty new clothes," said Ella. "And shoes, lots of shoes!"

Gold spotted Edgar Wertheimer approaching, an attorney appointed by the probate judge as guardian ad litem to protect Winston's interests. He was a former magistrate now in private practice, yet as he spoke, he sounded almost as if he were still part of the court system.

"The judge has instructed us to discuss this matter before the hearing, and I reserved a conference room where we can talk. Would you please come with me? Alan, please join us if you like." Without looking back, he turned toward the conference room. Millie and the family dutifully followed, with Gold bringing up the rear.

Inside a walnut-paneled room was a new, well-polished conference table and leather cushioned seats. On the longer wall, a large gold-framed portrait of the judge hung in classic style with a dark background and an unseen light shining upon his face and slick hair, broad-robed shoulders, and robust body evoking an aura of permanence, stability, and fortitude. Unlike other common pleas judges, the probate judge had his own floor in the courthouse. His was the only court that did not depend entirely upon county commissioners for funding. Instead, the probate fees it sets fund the court.

After brief introductions and explanations of what was to happen during the hearing, Wertheimer got down to business. "Now, as I understand it, the deceased—and let me express my condolences to the entire family—suffered a great deal before she died. Mr. Gold has been instructed to hold all monies until the court orders the distribution of funds. I am correct, am I not? She died leaving no will?"

"She had no will," said Millie.

"As I thought. It is my position that most of the money should go to the administrator for the benefit of Winston."

"Hold on a sec," said Duke. "What about us? We lost our sister. What about us?"

"Yeah, what about us?" asked Ella.

Miles asked, "How much are you talking about for Winston, and how much for us?"

"Well, I have not arrived at a final position, but I was thinking that 75:25 percent of the net proceeds would be a fair split. What is your suggestion?" asked Wertheimer.

"Who gets 75 percent?" asked Duke.

"75 percent to the estate."

Duke interrupted, "And we split just 25 percent? That ain't right. How about 40:60? He would still get more than any one of us."

"It is my opinion, at a hearing, the judge, under the circumstances, would agree with my percentages," Wertheimer said.

Miles questioned further, "Then you take a fee from Winston's share?"

"Yes, my fee would come from his share."

"Well, it's no wonder you want that much in the kitty," said Duke. "Ain't you got a conflict?"

"My fee must come from somewhere, and I don't think the court will determine this a conflict of interest any more than any other attorney would have. Please understand, I am willing to negotiate, but, if necessary, I am prepared to go to hearing and argue on behalf of the estate."

Ella said, "We ain't worried. Mr. Gold will fight for us like he did at that trial."

Gold interrupted. "Unfortunately, I cannot take part. My job was to recover money for all those with a valid claim. Because I was the attorney for claimants, each of you is my client. I can't argue on behalf of one of my clients against another, which is why I suggested you retain separate counsel."

"How could we pay for separate counsel?" asked Duke. "We ain't got no money. But Winston gets his lawyer for free. That don't seem fair."

"Actually," said Wertheimer, "because all of you are minors, your mother is your natural guardian. She speaks on your behalf. The court will recognize her words as yours."

All eyes turned to Millie, who had remained silent. "Can we talk to the judge?" she asked. "I have a few questions for him. We don't know much about this."

"I will see if the judge is available," said Wertheimer.

In a few minutes, Judge Russell Mudd entered the conference room wearing his black robe, followed by Wertheimer. Without instruction, each person rose as he entered. He glanced at the assembled as would a three-star general inspecting grunts. Few dared to look him in the eye; most looked down. He stood at the head of the table and looked around to be sure all were properly in position before seating himself, swirling his black robe in grand style. He nodded to the flock to take their seats.

Judge Mudd had presided over probate court for many years. Some attorneys in Franklin County had never known another probate judge, and unless they practiced in other counties, they were unaware that other judges did things differently. It just seemed like his way was the only way.

Over the years, Mudd had become a political giant and a consummate negotiator. Rarely did attorneys litigate cases before him. Instead, he would mediate for as long as necessary until he persuaded litigants to compromise. His success lay in finding the exact spot where no one was happy with his compromise but afraid of risking a trial and ending up worse.

Wertheimer began, "Your Honor, Ms. Rivers asked to speak with you prior to the hearing regarding the distribution of judgment proceeds. I do not object to this meeting. As you may recall, our counsel, Alan Gold, obtained a judgment from the city for $150,000 on our behalf. The defendants elected not to appeal, and the money is in his trust account, along with what is left from the prior settlements you approved. The jury verdict did not distinguish between survivor and wrongful death claims. Our hearing today is to determine the distribution of those funds.

"The deceased, Honor Wilson, died leaving a minor, Winston Wilson, around two years old. He resides with his maternal grandmother, Millie Rivers, and her children, although no adoption or permanent custody orders have been ordered. This court appointed her both as the administrator of Ms. Wilson's estate and on behalf of her family to pursue the lawsuit against the city of Columbus and others. Ms. Rivers and her children are present before you, as is Winston Wilson. Mr. Gold is present but not taking part. Honor was divorced. The clerk notified the child's father in Chicago, Illinois, uncertain who the custodian will be. He's not present today.

"Mr. Gold has applied for his fee, one-third of the gross plus costs, per his contingency agreement, approved previously by this court. On behalf of the estate, we have no objection to his fees and expenses being paid."

Alan sighed and the muscles in his neck relaxed.

"This morning," Wertheimer continued, "Your Honor, we—the family and I—discussed settlement under the new wrongful death act but have not reached an agreement yet. I have taken the liberty, Your Honor, of explaining to them that all survivor claims would go to Honor's estate, and wrongful death claims would be distributed according to this court's determination. Because Honor had no will, her minor son would inherit her entire estate. I leave it to them to explain their concerns."

The judge nodded and stared for a moment at his crossed hands on the table while he processed the attorney's words. He then glanced around the table until he found Millie's penetrating eyes returning his gaze.

"I am sorry for your loss," he began.

"Thank you."

"I read in the paper the jury award was the largest of its kind in Franklin County. You can be very proud of Counselor Gold's work."

"Yes, sir. We are very grateful."

"How is Winston doing?"

"Oh, he seems to be a happy little boy. He toddles and speaks a few words. He still looks around when he says 'Mama,' but I suppose he'll stop asking soon enough. He is getting along with his new family, well, not entirely new. He and Honor had been living with us for a few months before she died. After her divorce, she moved here from Chicago and was beginning a new life here."

"And these are your children?"

"Yes, sir."

"You are blessed, but it must be tough. My wife and I have no children."

He gestured toward Duke. "You, sir. Tell me about your sister, Honor, and what her loss means to you if you can."

Duke crossed his arms and stared at the table. "Mama works all the time. She sometimes took a second job. When she worked, Honor was my mama. Then she married and moved away. When she came back, she had her own baby, but she still was my second mama. Well, Mama still works, but Honor's not there for me anymore. But I'm cool with it," he said, wiping his eyes.

Judge Mudd took in what he heard and turned to Billie, "And what about you, young lady? How old are you?"

"Ten."

"What did you like about your sister Honor?"

"Well," she paused and adjusted her dress. "I liked when she was with me. She took us to the library when Mama couldn't. I don't like it now. It feels yucky to see Winston without his mommy. Say, you're a big judge. Can't you sign something to bring her back to us? Can you make it right, Your Justness?"

"I wish I could. I really wish I could. Ms. Rivers, have you spoken with Honor's father about this distribution?"

"Yes, I have, Your Honor. He's a musician, and he's on the road a lot. He got the notice at his home in Chicago. He told me he didn't want any money and couldn't come to the hearing. He's got a gig in Gary, Indiana, tonight."

"Well, as Mr. Wertheimer explained, monies paid to Honor's estate will be placed in trust for the care and maintenance of her son. Monies distributed as wrongful death payments for losses suffered by family members will go directly to them if they are adults or to their guardians if they are minors.

"You are their natural guardian. You've had time to think about an arrangement among the claimants. You should know that while not all the money might go to the estate, I will not allow the estate to receive nothing. May I ask you, Ms. Rivers, what are your thoughts about distribution?"

"Judge, it's not natural for a mother to bury her daughter. I would have let the city cut off my arms and poke out my eyes before letting them do what they did to my Honor. I've got a wound in my heart that eats at my soul. I feel empty. I come home from work, knowing she's gone forever. But we have to move on. Now, we'll raise Winston as one of us. The Lord did provide.

"I filed the case not only to get money for him but also to prove to everybody that Honor was not an addict like it said in the paper and to show my family to be good people. With Mr. Gold's help, we did just that. It may not be much in the city's history, maybe only a footnote. But, Your Honor, it's our footnote. I hope it's gonna change some things around here. Now what?

"My kids have been making wish lists like it was Christmas. I want nothing for myself. They are excited but not old enough to understand what this all means. I've been thinking of this day since the verdict. Finally, it came to me after praying for guidance. I have made a decision. Children, please listen to me.

"I want all the money to go to Winston. But with a catch. While he is a child with us, he will get no more than the other kids, and mine will have no less. All will be treated the same. Winston has no mother now, and even though I am getting a little older and a little tired, I will try to raise him as good as my daughter did and always consider what is in his best interest.

"Let him get the rest of the money when he goes to college or turns 18. That is what I would like, Your Honor. My question to you, sir, is whether your legal people can make this happen. And my question to you, kids, is whether we can abide by it?"

The initial ripple of discontent among the children ebbed into a quiet pond of acceptance and contemplation: a future without flashy cars or fancy shoes, a future premised on giving instead of receiving. Eventually, they stopped demanding and began dealing with the new reality. They didn't like it, but they knew Mama was right, as usual.

Judge Mudd looked for consensus in the eyes of each of her children. What he saw pleased him. He said softly, "Ms. Rivers, in my entire career on this bench, I have never received a suggestion as you are making. I will sign an order complying with your wishes. Children, treat Winston as your new brother. This hearing will be continued. I will sign an agreed judgment order once you approve, Ms. Rivers." The judge wrapped his majestic black robe around him as he withdrew from the room, humbled.

CHAPTER 73

"Hi, Mama. It's Reginald. I'm in Chicago."

"I'm not your mama, and I know your voice, Junior. What do you want?"

"I'm calling about my boy. How's Winston doing?"

"How's he doing? His mother is dead. After the funeral, you ran back to Chicago so fast you didn't take time to pay a little support for your son. I always work, raising my family, including my grandson, with no help from you. And you ask me how he is doing? He's a motherless child, Junior. Now up and comes his father, who suddenly calls from Chicago to check in like he was calling to see if his laundry is ready."

"Well, that is what I was calling about. I've been talking to my mother, and she's been thinking about how she could help. It's true I have not done right by my boy. But I think I can now. I want to try, Mama, and I am ready to be his father. You have enough to do, Millie, and we appreciate what you have done for him. Me and Mother want to take him off your hands. You understand. She has no other kids at home and is willing to take care of him. I mean, we are willing. We have an extra room, and with Mother not working, she has time for him. What do you think?"

"So, you heard about the lawsuit, huh?"

"This isn't about a lawsuit."

"I bet."

"This is about my boy. I'm his daddy and want him by my side."

"So, suddenly, you're his daddy. You weren't his daddy when he got sick, and you don't send money like a daddy would. When Winston moved in with us, where were you? Have you been there for him since she died? Tell me, Junior, when did your mother decide it was time for you to stand up and be his daddy? Can you smell money all the way from Chicago, Mr. Daddy?"

"My mother didn't make this decision for me. I made it. We discussed it for sure, and she agreed. But I decided. And we know nothing about a lawsuit. I think it's time for me to take responsibility for my child, my only child."

"Do you expect me to believe you, Junior? You didn't take responsibility when you married my daughter to provide food on your table or a roof over your head. You didn't take responsibility for her after the divorce, and you have done nothing for your boy except a few birthday gifts. Why should I believe you, Junior, an unrepentant prodigal son right out of the Bible? Why should I think you will suddenly become Winston's daddy?"

"I've grown up. You don't realize the changes I've gone through. I want to do right by Winston."

"Well, how can I realize changes I don't see? Winston needs a family. He needs to be with those who care about him. He needs a real father, not his grandmother's little boy. As far as I can tell, you're still little Junior, and that's not saying much! You might as well go on about your business and just call me once a year if it will satisfy your father urge and leave Winston well enough alone with us."

"I got rights, Ms. Rivers. You know I do. So, I'm telling you, plain as I can make it, me and my mother want my child back."

"Winston is part of our family now. Be careful what you ask for, Junior. Daddy is a lifetime profession. You haven't stayed with any job till the sun goes down. Let it pass, Junior. Let it pass."

Millie put the phone back in the cradle and went up to her room. She shut her door to read scripture for her bible class. She chose Luke 15.

CHAPTER 74

A FEW DAYS LATER, HER phone rang.

"Hi, Millie, how's it going? It's Alan."

"Doing OK. Getting ready to go to work. The kids are doing well. Duke was promoted at Wendy's, and Ella will be bussed to North High School this year. Duke says he wants to be a civil rights lawyer because of you. Say, I've wanted to ask you, how are you doing since we won?"

"I'm doing OK, but you know, I sort of expected more. At first, I was so excited by all the attention we got. Then after the cameras went away, the news stories stopped, and the chatter died down, I started thinking of Peggy Lee's song "Is That All There Is?" You know, she got a Grammy for that. But anyway, new clients are calling. Some have real potential, so I guess I can't complain."

"Yeah, neither can I. At the nursing home, people were always talking about me, like I was somebody special. But now it's just day to day, and I kind of like that."

"But that's not why I called, Millie. This morning, I got a call from an attorney friend who says she's filing suit against you."

"Yeah, I know. Junior and his mother want to take Winston from us."

"How did you know?"

"Junior called me. He said he wants to be the father he never was. But I think his mother wants a child she never had, and he's never had the gumption to make a sandwich."

"Now, Millie, we can't take this lightly. In Ohio, the law favors parents over grandparents. The attorney informed me that the court scheduled an emergency hearing next Monday, and they're coming in for it. I've been doing some research, and, honestly, it's not encouraging."

"The only thing Junior has ever put into Winston was his seed. He hasn't paid to support him, never comes to see his child, and still can't figure out which way a diaper goes on. Now, how can the law take Honor's baby from me and give him to another baby? Lord have mercy! Any court that turns a child over to Junior is committing child abuse."

"I understand what you're saying. We can present that view to the juvenile judge. But remember, under Ohio law, because the law presumes the parent is the proper person to raise a child, we'll have to prove not just you would do a better job than him in caring for Winston, but that he is unfit to care for the child. That, Ms. Rivers, will be very difficult to prove."

"But he won't be a father to him. He'll dump Winston on Maureen, his mother, just as sure as I'm talking to you."

"Perhaps. But the court would probably interpret that to mean Reginald would provide for his son by employing his mother's services to care for her grandson—much like a rich family hires a nanny."

"That's not right. He's not her son; Junior's just doing Maureen's bidding. It's like she found a way to buy a child instead of adopting one."

"The law is often a question of perspective, I guess. I will do my best to fight for you. I need you to know our hill is very steep."

CHAPTER 75

MILLIE WAS UNUSUALLY QUIET that evening when the family prepared dinner of rice and vegetables and a sweet bean pie. She was serving a vegetarian entree to her family for the first time and wanted to see their reactions. Despite inherent contradictions, Millie was always doing something new or transforming herself, like a model changing her wardrobe.

The kids were uncertain about what to do with so many vegetables. Millie hadn't bought them; she rarely did. Because she often came home late, they ate mostly quickly prepared meals, mainly meats, and starches. The other day, the cook at the nursing home gave her some extras she had: raw carrots, celery, and peas. She decided to give them a try. She showed Ella how to prepare each dish while Millie concentrated on her sweet bean pie. Her recipe called for white navy beans and a few tricks to give it a smooth consistency. Despite her efforts to focus on her pie, she could not stop thinking about her phone calls with Junior and Alan.

Winston was adjusting after his turbulent past—from married parents to divorce, from Chicago to Columbus, from young Honor to older Millie, from being an only child to the youngest of five. All that tumult before he turned four. Catastrophes had covered his life like lava flowing across a tiny isle. Millie hoped chaos was behind him so he could look forward to the rest of his childhood in peace.

As the pie baked, she mulled over her call from Junior. *Maureen put her son up to it. What was she thinking? Winston is settled now. He has a place surrounded by kids who love him. Oh, her house in Bronzeville is much nicer than ours and is without the hustle and bustle of so many of us in this small apartment, but what kind of life would he have living with a neglectful father who can't hold a job? But Maureen has a big, quiet house, lots of retirement money, and time to devote to him. With her connections, she could get him the best schooling. Then again, looking at that son of hers, would Winston become another Junior? Our small house is filled with noisy love, not stuffed with quiet money. But I am getting older.*

Back and forth she went, looking at the pros and cons without coming to any conclusions as she imagined so many scenarios. Suddenly, she was brought to the kitchen when Ella asked, "What am I supposed to do with peas?"

When the meal was finally on the table, Millie confronted an uproar: "Where's the meat?" "These vegetables are lousy!" "Where is real food?" Such griping was nothing new to her. She hoped it would go away after they tasted her sweet bean pie. Winston was in his makeshift highchair at the end of the table, eating what the others gave him from their plates.

After they were done complaining and had tasted a few dishes, Millie began.

"I got a call from Junior the other day," she said.

"Did he ask about Winston?" asked Miles.

"Yes, he did, but only a little. He talked mostly about himself and how he had changed."

"When I saw him at the funeral, he didn't look different to me. What's changed about him?" said Miles.

"Well, he says he is becoming more of a man and wants to be a father."

"You mean he's got some girl pregnant?" asked Duke.

"No, I mean he wants to be a father to Winston."

"I don't get it," asked Miles. "How can Uncle Reggie be a father to Winston when he's in Chicago and Winston lives with us? Is he moving here?"

THE MATTER OF HONOR

Millie's barren face was silent. Suddenly, there was an uncomfortable lull at the table as if they were trying to find the answer to a parlor game.

"No, oh no!" cried Ella. "Mama, does he want to take Winston away from us?"

Millie stopped looking at them and dropped her eyes. "Yes, that's what he said." Billie dropped her fork, and Duke pounded his fist on the table. After their clamor died down, they sat silently, not knowing what to say.

"Why, Mama? Why would he take little Winston from us?" asked Ella. "He's like my little brother, and he don't even know Winston."

"Do you think he is after Winston's money?" asked Miles.

"Of course," said Duke. "Why else would he lift a finger for him? We'll fight this, won't we, Mama? Have you talked to Mr. Gold? What does he say?"

"Mr. Gold said courts like parents more than grandparents. We have to prove Junior would be unfit to be a parent."

"Well, that shouldn't be hard," said Duke. "He ain't never acted like a parent."

"I'm not a lawyer," said Millie. "Mr. Gold told me it would be very hard to win. Junior's family has money and a nice big house for Winston. I guess Junior is counting on his mother to raise Winston. Well, the Lord will provide." Her voice cracked.

CHAPTER 76

GOLD PREPARED A RESPONSE to the motion of Reginald for a change of custody. The law in Ohio was tough on grandparents, as he had already discovered. Parental rights trump all others in custody cases, and the only exception is when a parent is unfit. To his surprise, he discovered that courts could not apply the general standard of 'the best interest of the child' until a parent is proven unfit.

He tried to find a way around this barrier. Gold's brief asked the juvenile court to do what he claimed to be the "right thing." Gold had not done his own research and preparation since Frank left to finish law school and go on to other things.

First, he laid out why Reginald was not fit. He cited his past behavior: no calls, visits, or child payments. If that didn't work, and knowing a judge must follow the law, he changed the narrative to portray Reginald as his mother's agent, who would be the de facto custodian. In that circumstance, he contended the actual plaintiff was Maureen, Reginald being only her surrogate. Therefore, he concluded the hearing was not a father vs. grandmother contest but one between grandmother and grandmother.

Then, he suggested that the court could apply the child's best interest, which, he contended, favored Millie. She had cared for Winston since his move from Chicago. Maureen had never cared for him, even when he lived near her. It would be in Winston's best interest to be with Millie. His argument was completely logical.

He continued that at the hearing, they would prove disruption, emotional trauma, personality dislocation (and anything else he could think of) to prevent the court from taking Winston away from Millie. He praised the tight living conditions among Winston and his aunts and uncles, contrasting it with his living in Chicago as an only child. Although custody cases were not his forte, Alan was satisfied when he finished—cleverly done, despite the law being to the contrary. He was not the first attorney beguiled by his own words.

* * *

Millie was folding laundry after an aide hadn't shown up for work, thinking about the upcoming hearing. *Can we prove that Junior is unfit, or if we were lucky enough to get the judge who would agree that the battle is really between the two grandmothers, can we prove I would be better than Maureen? She has money, prestige, and position; I don't. Her house has a separate bedroom for him; My apartment doesn't. She can get him into college; I can't. All I have is lots of kids and bills. And she is much younger than me.*

On the other hand, with all her money, Maureen never lifted a finger to help Winston. With the settlement, can't we say that money is no longer the most important factor? If a judge takes away Maureen's edge on the money issue, can't we show we have done more and would do more for Winston than she could? Did I make a mistake in what I agreed to with that probate judge?

What kind of woman is Maureen? She always seemed aloof to me, like she was from another world, one better than mine. We hardly spent any time alone together since they married. She would have more time to care for Winston: I always work. But Winston would be without other kids at her house. Will it make a difference that Winston has been with me for less than a year?

She thought her brain was about to turn to cheese, thinking of all the ways to look at the case. Mr. Gold can argue how things should be but can't overcome what is. She carried the clean towels in her arms and her troubles on her shoulders.

***

Gold called a meeting with the family to review what they would say at the Monday hearing. He prepped each family member to understand and describe what they would do for Winston and what Winston meant to the family. He asked them to recall tender stories about Winston and their relationships with him. After working with Millie, he was confident she would articulate her responsibilities and challenges well, her ways of rearing Winston, and why she would be the better choice. He also prepared his attack on Reginald's fitness.

The rest would be up to the newly appointed juvenile magistrate. Alan hoped she might recognize an exception to the general priority rule of parents over grandparents.

CHAPTER 77

ON MONDAY, MILLIE INSTRUCTED her children to wear the same clothes they had worn for Honor's funeral, and she donned her only suit. As they walked down the hallway of the county building used for juvenile hearings, Millie looked with pride at her flock. They marched unwavering in support of their nephew. She looked toward Gold at her side, who likewise displayed that aura of confidence she had grown accustomed to whenever he found himself in a tight situation. All were prepared to fight for Winston.

While she was looking at them, Alan also glanced toward Millie, trying to assure himself that she, too, was ready for the fight. He was surprised by what he saw. The resolve in her that steadied him throughout Honor's trial he felt was missing. She seemed distant, thinking about something else. Maybe it was just his imagination.

When they entered the courtroom, he placed his papers, law books, and notes in their proper places on the counsel table. Ella sat behind him, holding Winston. Millie had him dressed in a light blue outfit that perfectly complemented his caramel skin. Millie sat beside him but was elsewhere, but where?

Gold glanced up from his notes when he heard footsteps. Reginald, Maureen, and their lawyer walked into the improvised courtroom to the adjacent table. Millie's children mumbled under their breath, causing Winston to stir from his morning nap.

Maureen, at the other table, wore a finely tailored pink suit, matching pink pumps, and an elegant leather purse with gold adornments. When the kids' murmurs died down, Winston returned to the sleep of the innocent.

Alan walked to the other table to shake hands with Reginald's attorney. After a few perfunctory pleasantries, she said to Alan, "Before we start, my client's mother would like to talk with Millie ... alone. Is that okay with you?" Alan had only an instant to respond.

He knew allowing clients to talk directly to each other was risky. Sometimes parties would reach impossible settlements leading to more litigation or become entangled in heated discussions that broke down mutual respect, causing bitterness and irreconcilability. Alan glanced at Maureen, who was staring at him with open eyes showing innate sincerity, and then at Millie, looking straight ahead.

"Let me check with my client." He asked Millie to step outside for a moment, and they talked in the hall. She agreed to listen to Maureen, and Gold advised her not to disclose any facts that might harm their case.

After asking the bailiff to delay the hearing, the attorneys walked their mute clients to a small conference room while they chitchatted, avoiding an unhealthy silence. Alan opened a door into a room just large enough for a small table and four chairs. The two grandmothers took seats across from each other, both with arms crossed, as he closed the door.

After a while, Millie looked up from the table to find Maureen staring at her, searching for the right words to begin with.

"Thank you for inviting us to the funeral, Millie. It meant a lot that you included us. I still can't believe she's gone. I know you were very proud of her. I'm not sure Reggie realized how lucky he was to have a wife like Honor. He learned a lot from his loss but has a long way to go. As an only child, he never learned to share or give as his wife did. Perhaps that's my fault. I was an only child too. He is learning now.

"You and I haven't taken time to get to know each other over the years. You always seemed so busy with your family; I never wanted to disturb you. My life seems simple compared to yours. Since my husband Reginald died young from high blood pressure, I've kept to myself. I visit my people in Tugaloo, Mississippi, where I'm from, but other than that, I stay home.

"Reggie was too young to remember, but I, too, lost a child, a baby girl. She died in her crib, and I never knew why. All the books I read while studying literature at Tugaloo couldn't help me understand my loss. Nobody was there to help me. Reggie was too young, and my husband was too busy. I didn't have many friends to help me. I'd lost touch with those I used to be close to when I worked as an editor at *Ebony*.

As Millie looked across the table, she saw, for the first time, how strikingly beautiful her ex-in-law was, sitting straight, long legs crossed as if posing for a photo. She spoke crisply, like the sound of eating celery, without a Chicago twang. Now she knew why. She went to Tugaloo College. Millie realized, *I never got to know this woman; she is not at all who I thought she was.*

"Reggie is a good boy; he's just young. He always has been. He's been trying to do better lately. Recently he got a little job working for the University of Chicago. It's not the job I hoped for him, but it's a start. My husband and I worked hard to educate Reggie and prepare him for a place of leadership within our Bronzeville community. He attended the Chicago Lab school, and we introduced him to the brightest minds in the city. We're very proud of our community in Chicago, though it has been slipping since the days when some of our most successful people in the nation lived there. We did all we could to make Reggie a part of it. But, as you know well, kids go their separate ways. Nothing in life went as planned, I suppose, for either of us," she sighed. "There is something I've always wanted to tell you, Millie. I admire you."

"You admire me? Whatever for?"

"Because you're so strong. Others might have quit in despair by now. You faced so much, yet you kept your family intact and their lives focused. You are surrounded by beautiful children who love you. Frankly, I don't see how you have had time to do it all. When do you sleep? You're amazing."

"Do I understand that you want to take Winston so you, too, will be surrounded by beautiful children? Is that what this is all about?" Millie said, tapping her fingers on the old table.

"Of course not. It's about Winston. Our grandson. We both want the best for him, don't we? I can provide for him in ways very different from yours. I want to do it for him and me. Yes, for me too. When he was in Chicago, the few times Honor brought him to my house, Millie, my heart was filled with the same joy as I felt holding my daughter. Yet, I didn't do more, hoping my son would step up, and frankly was afraid to get too close for fear of losing him later as I lost my daughter.

"I don't deserve Winston; I know that. It's not like I have earned your trust or his love. I've had my issues over the years. And I won't try to tell you my son is a new man yet, or that we would be perfect in raising Winston. But I want to say this to you from the bottom of my heart. I promise I will do my best to raise, guide, and nurture him in ways that will make you proud—not of me, but of him. If only you will let me. Will you think about it?

Millie's face paled in shock by Maureen's words, and she squinted her eyes as if she had been blinded by a sunbeam.

Maureen continued. "Let's not make this about the past. You can provide him with many things that I cannot. The same is true of me. I can do for him in ways that you can't. But I want you to know my heartfelt desire to care for him and how highly I regard you. I don't just want your acceptance. I am asking for your support, not today but throughout his life. I want to avoid this hearing and instead take this time for you and me to plan his future together. Will you give me a chance? I promise to try my best and raise him with your guidance."

The Matter of Honor

When Millie saw tears in Maureen's eyes, she was helpless to dam the ducts in her own. After some weeping, Maureen reached out her slender sienna fingers and grasped Millie's solid umber fist. Their hands remained intertwined for a while before they arose, arm in arm, to plan the future of the child of Honor.

CHAPTER 78

AFTER THE CUSTODY CASE CONCLUDED, Alan and Millie didn't talk much, except when she called him to announce proudly that Pastor Jenkins had honored her and her family by naming the church preschool The Millie Rivers School of the Future, which *The Call and Post* heralded on its front page, after Winnie's first day at an exclusive preschool in Chicago, and when Duke began college majoring in pre-law.

Gold was proud of all he had done to change the Safety Department. Before his defeat, Mayor Blandford fired Haskell Gross and nurses Kratz and Hill and canceled the contract of Dr. V (who moved back to the Philippines). The City Council later (after Lex Baer was voted out) closed WCI and, with Franklin County, built a joint facility with first-class staff.

Gold had changed as well. Before leaving for a new job, his secretary Frannie told him she saw something new and truly remarkable in Alan. "It's your eyes," she said. "When I started working for you, I remember how blank they were. Now, for some reason, they have color in them, like they're full of life."

But changes in the Safety Department didn't last very long. One day, Gold read in the *Dispatch* that a pretrial detainee at the men's prison facility had died from type II diabetes. A new underpaid nurse had failed to follow up on his vital medications and refer him to the new part-time doctor. The new superintendent had paid no attention to his medical section.

Gold became intrigued when he read further that the new mayor was calling for a blue-ribbon commission to study this new problem and to report back promptly... after his reelection.

Gold smelled something but didn't know what it was.

Was the mayor cooking Terry Prince's old Masserole?

THE END
(not really)

ABOUT THE AUTHOR

Author painted by Evan Moore (2023)

BEFORE HE WAS AN ARTIST AND WRITER, A.S. White practiced law. He received scholarships to undergraduate (BA Economics, The Ohio State University) and law school (JD American University). Before he practiced law full-time, he was a parole officer with the Ohio Adult Parole Authority. During his 51-year law career, he was Chief of Legal Services Ohio Department of Urban Affairs and Ohio Department of Development and City Attorney for the City of Gahanna, Ohio.

His experience in journalism includes editor of a teen page in a local newspaper and editor of his law school paper. He has interviewed legal luminaries, including a U.S. Supreme Court justice, and has moderated published discussions.

Arnie is working on his second book, a dystopian novel. A short piece of his was published in the *Jonestown Review* (San Diego State University) and another in the law school paper, the *Arizona Advocate*. His art has been exhibited and can be viewed in homes in Columbus, Pittsburgh, San Rafael, and Nantucket.

A. S. WHITE

He was twice a candidate for office (Franklin County Commissioner and Judge, Franklin County Court of Appeals). Diagnosed with multiple myeloma during his second campaign, he received a successful donor-based bone marrow transplant in 1990, making him one of the longest-surviving transplant recipients suffering from that form of cancer.

Arnie is also a member of the Harmony Project, a 550-member choir that requires all singers to donate hours to community service. He has been married to Susan since 1971. They live in Columbus and have four children and six grandchildren.

The author can be reached at aswhiteauthor@outlook.com

Printed in the USA
CPSIA information can be obtained
at www.ICGtesting.com
LVHW030719110924
790750LV00003B/63

9 798990 820302